Boiotia and
the Boiotian L  ,
432–371 B.C.

Boiotia

and the **Boiotian**

League,

432–371 B.C.

Robert J. Buck

The University of Alberta Press

First published by
The University of Alberta Press
141 Athabasca Hall
Edmonton, Alberta, Canada T6G 2E8

Copyright © The University of Alberta Press 1994
ISBN 0–88864–253–9

Canadian Cataloguing in Publication Data

Buck, Robert J., 1926–
  Boiotia and the Boiotian League, 432–371 B.C.

  Includes bibliographical references and index.
  ISBN 0–88864–253–9

  1. Voiötia (Greece)—History. 2. Boeotian League.
I. Title.
DF261.B5B83 1994   938'.4   C93–091822–3

Printed on acid-free paper. ∞

Printed and bound in Canada by
Quality Color Press, Inc., Edmonton, Alberta

To my wife *Helen Buck*

Contents

Abbreviations

A&R	*Atene e Roma*
AHB	*Ancient History Bulletin*
AJA	*American Journal of Archaeology*
AJAH	*American Journal of Ancient History*
AJP	*American Journal of Philology*
AncW	*Ancient World*
Andok.	Andokides
ANRW	*Aufstieg und Niedergang der Römischen Welt*
BCH	*Bulletin de Correspondance Hellénique*
BSA	*Annual of the British School at Athens*
CAH	*Cambridge Ancient History*
CISA	*Contributo dell'Istituto di storia antica del Università del Sacro Cuore, Milano*
ClasAnt	*Classical Antiquity*
CP	*Classical Philology*
CQ	*Classical Quarterly*
CR	*Classical Review*
CSCA	*California Studies in Classical Antiquity*
Diod.	Diodorus Siculus
FGrH	F. Jacoby, *Fragment der griechischen Historiker*
GdA	E. Meyer, *Geschichte des Altertums*
GRBS	*Greek, Roman and Byzantine Studies*
Hell. Oxy.	*Hellenica Oxyrhynchia*
HCT	*A Historical Commentary on Thucydides*

Hdt.	Herodotus
IG	*Inscriptiones Graecae*
Isok.	Isokrates
Paneg.	*Panegyrikos*
Plat.	*Plataikos*
NC	*Numismatic Chronicle*
Paus.	Pausanias
PdP	*Parola del Passato*
Plut.	Plutarch
Ages.	*Life of Agesilaus*
Arist.	*Life of Aristides*
Comp. Pel.	
et Marc.	*Comparison of Pelopidas and Marcellus*
Comp. Phil.	
et Flam.	*Comparison of Philopoemon and Flamininus*
de Gen. Soc.	*de Genio Socratis* (*On the* daimon *of Socrates*)
Lys.	*Life of Lysander*
Pel.	*Life of Pelopidas*
Polyb.	Polybius
QS	*Quaderni di Storia*
RE	*Paulys Real-Encyclopädie der klassischen Altertumswissenschaft*
REA	*Revue des études anciennes*
REG	*Revue des études grecques*
RhM	*Rheinisches Museum für Philologie*
SEG	*Supplementum Epigraphicum Graecum*
SIG	*Sylloge Inscriptionum graecarum*
Symb Oslo	*Symbolae Osloenses*
TAPA	*Transactions of the American Philological Association*
Thuc.	Thucydides
Xen.	Xenophon
Anab.	*Anabasis*
Cyr.	*Cyropaedia*
Hell.	*Hellenica*
YCS	*Yale Classical Studies*

Author's Note

The perennial difficulty of the transliteration of Greek into English has been thoroughly burked. Ideally it would be the best to go directly from the Greek, as in Boiotia, Koroneia, Orchomenos (or Orkhomenos). But Thebes, Thrace and Thucydides are far more acceptable forms to most than Thebai, Thrake and Thoukydides, and I prefer Chaos to Khaos, Plutarch to Ploutarkhos. Therefore Agesilaus and Thebes share these pages with Kleombrotos and Thespiai. Ismenias is called in his own dialect *Hismenias*, but I have used the Attic literary version that even Plutarch used.

This book has been published with the help of a grant from the Canadian Federation of Humanities, using funds provided by the Social Sciences and Humanities Research Council of Canada, to both of which bodies I wish to express my thanks.

I should also wish to express my appreciation for the assistance and criticisms of my colleagues, Professors John Fossey and Albert Schachter, fellow Boiotians, and of the anonymous referees for the CFH. Any errors and mistakes are mine.

Introduction

The period of Boiotian history from the outbreak of the Peloponnesian War in 432 B.C. to the Battle of Leuktra in 371, when the Boiotians embarked on their decade of conquest, is the subject of this book. It fills a gap in studies in the English language, since my *History of Boeotia* stopped at 432, and John Buckler's *Theban Hegemony* begins at 371.

The description of this period is governed by the nature of the source material available. The literary sources are largely concerned with individuals, wars and politics. The epigraphical material is sparse though important; the coins have not been analysed by numismatists for about a century; the archaeological remains are in general not well published. This study concentrates on the Boiotian League and looks at this period of history from the point of view of Boiotia: the emphasis is throughout on the League, its changes in politics and structure, its relations with its neighbours and especially with Sparta, how its activities affected events, and how it in turn was affected by the activities of other powers.

The Boiotians seem to have had a class-structured society, but one receptive to the introduction of new ideas. By the outbreak of the Peloponnesian War it had undergone much modification from the rigidity described by Hesiod some centuries earlier, but we do not have the evidence to analyze it in detail.

Ancient Sources

The ancient sources dealing with this period of Boiotian history vary widely in quality. Thucydides is excellent and the standard against which all others are measured. Unfortunately he goes down only to 411. After that we rely principally on Xenophon's *Hellenika*, Diodorus Siculus, various *Lives* and selections of the *Moralia* from Plutarch, the Oxyrhynchus Historian, Nepos, Pausanias, and various Athenian orators. Beyond them are a scattering of other references. Unfortunately all too often the principal sources contradict one another and present widely divergent versions of events, crediting different motives to different people who do different acts at different places at different times. All this makes for much confusion in sorting out Boiotian history.

Whatever Xenophon's virtues may be, such as stylistic elegance and profound knowledge of contemporary tactics, he is universally recognized to have had a deep and abiding antipathy for the Boiotians in general, the Thebans in particular, and especially the great leaders Epaminondas and Pelopidas. As a consequence he omits many matters that we must pick up from other sources, such as the activities of both Epaminondas and Pelopidas, and their importance to Greek history in the 370s and 360s; various incidents, such as the interesting Battle of Tegyra; and matters no doubt painful for him to recall, such as the precise way that Boiotia was reunited, or the story of the formation of the Second Athenian Confederacy. The two Leagues were the main instruments that ultimately brought Sparta down. He is a great admirer of the Spartans and of Agesilaus in particular. He normally omits the name of any Spartan commander who gets disgraced. Although he is guilty of *suppressio veri*, he never, as far as we know, deliberately tells lies. There are occasional lapses of memory, but no real falsehoods. "His primary purpose is the moral one of depicting virtue."[1] The general rule is that when there is a discrepancy in the facts as related to us by Xenophon and by another historian, Xenophon is usually to be preferred, unless there are compelling reasons to the contrary. If there is a gap in the evidence as relayed to us by Xenophon, then the other historians may be used to supplement Xenophon's narrative, but with caution.

The Oxyrhynchus Historian is usually regarded as the principal exception to this rule. Whoever he was, he is generally considered a very good and careful historian, superior to Xenophon, though there are some recent attempts to rehabilitate the latter's standing again.[2] The Oxyrhynchus Historian seems to have used good, accurate sources and to have published a careful and precise relation of events, with invaluable background, such as his report on the Boiotian Federal constitution of 396. He seems to be the principal source for the Greek material for Books 13 and 14 of our next author, Diodorus Siculus. Here the events as related by Diodorus' source, when not too truncated or mangled chronologically by Diodorus, are usually to be preferred to Xenophon, if there are discrepancies, as in the campaign of Agesilaus in Asia Minor in 395, where Xenophon has surprising omissions, such as a major battle.

Diodorus Siculus was a compiler of the middle of the first century B.C., and he is no better, and sometimes worse, than his sources. He exercises his own judgement, occasionally, on the material, but fortunately not to excess. He is unwise enough to equate Roman consular years, starting in January, with Athenian archon years, beginning usually in late June. He is fond of lumping sequences of events that form a unit and cover several years under one of his archon-consular years. All this leads all too often into confusion, and if his source is unreliable, his testimony may be useless. In the area under consideration he used the Oxyrhynchus Historian and Ephoros: the Oxyrhynchus Historian (apparently through Ephoros) in Books 13 and 14, and Ephoros (using other sources) in Book 15. The Oxyrhynchus Historian is quite reliable; Ephoros without the Oxyrhynchus Historian must be approached with great caution. Ephoros has been over-rated recently as "an indispensable counterbalance to the biased reporting of Xenophon."[3] This is wrong. It may be argued that the Oxyrhynchus Historian takes priority over Xenophon; Ephoros does not.

Plutarch in his *Lives* and *Moralia* was not interested in writing history, as he says. Like Xenophon his aim was moral: the presentation of virtue and its comparison with vice. He was a prominent Boiotian in the second century after Christ. He is eclectic in his use of sources, but generally seems to use good ones: Xenophon, the Oxyrhynchus Historian or someone close to him, Kallisthenes and many others, including Ephoros. Kallisthenes is an important source, though not the only one, for his *Life of Pelopidas*.

Isokrates, Andokides, Aischines and other Athenian orators provide some evidence occasionally, but they must be treated with suspicion.

They were not interested in history in itself or in getting at the truth or in moral instruction. They were constructing cases to persuade their listeners to certain courses of action, and if colouring and twisting their versions of events assisted or gained that end, they would do so. Their main interest was in the next vote, not the opinion of history. Whatever they may be for politics, for entertainment, for style, for rhetoric or for jurisprudence, for historical evidence they are unreliable.

Pausanias is, like Plutarch, eclectic in his sources, one of whom may be Plutarch himself, with Xenophon as another important one; he used several other historians, including Ephoros. He was not a historian, but the compiler of a guide book. It is sometimes thought that for his version of the Battle of Leuktra and its aftermath he relied on Plutarch's lost *Life of Epaminondas*, though some of the latest researchers are opposed to this idea. He sometimes provides evidence unobtainable from the other sources, usually reliable material.

Nepos is also eclectic, relying largely on Xenophon, though in one place he cites Theopompos, and his main value lies in his supplying the occasional detail. The remaining sources are sparse and of dubious quality in most cases.

Coins

There are numerous Boiotian coins that may date from this period, but they have not been methodically examined since the time of B.V. Head.[4] The interpretation of the coins and their sequence depends on Head's ordering of the coins and his interpretation of Boiotian history. In the absence of a thorough modern analysis there is a grave risk of creating circular arguments when one uses their evidence to interpret events.

Inscriptions

P. Roesch gives masterly surveys of the epigraphical evidence from Boiotia in his two important books, though by the nature of the evidence they treat the Hellenistic period more fully than any other.[5] A. Schachter has a useful index of cult inscriptions,[6] and J.M. Fossey includes a listing and index by site.[7] The relevant inscriptions are comparatively few in number, but they are of great importance for clarifying such matters as the calendar, the titulature and number of federal and local officials, federal and local cults and games, and, on occasion, shifts in political relations.

Archaeological Evidence

Comparatively little archaeological excavation has been done in Boiotia, and even less has been published.[8] Topographical studies and field surveys, however, have compensated in many ways, notably those of the survey team from the Universities of Bradford and Cambridge; they give a good picture of settlement patterns.[9] They promise to give new insights into Boiotian history. The studies and surveys of many researchers, as seen in the publication of Professor J. Fossey, *The Topography and Population of Ancient Boiotia*, which gives the most complete cataloguing of the known sites, show that there are an impressive range of remains. A. Schachter is publishing a full catalogue of the cults of Boiotia and their material remains.[10] The excavation of such sites as Ptoion,[11] Onchestos,[12] Kabirion,[13] Thebes[14] and Thespiai[15] are of only limited use for this period because of the lack of publications. Furthermore, there is considerable controversy about the precise location of such sites as the great sanctuaries of Athena Itonia[16] and Athena Alalkomeneia.[17]

Modern Scholarship

For this period Boiotia has been comparatively lightly studied by modern scholars, though the quality of their researches is usually high. Apart from the standard histories, such as Grote, Beloch, Meyer, Bengtson, de Sanctis, Hammond, Fine and the *CAH*, there is no single work that covers Boiotia during this period from 432 to 371 B.C.

completely. P. Salmon in his careful and critical study comes down to the Peace of Antalkidas.[18] N. Demand discusses Thebes in the fifth century.[19] P. Cloché has produced a general work on Thebes from the earliest times,[20] of deservedly high reputation. L. Prandi does the same for Plataia.[21] E. von Stern's two works[22] still repay study for their meticulous handling of the sources. J. Buckler gives a full treatment of the times after 371, and his introduction has valuable insights into the times before Leuktra.[23]

Several theses on Boiotian topics are available for study through University Microfilms or the National Library of Canada. These include Ph.D. theses by M.L. Cook, H.M. Hack, C.J. Dull, and an M.A. thesis by G. Clarke.[24]

There are many recent works touching on Boiotian history for this period which repay examination. They include books by Hamilton, Cartledge, Bruce, McKechnie and Kern, Accame, Ryder, Larsen, Cargill, and Henry. In addition there are several useful theses, in particular those of Rice, and Kagan.[25]

There are several recent articles, mostly concentrated about some of the *cruces* of this period. M.L. Cook has two important ones on political factions, especially Boiotian, before the Corinthian War.[26] Most of the others concentrate on matters in the period from 378 to 371, though an occasional one strays into the 380s. G. Cawkwell in a stimulating set[27] has prompted a considerable re-examination of the sequence of events from 378 down. J. Buckler wrote several touching on these years,[28] with his usual meticulous scholarship. Others come from C.J. Tuplin, A.P. Burnett, R.M. Kallet-Marx, M. Sordi, and S. Lauffer.[29] There are several older articles that are still useful, including those of W. Judeich, J.H. Thiel and G.M. Bersanetti.[30] Valuable insights into the topography, particularly of battlefields, come from W.K. Pritchett, and on other military matters from M.H. Munn and V.D. Hanson, as well as from the standard work on the fighting in this period by J.K. Anderson.[31]

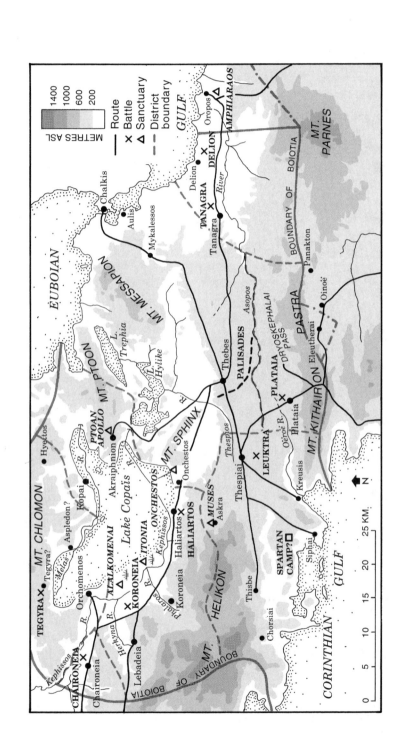

I   Boiotia and
the Boiotian League,
432–371 B.C.

Boiotia lies in the centre of Greece, between the Peloponnese and Thessaly, between Attica and Phokis. It
contains the main land routes between northern and
southern Greece and some of the important ports for
crossing by sea to the Peloponnese. It is separated from its neighbours
Athens, Phokis and Lokris by fairly easy ranges of hills or low mountains penetrated by many passes.

It was also on a crossroads for the spread of ideas, linking as it
did Delphi with Athens and the Peloponnese, and, despite the deri-
sion of its Athenian neighbours, it was a centre of some original
thought, notably in poetry and in political theory: Hesiod and Pindar
were both Boiotians, and there were several Boiotian women poets,
the best known being Korinna; its political theorists of the early Classical period deeply influenced oligarchic thought, not the least in fifth-
century Athens. It was firmly believed in Athens by 415 B.C. that a
rotating sovereign Council on the Boiotian model was a *sine qua non*
of a properly established oligarchy. This explains why the oligarchs
of the revolution of the Four Hundred in 411 B.C. proposed an elected
set of four Councils drawn from the Five Thousand and rotating in
turn (Aristotle, *AP* 30). The Thirty in 404/3 were supposed to establish a body of citizens who would take turns at providing the person-
nel for a council of councils. The influence is still apparent in the
fourth century, when the so-called Constitution of Drakon presented
a council with similar properties.

1

Though its own harbours were few, and the majority of these not particularly good, it is possible that Boiotia exported grain to Athens.[1] It was, however, in close contact with the Euboians, and through them it had wider links across the Mediterranean. Boiotian isolation and lack of direct overseas contact must not be overstated. Thebes and Carthage found it expedient in the fourth century to appoint *proxenoi* to serve one another's needs.

There was considerable construction of fortification walls and of buildings in the fifth and fourth centuries, much of it apparently in the period from 432 to 371.

Boiotia also produced at times good pottery and sculpture. All in all it seems to have been a lively and vigorous place, and, for Greece, wealthy and prosperous.

The boundaries between the various cities and subdivisions were seldom so marked by any prominent natural features that they could not be ignored, and so there were always boundary disputes. The Boiotians had an unenviable reputation for quarrelsomeness and mutual hatreds to the point of mutual destruction. Pericles remarked that they were like the ilex trees that knock one another down. Eteokles and Polyneikes, who fought one another to the death, though brothers, were Boiotians. Nonetheless the Boiotians were able to co-operate in some areas, notably in the maintenance of various shrines, of which there seemed to have been many. There were also numerous oracles and cult centres that attracted a wide following from across Greece,[2] from the shrines of Trophonios and the Muses to the Kabeirion and the Amphiaraion.

Early History

In the Archaic and Classical periods most of the inhabitants though at daggers drawn were a fairly homogeneous group, culturally speaking; they shared the same dialect, as well as various cult and other common traditions. They apparently lacked many of the usual Greek societal features, having, for example, no tribes or phratries. They were attached to various villages and to thirteen or so towns, of varying size and importance, from Thebes and Orchomenos down to such small places as Harma and Mykalessos. Since they were so quarrelsome, there were many wars recorded between the Boiotian cities; the hatred of Plataia and Eleutherai for the other Boiotians, and Thebes in particular, for example, was all too well known; Orchomenos and Thespiai seem to have nursed hostile feelings *vis-à-vis* the rest of Boiotia; most of the other cities seemed to have disliked one another.

In spite of this at some point in the last quarter of the sixth century B.C. the Boiotians managed to do something that no other Greek people quite managed to do, at least for several centuries. They formed a viable federal state. They also managed to avoid undergoing tyrannies, the sending out of colonies,[3] and most of the other activities associated with the "normal" political development of the better-known Greek states. Instead there was slow change from numerous independent communities to a series of eight or nine groupings, each group under its dominant town. In the very earliest phase of the formation of these groups there was annexation of territory by the dominant town and, often, transfers of population. Thebes, for example, incorporated the territory of Potniai into its own and moved the inhabitants to the Kadmeia. Thespiai annexed the territory of Askra, expelling the Askraians. It soon became apparent, however, that it was more advantageous to rule over one's neighbours, and not to incorporate or move them, to have them simply as *perioikoi*, as "second-class citizens" so to speak. In this status they would pay taxes and furnish troops, but they would have none of the privileges of citizenship except protection (an important consideration), certain cult links and probably the *ius connubii*. Thebes gained dominance over Aulis, Glisas and Skolos; Thespiai over Siphai, Thisbe and Chorsiai; and Plataia over Hysiai and Erythrai. Occasionally a reversal of this pattern occurred, as when Koroneia or Eleutherai preserved or regained a precarious freedom.

In general, then, there arose a number of dominant towns, each of which controlled a district, the inhabitants of which had a status subordinate to that of the ruling class of the dominant town. The ruling class formed an oligarchy. No doubt some individuals or important families from subordinate towns joined with or were co-opted into the ruling class, but the impression (as in Thuc. 5.31.6 and 3.62.3–4) was of tightly-knit groups running affairs, with the great majority drawn from and living in the dominant towns.

All the states of Boiotia were primarily agricultural. The arable areas of Boiotia, which were quite extensive, surrounded the (now drained) shallow and swampy Lake Copaïs. The survey carried out by the Bradford/Cambridge Universities Boiotia Project shows that there was "a formidable density of settlement" in the Archaic and Classical periods.[4] It has been estimated that by the fourth century it may have been as high as 85 persons a square km.[5] The great majority of rural sites were small farmsteads, though there were some rural hamlets as well. The general pattern seems to be of complementary town and rural farm settlement, rather than a nucleated hamlet/village pattern.[6] In the fourth century the amount of population was seriously beyond the capacity of the land to support it. The implications are still being studied, but clearly the Classical and Archaic settlement pattern means that the large number of farms permitted a large pool of hoplite-class farmers to be available for military service. The survey evidence has so far not revealed much about large estates.

As Aristotle notes (*Pol.* 1292 B 25–35), farmers and proprietors of moderate-sized holdings tended to be oligarchic. They were busy and preferred to hold a minimum of assemblies rather than to meet frequently. They were apt to leave the management of affairs to the larger landholders, the more leisured class (*Pol.* 1293 A 21–27). In Boiotia by the time of the Persian Wars very small inner circles had developed, notably at Thebes, as the ruling bodies, as oligarchies within their oligarchies. All the Boiotian states were oligarchic in the sixth century B.C. The pro-Athenian city of Plataia only turned to democracy sometime between 490 and 480 B.C.,[7] but even here an attempted oligarchic coup at the time of the battle of Salamis registered some discontent with the new style of government.

From early times the Boiotians had employed amphictyonies to care for various shrines and to superintend festivals.[8] These amphictyonies were probably organized on the usual pattern, with delegates drawn from the Boiotian areas to form the governing body, the Council, much in the manner of the amphictyony at Delphi or of the delegates to the

League of Kalaureia. These Boiotian amphictyonies were not, it must be emphasized, political or military organizations. They existed solely for religious purposes.

Several, though not all, of the Boiotian cities formed a political League in the last quarter of the sixth century under the leadership of Thebes. It was the first federal League in Greek history.[9] The League was apparently at first a defensive arrangement against Thessaly, but it was seen to be advantageous by most Boiotian states, particularly by Tanagra, Thespiai, Haliartos and Koroneia. Although most Boiotian states joined, it is clear that Plataia, Eleutherai and Orchomenos remained aloof.[10] An attempt to compel Plataia to join (probably in 519, but perhaps in 509) ended in disaster for the League forces, and Plataia and Eleutherai fell into the Athenian orbit for the next century. Orchomenos probably joined the League between 510 and 506 B.C., certainly by the time of the Persian Wars.

As far as can be ascertained, the new League followed and utilized the previously existing pattern of the older religious amphictyonies: a Council (called the *Halia* in Herodotus, 5.79) composed of delegates from the various areas, and no doubt drawn from the governing oligarchies, set policy. Answering to it were the military commanders, the Boiotarchs, who also were given other tasks. At some early stage the Council ceased to meet very often as a full body but divided itself into four sections. Each of these in turn, probably for three months, acted as the Executive Committee, consulting the other three sections only on matters of great moment. In this way Councillors were spared frequent attendance, and they were able to minimize the number of meetings and the burden of holding office. A Council of this type, not backed by any popular assembly, is certainly oligarchic in principle. How the Councillors were chosen is unknown; but it would be most likely that the local oligarchic Councils selected those of the hoplite class they wished. It is, perhaps no coincidence that one of the first acts of the Boiotian League was to mint coins, and that one of the few things we know about the federal Councillors is that they were paid.[11]

Nevertheless Thebes in reality controlled the League, presumably as much by *auctoritas* as by the support of the smaller districts. Thebes in turn was, as Herodotus (9.86) tells us, controlled by a small inner circle of noble families. After the Battle of Plataia the victorious Greeks took vengeance on the Boiotian League for Medizing. They besieged Thebes, which eventually surrendered. All that the Allies did was to arrest a handful of Theban leaders, prosecute a few of these and finally execute one or two. Since Boiotia got off so lightly, one may argue that the rest of Greece regarded it as ruled by this handful of Thebans.

The League was probably not dissolved after the surrender of Thebes, as some authorities think. All the evidence we have indicates that it continued in existence, but under another dominating state, perhaps Tanagra. No change of type of government occurred; pro-Allied or pro-Spartan oligarchies replaced the Medizers.

Changes in the type of government did occur, however, in the period after 458/7, after the Battle of Oinophyta, when Athens defeated the Boiotians and gained effective control of the area, as Thucydides (1.108) tells us. Several states, notably Thebes and Thespiai, became democracies, while others, it seems, replaced their previous regimes with pro-Athenian oligarchies. According to Aristotle (*Pol.* 1302 B 30) these new governments were not very popular and not very competent. They were eliminated after about ten years. A group of oligarchic exiles, mostly Thebans, seized Orchomenos by a *coup de main* in 447. The local populace joined them and helped to defeat an Athenian force near Koroneia. Shortly afterwards the Athenians evacuated Boiotia, and the oligarchs were left in firm control. Thebes regained its hegemony over the Boiotian League. Doctrinaire oligarchs were in control. The narrow inner circles seem to have lost power to a more broadly based oligarchy, the so-called hoplite oligarchy, Aristotle's first type, in which the majority of citizens are small property owners (*Pol.* 1293 A 13).

Some changes in the structure of the League were put into effect after 447. The local governments were so altered as to possess the same sort of quadripartite Councils as the League. Clearly the federal organs provided a pattern that was imposed upon the local governments. A few anomalies remained in the latter to demonstrate how diverse the old forms had been before they were standardized. Clearly these new changes were the products of application of oligarchic theory, a theory that held views about the virtues of quadripartite Councils.

Federal states all exist in a chronic condition of instability. This is nothing new, and it may be consoling to look at Boiotia from this point of view. But it would be more instructive to see how this federal state eventually embraced democracy, and how it tried to cope with both federalism and the rule of the People at the same time.

Boiotian Culture

Boiotia must have had a fairly high level of prosperity, especially in the period from 432 to 371. In the absence of excavation of stratified materials it is difficult to be precise, but there was construction at such towns as Plataia, Thebes, Orchomenos, Chaironeia, Koroneia, Thespiai, Tanagra, Siphai, Kreusis, and at the fortress at Mavrovouni. Though the archaeological evidence is restricted, the historical evidence makes it clear that the period from 432 to 371 was a time when many expensive public works were constructed, like the Theban palisades, the stoas and monuments erected after the Battle of Delion, the walls thrown around many smaller Boiotian towns, and many public structures, such as shrines, fountains and theatres. Even invading forces left their traces, if the suggestion that the site on Mavrovouni is the main Spartan camp is correct.

There was cultural contact with Athens that went in both directions. While Boiotian oligarchic political theories deeply influenced the Athenian oligarchs, democratic influence from Athens was widely felt in Boiotia. Besides the Boiotian pro-democrats who played a significant rôle in the early phases of the Archidamean War, the faction of Ismenias at the end of the fifth century had close and friendly relations with such strong democrats as Thrasyboulos. The faction supported the democratic counter-revolution, in 379/8, though there is no evidence that their relationships with Athenian democrats were translated into democratic practice until after the coup.

We know nothing about what plays were presented in the many Boiotian theatres constructed in this period, nor what poetry, if any, was created. No Boiotian prose authors from the time are extant, though we know the names of a few historians.

The general impression is one of a prosperous area, inhabited by a tough, quarrelsome, rather bucolic population, one interested in politics and well versed in them, enjoying drama and the arts but not producing much original in those fields. A land power that could afford a navy obviously had wealth to spare. They were not quite the stupid, cloddish Philistines that the Athenians alleged.

The problems faced by the Boiotian League are those faced throughout history by federal states: union as opposed to particularism; patriotism and disaffection; federalism as opposed to secessionism; reconciliation of unity with the aspirations of the constituent parts; equitability of representation by size of population against the rights of the smaller states. The handling of some of these problems is interesting and even instructive. For these reasons the study of this period of Boiotian history is particularly useful.

II Boiotians in the Peloponnesian War, 432–404 B.C.

Boiotia took an active part in the Peloponnesian War,[1] and the general opinion is that it was a steadfast Spartan ally.[2] The Boiotian League, however, had its own agenda and its own interests, and both of these diverged from Sparta's quite frequently. It was an important state, and Sparta departed from its usual policies by making an alliance on equal terms with the League because of its value as a counterpoise to Athens.[3] Shortly after the end of the Peloponnesian War Boiotian-Spartan relations became very cool, but there had been differences before. There are also the widely held views that the League was under the firm control of Thebes, and that this control was tightened and strengthened during the War.[4] Neither seems to be strictly true.

Boiotian Oligarchies

Oligarchic exiles were the leaders in the overthrow of the Athenian domination of Boiotia,[5] and so it is reasonable to infer that an oligarchic rule was established in Boiotia in 446 and continued on until 387. If it was similar to the one described by the Oxyrhynchus Historian, as is normally held to be the case, then it was dominated by the hoplite and cavalry classes. Only they (and perhaps not all of them) held full citizenship and were the voters.[6] The oligarchy was not a narrowly based *dynasteia* like the one that controlled the League to the end

9

of the Persian Wars, or the one at Thebes during the Spartan occupation, but it did have a restricted electorate. The number of hoplites and cavalry was, according to *Hellenica Oxyrhynchia*,[7] at least 12,000, but not all of them were necessarily voters.

Hellenica Oxyrhynchia says that the League was divided into eleven units of about equal population, districts, μέρη. Thespiai and Orchomenos had two of these units each, Tanagra one, and Koroneia, Haliartos, Lebadeia, Akraphnion, Chaironeia, and Kopai one-third of a unit each, so that the six small towns made up two units. Thebes originally had two units, but then four after the annexation of Plataia and the two allotted to it. Each unit provided 1000 hoplites, 100 cavalry, and various light-armed troops to the Federal army and equal sums to the Federal Treasury. Each unit elected one Boiotarch, sixty representatives to the Federal Council, an unknown equal number of dikasts for the Federal Court, and equal numbers of other officials as required. The Council of 660 men was divided into four 165-man committees. Each consisted of fifteen men from each of the eleven districts; each committee of 165 presided in turn over the other 495 and acted as an executive council, bringing matters to the attention of the others. Whatever was resolved in all, this was final.[8] How the voting was done, by majority of the councillors or by majority of districts or however, is unknown. How each district selected its Council members and other officials also is unknown. It has been suggested that the second district in Thespiai and Orchomenos, and the third and fourth in Thebes were in some way subordinate, and their representatives selected by the dominant classes of the ruling city.[9] It may or may not be the case.

This hoplite oligarchy, as we may term it for short, seems to have had a certain missionary zeal for spreading the ideology of the oligarchic system to other peoples of Greece. Among them were the oligarchic circles at Athens. These borrowed from the Boiotians their concept of an elected set of four Councils drawn from the Five Thousand and rotating in turn, which they employed for the constitution that was to be introduced by the revolution of the Four Hundred in 411 B.C.[10]

Plataia

Boiotian zeal also lies behind the attack on Plataia that triggered the Peloponnesian War. It is sometimes forgotten that this assault was made at the invitation of some prominent Plataians (οἱ πρῶτοι καὶ χρήμα-σι καὶ γένει [Thuc. 3.65.2]), led by one Naukleides, who had hoped to gain power for themselves, so as to destroy their opponents and to attach (προσποιῆσαι) their city to the Thebans.[11] There had long been an oligarchic sentiment in Plataia, causing trouble as far back as the Persian Wars.[12] Thus it is a reasonable inference that Naukleides' idea was to make Plataia a hoplite oligarchy, too.[13]

The presence of two Boiotarchs with a small invading force of 300 men leads to two other inferences. First, that the attempt at Plataia was under League auspices; it was not simply a ploy by Thebes; Plataia was, in spite of Thucydides' turn of phrase, to be brought into the Boiotian League, not simply made a part of Thebes.[14] Second, the small size of the force meant that it was symbolic: no resistance was really expected, and a considerable measure of support was anticipated.[15] Quite a few Plataians seem to have sided with the invaders. When the Plataian oligarchs and the pro-League inhabitants of the areas originally controlled by Plataia were moved to Thebes for security in 425 (along with the inhabitants of various unwalled Theban towns), the population of the city doubled.[16]

The attempt at taking over Plataia nearly succeeded, according to Thucydides, and it was only the softness of the Boiotarchs, who decided not to kill the democratic leaders, even though requested to do so by Naukleides and his friends, that led to Plataian democratic counterattacks and the eventual massacre of the Thebans.[17]

One of the prominent figures among the attackers, though not a Boiotarch, was the Theban Eurymachos, the "most powerful" man at Thebes (Thuc. 2.2.2). His father, Leontiades, had been one of the Theban leaders in the Persian Wars.[18] Eurymachos was clearly of a leading family and the head of a dominant political faction.

Boiotian Factions

A faction, a *hetaireia*, is a very different thing from a political party, as recent discussion emphasizes.[19] One of the definitions in the *OED* (*s.v.* "Faction," 3.c.), referring to Irish peasantry, seems *à propos*: "certain mutually hostile associations . . . , usually of the members of one particular family (which gives its name to the faction) and of their relatives and friends." Strauss in discussing Athenian factions gives another: "a small unit of political competition loosely organized by a leader through a variety of one-to-one ties with his followers and aiming at winning power."[20] There is no permanent organization, but instead shared interests; there is common association and common outlook, but no necessity for any continuity of policy beyond that required for the continuity of personal ties. Strauss has argued that unlike other political groups a faction depends upon its leader for its organization. Its membership is recruited by him on his nexus of personal connections: patron-client relationships; educational ties; local origins; religious ties; kinship ties; politico-economic ties; shared interests or philosophies; or any combination of them.[21] Herman emphasizes how such a faction may extend beyond a city on the basis of *xeniai*, guest-friendships.[22]

A faction can vary in size considerably. It is usually argued that a *hetaireia* must be small, not much bigger than the membership of a dining club: either the limits were the size of the leader's personal connections; or there were as many as could be held together by mutual trust.[23] The evidence does not necessarily bear this out. Herodotos (5.66.2) says that Kleisthenes brought the whole Athenian Demos into his faction (προσεταιρίζεται). With its support he prevailed. If it is argued that Herodotos was making a joke or a rhetorical exaggeration, there is some evidence for the size of Boiotian factions that indicates that they were somewhat larger than dining clubs. When Thebes was seized by the Spartans and Leontiades in 382, over 300 members of the faction of Ismenias went into exile at Athens,[24] and they were not the whole membership; several more, including one of the leaders, Galaxidoros, stayed in retirement in Thebes; at least 150 others ended up in the Theban jail.[25] At the Battle of Haliartos in 395 most of the 300 hoplite casualties on the Theban side were members of the faction of Leontiades, who were desperately trying to prove their loyalty.[26] These were merely the Theban members of their factions. Those from outside Thebes are not included; until the Peace of Antalkidas of 387 the factions were League-wide, as *Hellenica Oxyrhynchia* (17.2) makes clear.

However big the membership the leadership of a faction was probably concentrated in the hands of a small group of aristocrats. If it resembled the leadership of the factions in 396, it contained leaders from other parts of Boiotia, too, not exclusively Thebans. *A fortiori,* the membership must have been widely spread throughout Boiotia.

Though the Boiotian factions were not political parties, they were something more than personal entourages or clusters around various leaders. Continuity of policy was quite important. The faction of Leoniades had a general policy of supporting Sparta, while that of Ismenias assisted the Athenian democrats. With fairly large numbers and an agreed basis in policy they were more than just followers of a leader or a company of friends. They were organized to seek power.

Even so it is doubtful if any faction could seek to dominate Boiotia by filling the majority of seats in any elected council, or other organ of state; rather, it apparently used its *auctoritas,* its "clout," to gain acceptance of its ideas, to get a few men into key posts, to defeat its enemies and to keep power. In Boiotia as long as it had the confidence of the majority of the members of the Council, a faction could in effect control the state. To put it another way, as long as it expressed views and advanced measures acceptable to the majority of the voters, it could guide the state. Such a faction would dominate policy as long as it commanded the support of the majority of the voters in Boiotia, not simply of those in Thebes.[27] There were, however, limits to what even a dominant faction could do.

There is no evidence for any political parties in Greece, even in Boiotia, where if anywhere they might have existed,[28] although there was more continuity in Boiotian factions than has been admitted. On the death of Eurymachos his son Leontiades was able to assume his leadership and his nexus of associations, very successfully. He and his faction played a dominant part in Boiotian politics for many years.

The faction headed by Eurymachos and then Leontiades was by and large pro-Spartan and anti-Athenian. There was also enough pro-democratic sentiment to give rise to another faction (or perhaps several factions) in various Boiotian cities. It or they were not very successful. Many of the leaders ended up in exile, like Ptoiodoros of Thebes (Thuc. 4.76.3). Nonetheless, the pro-democrats were of sufficient importance to have influence on Boiotian politics and on Athenian strategic thinking.[29]

The Early Stages of the War

When the news of the attack on Plataia reached Athens, the Athenians interned their resident Boiotians and sent troops to Plataia to evacuate the women and children (Thuc. 2.2–7). The Boiotians in reprisal for the massacre sent a contingent of cavalry and infantry to join the forces of the Peloponnesian League, their allies, while the remainder of their troops laid waste the territory of Plataia (Thuc. 2.12). There was a skirmish at a place called Phrygia[30] between Athenian and Boiotian cavalry, settled in favour of the Boiotians when the infantry intervened (Thuc. 2.22). It is remembered chiefly because the dead were among those whose burial was the occasion for Perikles' great funeral speech.

The Boiotian League probably participated in the Peloponnesian invasion of Attica in 430.[31] After 429, however, its main effort was concentrated on the siege of Plataia until its capitulation in 427. This led to the judicial murder of the 200-odd men of the Plataian garrison, in recompense, one might think, for the slaughter of the 300 Thebans.[32]

The number of pro-League Plataians was fairly large, although precisely how many there were is unknown. Several of them (ὅσοι τὰ σφέτερα φρονοῦντες) even cultivated and inhabited their lands during the siege and for some time after the surrender of the town (Thuc. 3.68.3). They were, especially after the conclusion of the siege, joined by Thebans who held some of land confiscated by the League (δημοσιώσαντες) on ten-year leases. When these Plataians, like the inhabitants of Skolos and Skaphai, moved to Thebes for security in 425 in a kind of synoecism, it did not mean that Plataia as a political unit ceased to exist. The People were still the People of Plataia, though residing in Thebes temporarily.[33] A decade later, when the Athenians claimed Plataia, the Thebans pointed out that it had voluntarily joined the League (Thuc. 5.17.2). They were not lying, at least in their own view: the People (i.e., those recognized as such) *had* joined the League; where the legally constituted Plataian Demos resided was presumably a matter of indifference.

In the meantime a Boiotian, Hermaiondas, joined the Spartans in their mission to Mitylene in 428 at the time of the revolt on Lesbos (Thuc. 3.5.3).

The Athenians attempted a combined operation against the Boiotians in 427/6.[34] A landing by the hoplites of the Athenian fleet in the territory of Tanagra was coupled with an invasion by the full Athenian army. Whether or not it was counter to the advice of Perikles to avoid land campaigns against the Peloponnesians (Thuc. 1.143), it was successful. A Boiotian League force of Tanagraians and Thebans was met and defeated. There were no Peloponnesians present. The Athenian aims, if any, in the operation remain unclear. One may infer, however, that it did alert the Boiotians to weaknesses in their own mobilization system, ones that were quickly rectified, to judge by their swift reaction a few years later at Delion.

Herakleia

Boiotia seems to have supported, or at least not opposed, the Spartan foundation of Herakleia in Trachis in 427/6. At first the colony did nothing except irritate its northern neighbours and give the Boiotians a buffer between themselves and their ancient enemy Thessaly;[35] but it gave Sparta a foothold in an area where Spartan and Boiotian interests might not necessarily coincide. Its garrison protected Phokis, a neighbour and long-time enemy of Boiotia. There was a difficulty a few years later in 419 when the Boiotians took over the colony and expelled the Spartan governor for incompetence. They did this, they said, because they wished to forestall any Athenian initiative here; they caused great offense at Sparta (Thuc. 5.52). The expedition of Agis to the Malian Gulf six years later, in 413, is in some way to be connected with repercussions arising from this incident.[36] Herakleia in Trachis, then, was a spot that saw friction arise between Sparta and Boiotia quite early on, even when the pro-Spartan faction of Leontiades was guiding affairs.

In 427/6 Boiotia was the objective of an over-ambitious Athenian plan, one undertaken by Demosthenes. It failed, but it is of significance that an attack on Boiotia from the west was thought feasible (Thuc. 3.94–98). Nothing is known of Boiotian activities for the next few years.

In 424/3 the Boiotians sent a force of 2200 hoplites and 600 cavalry to help secure Megara for the Spartan alliance. There had been an attempted democratic coup, one undertaken with Athenian aid. The Boiotians arrived well before Brasidas and the Spartans (Thuc. 4.72).

The Delion Campaign

Later in the same year the Athenians launched an elaborate plan of concentric attacks against Boiotia, which it was hoped would take it out of the war and permit the victors to democratize it. The plan relied heavily on the assistance of pro-democrats, whose efforts the Boiotian government also took seriously.[37] The Athenians were to land on the south coast at Siphai, which was to be betrayed to them by democrats, presumably local Thespians. They were to receive Chaironeia in the west from the Phokians and local Orchomenian democrats, who were to be aided by mercenaries hired from the Peloponnese by wealthy Orchomenian exiles. Finally, the Athenians were to invade the eastern areas with their full levy and occupy and fortify the sanctuary of Delian Apollo as a base for further operations. The success of all these attacks depended upon precise timing; all were to be done on a fixed day. In this way the Boiotian League would have to split its forces and be fatally weakened. (Of course, the Athenians would have to split their forces, too, but this was apparently not considered much of a hazard.) Demosthenes was in command in the west and Hippokrates in the east.

The names of a few Boiotian democratic leaders are known, including the Theban exile, Ptoiodoros (Thuc. 4.76.3), who played a key rôle in negotiations, and two Orchomenians, who were honoured by Athens, Potamodoros and his son Eurytion.[38] The fact that some of the exiles were wealthy enough to hire mercenaries leads to the inference that there were factions supporting democracy with members in the highest reaches of Boiotian society, or at least in the top census classes. One might expect that even democratic Boiotians would be led by aristocrats.

Apparently some months were consumed in the negotiations and the planning, and there were serious leaks, most notably by a Phokian, Nikomachos, who told all he knew to the Spartan authorities. They in turn told the Boiotian government. This led to the crushing of the Orchomenian and Thespian democrats and consequently of the possibility of undisputed occupation of Siphai and Chaironeia. A rapid deployment of troops in Siphai and Chaironeia, doubtless backed by the arrest of key democratic figures, cowed the democrats into inactivity (Thuc. 4.89).

There was still a chance, however, that the Athenian assaults might succeed. This was made impossible by a mistake in the timing; Demosthenes made his attempt on Siphai several days too early. He was met by the whole League army and decided not to attempt an opposed landing. He withdrew, and the army marched off to Delion, where they trounced the Athenians very handily by themselves. No Peloponnesian forces helped in the battle, though some arrived in time for the siege and assault on the Athenian fortifications at the sanctuary. If the Athenians had made no errors, the Spartan forces would have come to the rescue far too late to do any good, a point presumably not lost on the Boiotians. They, like the Athenians at Marathon, never forgot their victory; they embellished their towns with stoas and monuments, and they established a special festival called the Delia.[39]

Just before the battle, when the main Athenian force was withdrawing into Attica, the Boiotarch Pagondas[40] referred the question of whether to engage the enemy (surely a key point of policy to a Greek state) to the hoplites after the Boiotarchs had disagreed. He canvassed their opinion *lochos* by *lochos*, and obtained their opinion in the same way, as if the Boiotians voted by units, like the equally oligarchic Romans in their *comitia centuriata*.[41] Whether the Boiotians ever voted by *lochoi* for other purposes is unknown.

The battle has been well analyzed,[42] and among the main points of interest are the claim that the tactics later employed at Leuctra were first adumbrated here, and the idea that the Sacred Band was used as a stiffener for the front rank.

Thespiai and the League after Delion

Delion was a hard-fought battle, and the Thespian hoplites on the left wing had suffered heavy casualties, apparently most of their contingent (Thuc. 4.96.3, 4.133.1). Shortly thereafter, in 423, the Thebans tore down the walls of Thespiai. Βουλόμενοι μὲν καὶ αἰεί, παρεσχηκὸν [παρεστηκὸν codd.] δὲ ῥᾷον ἐν τῇ πρὸς ᾿Αθηναίους μαχῃ ὅτι ἦν αὐτῶν ἄνθος ἀπωλώλει. "They had always wanted to do this, and a justification was readily provided, as the flower of the Thespians had perished in battle with the Athenians" (Thuc. 4.133). This action is often taken as an example of Theban imperialism: they gained 6/11 of the offices necessary to control the League with 2/11 of the expenses.[43]

There is, however, another possible interpretation of Thucydides: he sometimes uses "Theban" as synonymous with "League." The majority of the Thespian hoplite class had supported the Federal (rather than just the Theban) regime, and probably Leontiades' faction as well. The matter of the walls did not become urgent until after Delion. When most of the Thespian oligarchs were killed, support for both the League and for Leontiades' faction was drastically weakened.[44] This in turn implies that an important segment of the Thespian population was anti-League (or anti-Theban) or at least liable to support democracy. They demonstrated all these in their revolt in 414. What is really meant by Thucydides here is that the League, not just the citizens of Thebes, had long desired the demolition of the Thespian walls. League security rather than Theban imperialism seems to be the end in view. Synoecism with Thebes, on the pattern seen with Plataia, with a union more like a unitary state eventually ensuing, could have been the eventual result. Thucydides in confusing the League with Thebes probably was following a common Hellenic sentiment.

There are two pieces of evidence that support this interpretation of Thucydides. First, the circumstances of the massacre of the inhabitants of the Theban town of Mykalessos by Thracian ex-mercenaries of Athens in 413 (Thuc. 7.29.4). The Thracians easily passed through the ruined and unrepaired walls (unrepaired in wartime!).[45] The population had probably been evacuated to Thebes in 425, but had returned after the Peace of 421.[46] That is, they had been temporarily synoecized to Thebes. The walls were neglected for the same reason that led to the pulling down of the walls of Thespiai: to allow for quick entry by Federal hoplites in case of trouble from democrats or other anti-League subversives.

Second, Oropos was captured by the Boiotians in 412/11 with the aid of the Oropians (Thuc. 8.60.1). Its hoplite class after a few years was unwilling to remain in the Boiotian League, and the town withdrew, perhaps about 409; apparently the League did not oppose its withdrawal, and there was little or no Athenian interference in the matter. Oropos, according to Diodorus and Theopompos, rejoined the League in 401 or so, when its hoplite class requested help from the Boiotians against the "Demos" during *stasis* in 402/1.[47] It is, however, not mentioned by the author of the *Hellenica Oxyrhynchia* in his description of the eleven districts. For this reason many authorities doubt that it actually did rejoin, and they reject the testimony of Diodorus. On the other hand, *Hellenica Oxyrhynchia* does not mention Mykalessos, Chorsiai, Anthedon and various other minor Boiotian towns, either. Oropos could have been taken under the protection of the League in some subordinate position, one comparable to that of any of these. Or it could have been given a category like that of Orchomenos in 371.[48] There are not strong enough grounds to reject the testimony of Diodorus' source, *Hellenica Oxyrhynchia*, here. Whatever its precise relationship to the rest of the League, Oropos was in the League, probably in some subordinate status. It may also be inferred that its admission into and its withdrawal from the League was accomplished with the consent of the majority of its hoplites: it seems reasonable to conclude that the same rule applies to each of the other cities. If this is so, it means that although Thebes was certainly the leader of Boiotia, it was not the dictator.

The Peace of Nikias

Skirmishes had doubtless continued throughout the Archidamian War along the Boiotian-Attic border, but during 422 the Boiotian seized the important Athenian border post of Panakton and took some prisoners (Thuc. 5.3.5). Nothing more is recorded until the Peace of Nikias in 421.

One of its main provisions was the restoration of the *status quo ante bellum*; it is not surprising that the Boiotian League, along with the Corinthians, Eleans and Megareans refused to sign (Thuc. 5.17.2). The League had, shortly after the Peace, arranged for an armistice with Athens, renewable every ten days.[49] The Boiotians and the Megareans, the hoplite oligarchies north of the Isthmus, began to pursue a common policy, one that diverged from that of Sparta. Nonetheless, they refused to go along with Corinth and Elis and make an alliance with Argos, stating that "the Argive democracy would be less advantageous to them, since they were oligarchies, than the Spartan system of government" (Thuc. 5.31.6). This clearly shows that the Boiotian League, or at least the majority of the members of the Federal Council, still had ideological views about oligarchy and oligarchic solidarity. Even if they were having their differences with Sparta, these were not a sufficient reason to make up to any democratic state.

Boiotia's and Megara's policies were not distinct enough from Sparta's to lead to hostilities and reprisals,[50] but different enough to cause anxiety and anger at Sparta, as the incident over Herakleia in Trachis makes clear. Sparta began seriously to attempt to get Boiotia to join the Peace. With some naïveté[51] Sparta urged Boiotia to hand over both Panakton and the Athenian prisoners, so that Sparta could trade them for Pylos. The simplicity of this suggestion, repeated twice in Thucydides (5.35.5 and 39.2), has caused some incredulity in the minds of many scholars.[52] Probably Gomme and Dover are right in concluding that Sparta was simply arrogant.

An incident in the next winter underlines the fact that there were limitations on the power of Leontiades' faction (Thuc. 5.36). The Ephors Kleoboulos and Xenares, who were opposed to the Peace of Nikias, asked the Boiotian and Corinthian envoys at Śparta to make an alliance with Argos. They hoped that it might lead Argos ultimately to become an ally of Sparta. This would do two things: first, it would ease pressure on Boiotia and Corinth to join the Peace of Nikias, since an alliance with Argos by Sparta would lead to trouble with Athens; and, second, it would stop any Athenian activity in the Peloponnese. Under Hyperbolos Athens may already have been negotiating with Argos.[53]

The Boiotian envoys on their way home met some high-ranking Argives, probably by no accident.[54] They soon settled on mutually satisfactory terms of agreement. The Boiotians brought these to the Boiotarchs, who also liked them. The latter, like the envoys, were presumably under the influence of Leontiades' faction. They had, however, to refer the matter to the quadripartite Federal Council, "which had the supreme power." The Council, however, refused to accept their advice, "fearing to go in opposition to Sparta" (Thuc. 5.38.2–3), not unreasonably. In other words the Council did not go along with the advice of the envoys and the Boiotarchs and presumably the faction of Leontiades. If it is considered along with the point about Boiotian oligarchic views made by Thucydides in 5.31.6, the Council's refusal further emphasizes the fact that although it was oligarchic in sympathy and ideologically solid, it was not blindly following the lead of the leaders of Leontiades' faction.[55] The Federal Council had the ultimate say, the κῦρος. Since it was chosen from across Boiotia, clearly its ideological views on oligarchy and oligarchic solidarity were Federation-wide. This oligarchic set of views was normally the foundation of support for the faction of Leontiades against any pro-democratic groups.

Sparta was now so anxious to get the prisoners in exchange for Panakton that they finally agreed to the Boiotian price: a separate alliance against Athens (Thuc. 5.59.3). The Boiotians in this way negated any hope for progress by the Spartan peace party: they turned over the prisoners to Sparta and prepared to turn over the site of Panakton to Spartan commissioners, with the walls demolished.[56] Athens was not mollified by obtaining a ruined site, and this, together with the news of the Spartan-Boiotian alliance, which contravened the Peace of Nikias, was a major factor in inclining the Athenian people towards concluding an alliance with Argos (Thuc. 5.46.2). Sparta had little choice but to stick with Boiotia rather than to try to improve relations with

Athens. All in all Boiotia did quite well out of her manoeuvres. The Council seems to have foreseen the results with more perspicacity than the Boiotarchs. The separate alliance meant that Boiotia became an ally on equal terms rather than a subordinate, the norm in the Peloponnesian League.[57]

The incident at the Olympic Games of 420, when a Spartan, Lichas, son of Arkesilas, gave the credit for his victory to the Boiotian People, at least indicates some closeness between various elements in the two powers at that time (Thuc. 5.50.4). The occupation of Herakleia in 419 apparently dispelled any amicable feelings briefly, but the efforts of Athens and Argos drove them together again. In 418 the Boiotians sent a strong contingent to the levy of Sparta's allies, 5000 hoplites, 5000 light-armed, 500 cavalry and 500 *hamippoi*. This was twice the size of the Corinthian force (Thuc. 5.57.2).[58]

The Sicilian Expedition

In 415, at the time of the despatch of the Athenian expedition to Sicily, the Boiotians massed their troops on the frontier with Attica,[59] and a small Spartan force was despatched to help them in accordance with the Boiotian-Spartan agreement (Thuc. 6.61.2). It got as far as the Isthmus before it was halted; its advance caused a considerable uproar at Athens, in which Alkibiades was accused of inviting them so as to betray the city to them. Probably the Spartan Government had decided to go to war with Athens (Thuc. 6.93.11), but not as yet, and it stopped the force at the Isthmus before trouble began. The Boiotian reaction to the cancellation of Spartan support is not recorded.

In 414, the "Demos" of Thespiai (the pro-democratic section of the populace) tried a coup against the ruling oligarchs (Thuc. 6.95.2). Since the walls were demolished, Theban hoplite forces were able to rescue the Thespian government, arresting some of the revolutionaries and expelling others. A Thespian contingent of hoplites was part of the force sent by Boiotia to Sicily in 413 with a Thespian Boiotarch (Thuc. 7.19.3). Probably this could only be done because the democratic and anti-League faction was so crushed that there was no risk to the Thespian government and to the unity of the League. The oligarchies under the rule of the hoplite and cavalry classes supported one another.

The Dekeleian War

When hostilities commenced in Greece after the Athenian raids on the Peloponnese, the Boiotians gained a great deal of booty over the next decade by their assiduous ravaging of Attica.[60] In 413 they sent a contingent of 300 hoplites to Sicily with three Boiotarchs, two Theban and one Thespian (Thuc. 7.19.3). Presumably the troops were Theban and Thespian in proportion; the latter had a narrow escape from the Athenian blockading patrols but eventually arrived safely at Syracuse (Thuc. 7.25.3–4). The force was intended to be symbolic, like the one at Plataia, but it did useful service (Thuc. 7.43.7). The Boiotians were a major power on the Spartan side, as they said themselves (Thuc. 3.62.5), and as they demonstrated by the size of their forces in the Peloponnese and the fact that they were asked to provide 25 ships for a new 100-ship navy, an amount equal to the contribution of Sparta itself (Thuc. 8.3.2). They were also able to provide ten triremes for the Lesbians (Thuc. 8.5.2).

In 412/11 the Boiotians captured Oropos, thanks to aid from the Eretrians and the Oropans themselves, with no Peloponnesian assistance (Thuc. 8.60.1). This was followed the next summer, in 411, by the capture of Oinoë sometime after the fall of the oligarchy.[61] Boiotian ships were involved at Kynossema (Thuc. 8.106.3). In 408 a Boiotian force served at Byzantium, where their commander, Koiratadas, was captured. He was probably a prominent member of Leontiades' faction, and by 395 was one of its leaders.[62] A 900-man cavalry brigade joined in Agis' attack on Athens in that year.[63]

At Arginousai in 406 the left wing of the Peloponnesian fleet was under the command of Thrasondas of Thebes.[64] At Aigospotamoi the Boiotian commander was Erianthos of Thebes, the one who later proposed the destruction of Athens.[65]

Though the Boiotians were gaining much booty, especially in Attica, there are hints that relations were becoming somewhat strained in the latter part of the War, in spite of the prosperity accruing.[66]

Boiotian Factions: Ismenias

Hellenica Oxyrhynchia says in the context of 395 that two factions, one under Ismenias, Antitheos and Androkleidas, and another under Leontiades, Asias and Koiratadas (no doubt the one captured at Byzantium), had quarrelled over the question of relations with Sparta. Both factions were not simply Theban groups, but were federation-wide. *Hellenica Oxyrhynchia* says that Leontiades' group, though not in power in 395, had previously been in the ascendant "for a long time" (χρόνον συχνόν).[67] It had clearly been dominant since before the Peloponnesian War, when it was first headed by Eurymachos and then by Leontiades. Leontiades' group was accused of being too friendly with Sparta, while Ismenias' was charged with being soft on Athens.[68] The latter group was anti-Spartan, wishing "to avoid destruction at the hands of the Lakedaimonians"; they were alleged to be anxious to involve Boiotia in an war with Lakedaimon.[69] The comments of the author of the *Hellenica Oxyrhynchia* (17.1) unfortunately contain a lacuna, but the phraseology of what is left indicates that Ismenias' group was not really pro-Athenian. Although Pelopidas and other founders of the democracy after 379 were members,[70] any links with earlier pro-democratic factions are not demonstrable.[71] A financial windfall that Ismenias received at some point before 400 enabled him to become the leader of this new faction.[72] It took power "a little earlier" (μικρῷ πρότερον) than 395. The term is elastic, and there has been much dispute over when the changeover happened, with suggestions varying from 404 to 397.

The Cooling of Boiotian-Spartan Relations

The faction of Eurymachos and Leontiades remained in a dominating position in the state down at least to 404. The first unequivocal evidence that the Boiotian-Spartan alliance was heading for trouble comes from the meeting of the Council of the Allies in the winter of 405/4, after Aigospotamoi. The Corinthian and Boiotian delegates argued for wiping out (ἐξαιρεῖν) Athens, but the Spartans said they would not agree to this, because of the great Athenian services to Greece against the Persians. This was a severe snub, especially for Thebes, which had fought on the Persian side and had not rendered any services to Hellas after Thermopylai. Probably the real reason for the Spartan action was to curb the aggressiveness of the Boiotians.[73] The Boiotian delegate, identified in Plutarch (*Lys.* 15.2) as Erianthos, was later alleged to have exceeded his instructions.[74] Erianthos had held a senior command during the battle of Aigospotamoi, and so as a high officer, a navarch, he should have been a member of or involved with Leontiades' group. The rejection by Sparta would have been a defeat for both the League and the faction of Leontiades: the repudiation of Thebes (and Leontiades) by the leader and ideological model, as well as the intrinsically barbarous inhumanity of the Boiotian proposal, could both be capitalized upon by any opponents, such as the members of the faction of Ismenias. It was similar Spartan behaviour in the 460s to the Athenians that had given his rivals the chance to bring down the great leader Kimon. The allegations that Erianthos exceeded his instructions sound like the defensive explanations of a beleaguered administration.[75]

Sparta's attitude indicated that Boiotia should look to her own interests even more than before. For the Boiotians a policy that encouraged *stasis* among the Athenians, such as one that supported a dissident faction, would be very useful. If it won, then a friendly group in power might be grateful and even repay favours. If it lost, the quarrels might keep Athens weakened indefinitely, especially if it had commanded popular support. In the spring of 404 came the conditional peace with Athens and shortly thereafter the rise of the Thirty Tyrants.

By the summer of 404 the change in Boiotian policy becomes apparent. The Boiotians demanded a tithe of the booty from Dekeleia for Ptoan Apollo.[76] By making this claim they gave a severe diplomatic insult to King Agis, almost as harsh as the one against Agesilaus some years later.[77] The Spartans gave way, but even ten years afterward they still were bitter about it.[78] Then the Boiotians began to give aid and shelter to the Athenian democrats, at about the same time as or a little later than the tithe incident.[79] It is no coincidence that the principal support for these Athenians came from members of the faction of Ismenias. *Hellenica Oxyrhynchia* indicates that it was primarily a matter of political expediency.[80] Then the Boiotians in general, not simply the Thebans, gave open support for the exiles, and the League government (presumably under the influence of the Ismenian faction) refused to extradite them at the request of the Thirty and Sparta.[81] By the end of 404 the change was complete. Boiotia and Sparta, though still officially allies, were now coldly correct and unfriendly. Surely the change reflects some shift in factional relations, with the Ismenian group becoming more influential.

It is clear that the Ismenian group began to gain some authority, after a sufficient number of hoplite and cavalry voters, and Federal Councillors, looked to them for leadership. There are hints, too, that Spartan attempts to strengthen Leontiades' faction may have backfired.[82]

The support given to the Athenian democrats was in line with the Boiotian factional policies of self-interest, self-preservation and self-advancement. The Boiotians were careful to preserve their position as an equal ally of Sparta, and not to provoke Spartan reprisals and continued in this way for several years. After the defeat of Athens the general situation altered, as did the Boiotian view of Sparta.

III   Boiotia Between the Wars, 404–395 B.C.

 The history of this period is full of difficult problems. Among the most recalcitrant are the sequence of events leading up to the outbreak of the Corinthian War, and the initial stages of the war itself.[1] Part of the trouble is that the three main sources, Xenophon's *Hellenika*, the *Hellenica Oxyrhynchia*, and Pausanias, do not agree in crucial areas on what happened or why it happened, and there is a temptation to pick and choose from the sources whatever fits one's preconceptions.

Thebes and the Boiotian League had, from the end of the Peloponnesian War, grown increasingly hostile to their old ally, Sparta. They came out of the Peloponnesian War enriched and prosperous, with enhanced prestige and an enlarged territory.[2] The faction that had dominated the state for most of the War, that of Leontiades and his friends, was losing power and influence to another one, that of Ismenias. The process had begun shortly after the Battle of Aigospotamoi. Since both factions were found throughout Boiotia, and their leaders were not drawn simply from Thebes, we may conclude that the change in opinion was general throughout the League. Leontiades and his group were generally pro-Spartan, while Ismenias and his friends were generally anti-Spartan. They also displayed a fairly benign attitude towards the Athenian democrats. Their feelings toward Sparta were apparently reciprocated.[3]

Boiotia and Athens

The Boiotians, probably under the guidance of Ismenias' faction, refused a Spartan request to send a force against the Athenian democrats when the latter were occupying the Peiraieus in 404/3,[4] and they preserved a benevolent neutrality during all the complex manoeuvres that eventually led to the restoration of democracy and the elimination of the Thirty Tyrants. They did, however, seize two talents worth of goods from Attica in recompense for a defaulted payment.[5] It was apparently not taken too seriously.

The price of Boiotian support for the Athenian democrats may well have been Athenian noninterference at Oropos: this would explain the somewhat surprising "hands-off" attitude of the Athenian state towards the Boiotian annexation, which happened about 401.[6] Oropos controlled good lines of access to Boiotia from Attica, including the usual invasion route;[7] a success such as that of bringing the town into the League would bring much credit to the faction deemed responsible, presumably that of Ismenias.[8]

Eleutherai, too, may have been regained for Boiotia about this time, if not earlier. A recent study argues that the guard towers above the site of Eleutherai are of Boiotian pattern, not Athenian.[9] If the identification of the site of Gyphtokastro as Eleutherai and the conclusions about the type of towers are both correct, then Eleutherai could have become Boiotian by 401, if not at the time when Oinoë was taken, in 411.

Boiotia and Sparta

A small force of mercenaries went from Boiotia in 401/400 with Cyrus.[10] Whether or not it was authorized by the Boiotian federal officials is unknown, but the expedition had the approval of the Spartan authorities.[11]

The faction of Ismenias was probably in charge in 400/399, when the League, along with Corinth, refused to join the other Spartan allies in a campaign against Elis.[12]

In 399/8 the Spartans resumed control over Herakleia. The Lakedaimonians sent a military expedition, probably by way of Boiotia, to restore order and quell *stasis*. It was commanded by Herippidas, but Lysander may have accompanied him.[13] The Spartans expelled the inhabitants of the neighbouring territories, notably those of Oite, who had rebelled. These went as refugees to Thessaly; from here they were restored to their homeland by the Boiotians in 395/4.[14] To judge by an anecdote reported by Plutarch, there may have been some protest at the Spartan passage through Boiotian territory. The Boiotians "tried to play a double game (ἐπαμφοτερίζοντας)," and Lysander asked them whether he should march through their land with spears upright or levelled.[15] But there was no overt resistance, even if some unease.[16] Although the Spartans were clearly hemming the Boiotians in, apparently the faction of Ismenias did not feel itself in a position at this time to oppose the Spartans too vigorously.[17] Perhaps this incident helped to harden Boiotian popular opinion further against Sparta.[18]

By autumn 397 the faction of Ismenias, or maybe the Boiotian Council, felt strong enough to risk an open rupture with the Spartan government. The Boiotians refused to send troops to support the expedition of Agesilaus against Persia. In an effort to change their minds, Aristomenidas, one of the Spartan judges who had condemned the Plataians in 427, was sent to them as an envoy. He had "excellent relations" with the Thebans (especially, one may infer, with Leontiades and his group, the governing faction during most of the Peloponnesian War), but he returned empty-handed.[19] It was no doubt disappointing, as well as a cause for Spartan dissatisfaction, that the second most powerful state in Greece refused to follow its lead.

In the spring of 396 King Agesilaus and a few companions landed from a single trireme at Aulis[20] and wished to sacrifice as "Agamemnon had sacrificed before going to Troy" (Xen. *Hell.* 3.4.4).[21] The Boiotarchs sent junior officials (ἱππέας [Xen.] or ὑπηρέτας [Plut.]) to stop him and to make plain their displeasure at his acts. The ostensible reason (given by Plutarch [*Ages.* 6]) was that he had ordered his own *mantis* to perform the rites and not the regular one appointed by the Boiotians. A claim to use one's own *mantis* might have political dimensions unacceptable to Boiotia. Agesilaus was enraged, and the Spartans much annoyed. By this act the Boiotians rejected any implications of any Spartan claim to a Homeric-style pre-eminence or hegemony in Greece. They now had administered strong personal insults to two imperious Spartan kings, this time under the guise of protecting τὰ πά-τρια Βοιωτῶν.[22] No doubt in this way the Ismenian faction ensured voter support and checkmated its opponents.[23] Agesilaus departed for Asia Minor, and the Persians had a Spartan invasion to contend with.

It was no doubt expected by the Ismenian faction that there would be repercussions.[24] The Spartans, though seriously annoyed, were not ready to resort to arms against an ally, as yet. They had Herakleia, Phokis and a network of alliances blocking the Boiotians to the west and towards Thessaly, as well as a considerable measure of support in Boiotia itself.[25] The Boiotians had one ally, the Lokrians, although whether these were the Opuntian or the Ozolian Lokrians or both is unclear, since the various sources disagree. Cartledge has pointed out that certain conditions had to be met before there was any chance of fighting successfully: Sparta had to be so aggressive as to frighten various other states; she had to show signs of internal discord; there had to be financial backing; and Boiotia and Athens would have to ally themselves.[26] The aggression against Elis and other states was sufficiently frightening; the conspiracy of Kinadon must have become widely known and duly considered. The other two requirements were soon met.

The Outbreak of the Boiotian War

The sources all say that at some stage (though no one is quite sure when) Timokrates of Rhodes went to Greece on behalf of the Persians with 50 "silver talents worth of gold," to bring over various leaders against Sparta; that is, to buy a war and so get Agesilaus out of Persian territory. All our sources claim that the leaders of the Ismenian faction, Ismenias, Androkleidas and Galaxidoros, were bribed to get Sparta involved in a war in Greece.[27] They somehow engineered a conflict, the opening preliminaries of the Boiotian War, which in turn was the

opening round of the Corinthian War. What happened precisely is uncertain, since the sources, the *Hellenica Oxyrhynchia,* Pausanias and
Xenophon, go off in various directions. The disagreements at this point
are, however, so severe that even this part about the mission of
Timokrates and the bribery is open to challenge.

None of the three main sources agree (1) where precisely the initial
incident of the Boiotian War happened, (2) which states were involved,
(3) what incident started the fighting, and (4) how it all happened.

First, where did the initial incident happen? There was, as all agree,
some disputed territory. Xenophon (*Hell.* 3.5.3) puts it between the
Phokians and the Opuntian Lokrians; the author of the *Hellenica Oxyrhynchia* (18.3) says it was near Parnassos, which is nowhere near
Opuntian Lokris; and Pausanias (3.9.8) says only that it was near Phokis,
as one might expect if the Phokians were involved.

Second, which states were involved? They all have the Phokians as
one party, but Xenophon has the other as the Opuntian Lokrians; the
Hellenica Oxyrhynchia has the Hesperian Lokrians; and Pausanias says
it was the men from Amphissa. These last two were of course both
from western Lokris, but the difference in phraseology between Pausanias and the *Hellenica Oxyrhynchia* is indicative of their use of different sources.

Third, what was the incident was that sparked the fighting? Xenophon has the Opuntian Lokrians collect taxes from the disputed land;
the *Hellenica Oxyrhynchia,* very differently, has the Phokians attack the
Hesperian Lokrians over sheep-stealing; while Pausanias, differently
again, makes the Amphissans harvest grain as well as rustle sheep from
the disputed land.

Fourth, how it all happened is also very different. In Xenophon the
faction of Ismenias approached and persuaded the Opuntian Lokrians
to collect the taxes; in the *Hellenica Oxyrhynchia* the faction talked the
Phokians, not the Lokrians, into starting things, in this case by invading Hesperian Lokrian territory; and in Pausanias Ismenias and his
group persuaded the Amphissans to harvest grain and rustle sheep. It
is apparent that who did it and what they did are very different in the
various sources.

The escalation proceeds differently, too, in our three versions. In Xenophon the Opuntians' tax-gathering in the disputed territory provoked a Phokian invasion of Opous proper; the Opuntian Lokrians appeal to their ally Boiotia; Boiotia comes to their aid by invading northern Phokis; and the Phokians in turn cry for help to Sparta, which at that point comes to the rescue. In the *Hellenica Oxyrhynchia* the Phokians (persuaded by the Ismenian faction) invade Hesperian Lokris; the latter asks its ally Boiotia for help; the Boiotians mobilize; the Phokians at this point hastily withdraw, appealing to Sparta for help; the Spartans order arbitration; the Boiotians reject the command; all this before any Boiotian invasion. In Pausanias the Phokians, in revenge for the Amphissan harvesting and sheep stealing, invade the territory of Amphissa; the Amphissans appeal to Boiotia for help; the Boiotians invade Phokis; the Phokians in turn call on Sparta.

The three versions are a tissue of mutual contradictions, and it is not surprising that many modern authorities entirely reject all their testimony.[28] This is too drastic. Whatever else one may conclude from all this, it is clear that there was in the time of Xenophon a widespread belief that the faction of Ismenias was behind the outbreak of the Boiotian War. Ismenias and his gang somehow did it.

Why the faction of Ismenias should have chosen whatever way they did, but one certainly devious, for starting the war is also given differently in the three versions, too. Xenophon (3.5.3) says that the faction was in effect provoking the *Spartans* into fighting, and that the latter were glad to have the opportunity. The Oxyrhynchus Historian (13.2), however, says that Ismenias and his group were trying by trickery (ἀπάτη) to push the *Boiotians* into eventually fighting the Spartans.[29] Pausanias (3.9.8–11), different again, makes the intervention of Ismenias a straightforward *quid pro quo* for bribes from Timokrates, with a last-minute (and doubtless fictional) abortive intervention by Athens.

There are at least two kinds of inherent improbabilities in the versions given in the *Hellenica Oxyrhynchia* and by Pausanias, geographic and diplomatic. First, the geographic: as Lerat[30] long ago pointed out, the slopes of Mount Parnassos mentioned in the *Hellenica Oxyrhynchia*, the ones that bordered on West Lokris, are not Phokian. They belonged to Delphi, not Phokis. Any disputed area of the kind mentioned by Pausanias, between Amphissa and Phokis, would be well down toward Krisa, and it ought properly to belong to other west Lokrian towns, like Chalaion or Ditaia, not Amphissa.

Second, the diplomatic: an alliance made by the Boiotians with the West Lokrians rather than with their neighbours, the Opuntian Lokrians, is hardly credible. Thucydides reports (3.101.2) that the western Lokrians in general and the Amphissans in particular were terrified of making enemies of the Phokians; but the Opuntian Lokrians and the Phokians had fought recently (Thuc. 5.32.2). The Opuntians were close neighbours of Boiotia and old allies, and they were old-time enemies of Phokis. The campaign launched by Boiotia was in northern Phokis, an area where pressure would directly assist Opuntian Lokris, not Western Lokris. Furthermore, as Lerat pointed out, we know from other sources of one important area of dispute between Opuntian Lokris and Phokis, one that had nothing to do with Parnassos, the seaport of Daphnous.[31] The strip of land in which it sat bisected the East Lokrian territory, separating Opuntian from Epiknemidian Lokris, and it was the subject of much fighting. It is understandable that Boiotia would be willing to support its neighbour against the Phokians, especially if the League were feeling surrounded.[32] Finally, the idea in the *Hellenica Oxyrhynchia* of the Boiotians persuading the perennially hostile Phokians rather than the traditionally friendly Opuntian Lokrians to further their underhanded policies is intrinsically improbable.[33]

Cook[34] argues with considerable ingenuity that all these versions are complementary rather than inconsistent or contradictory. It seems better, however, to reject the testimony of the Oxyrhynchus historian and Pausanias and with it reject the motivations and reasons they give for the outbreak of the Boiotian-Spartan dispute. It is possible that the *Hellenica Oxyrhynchia* and Pausanias may have confused incidents of the Third Sacred War and the Amphissan War with happenings of the Boiotian War, as Meyer and Busolt thought,[35] though this does not seem likely, given the differences between the Wars.[36] The versions of the events leading up to the war in the *Hellenica Oxyrhynchia* and in Pausanias, and the motivations they present, each form a tightly-knit unit, and if any part of the unit is rejected, the whole of that version must go. That leaves us with Xenophon.

Xenophon (3.5.1–3.5.5) says that the Boiotian leaders were bribed by Timokrates with Persian gold to make war on Sparta. They then induced the Opuntians to exercise their claim to territory in dispute with Phokis (presumably Daphnous) realizing how the escalation would go. It went according to plan. The Phokians invaded Opuntian territory, the Boiotians mobilized a force that invaded Phokis, and the Phokians appealed to Sparta. Sparta, delighted, mobilized, and the war was on.

Xenophon, however, is notorious for his anti-Boiotian bias.[37] Pelopidas and Epaminondas, for example, are never mentioned, in spite of all they did, until Book 7 of the *Hellenika*, well after the Battle of Leuktra. His treatment of the Thebans is infamous for his ascription of the worst motives and lowest behaviour to them. His ready acceptance of the idea that the Boiotian leaders were bribed into anti-Spartan behaviour is, I conclude, a case in point. Bribery is a standard fourth-century accusation against any politician, but I do not think that Ismenias and his friends really needed much bribing. They had been anti-Spartan for years, as the author of the *Hellenica Oxyrhynchia* (7.2) is careful to point out. No doubt Timokrates came around; but it seems more reasonable to believe that he promised Persian funding for military operations, with the gold as a guarantee that he was on the level, with a little something for the leaders as a "gift." The Boiotians, like their other allies, did receive large Persian subventions during the Corinthian War, as the author of the *Hellenica Oxyrhynchia* points out (18.1); the Persians did indeed buy a war in Greece, even if their payments were somewhat slow and irregular.[38]

The inconsistent stories of how Ismenias and his followers were bribed, and what they did to carry out their part of the deal should be rejected. It is reasonable to suggest that they all stem from the same dubious source: the charges and accusations made during the trials and purges of Ismenias and the Ismenian faction after the Spartan occupation of Thebes in 382.[39] We know that Ismenias was then tried by a Spartan tribunal for Medism, taking bribes, collaborating with the King and instigating the war. He was, of course, found guilty and put to death.[40]

We of this twentieth century have seen too many "trials" of that type to put much credence in their character-blackening evidence. Perhaps in the face of persistent opposition from the Orchomenian representatives on the Federal Council, abetted by Spartan intrigues, as well as from the efforts of the faction of Leontiades, Ismenias and his group may have felt that they had to work through their Lokrian allies.[41] It is also possible, though on the evidence I doubt it, that the flare-up had nothing to do with Boiotia, but was something that arose from Opuntian-Phokian relations and led the Lokrians to invoke their alliance with Boiotia and the Phokians theirs with Sparta.

The Persians guaranteed funding for what everyone recognized would be a long and hard war. Assured of financial support and given a down payment the Boiotians seized upon one of the long-standing disputes between their ally Opuntian Lokris and Phokis, in order to support the Lokrians vigorously. When things got hot, they invaded northern Phokis and relieved pressure on their allies. Whether Daphnous remained in Phokian hands is unknown.

The Boiotian War

The *Hellenica Oxyrhynchia* (18.5) gives the only detailed account of the course of the early part of the "Boiotian War,"[42] one rather neglected by most authorities and rejected by Busolt on insufficient grounds.[43] The area of operations was the upper Kephissos valley, immediately adjacent to Opuntian Lokris. One might infer that it was a successful Boiotian attempt to relieve pressure on their allies by attacking at harvest season and ravaging the land of the towns from which, presumably, most of the invaders of Lokris had come. Whether or not the Boiotians intended to occupy the area is impossible to say, but if any of their assaults on the fortified towns had succeeded, no doubt they might have given some consideration to annexation.[44] Since, however, a Spartan reaction was to be expected, it seems not unlikely that it was simply a "smash-and-grab" raid, especially as the force was mobilized διὰ ταχέων, which may well mean "hastily gathered, not the full levy."[45] The Boiotians marched into Phokis from their forward base at Orchomenos ravaging the land and eventually withdrawing. Their route took them back by way of Hyampolis to Orchomenos, where they no doubt disbanded.

The faction of Leontiades, Asias and Koiratadas was, as we have emphasized, usually pro-Spartan; it was doubtless supported by Sparta. But foreign policy surely did not form the only area for factional disputes in Boiotia. There was undoubtedly support at home for this faction on other political aspects. At this time it seems to have been less in favour of a strong, centralized League than the Ismenian faction, to judge from its behaviour, as in its treatment of Oropos in 409 and in its acquiescence in the dissolution of the League after the King's Peace in 387.[46] Such a faction might well be more popular in such areas as Orchomenos, which since 447/6 seems to have been strongly pro-oligarchic, and not particularly pro-League. The destruction of Orchomenos in 364 was the result of its involvement in an oligarchic attempt at an anti-democratic and anti-League coup.[47] Perhaps also Sparta had been intriguing with Orchomenos to hamper the furthering of Ismenias' policies.[48]

If Orchomenos were a centre of anti-League sentiment, as well as being a strong supporter of Leontiades' faction, its behaviour in seceding becomes more understandable. Orchomenos will have been a permanent base of opposition and by the time of the Boiotian War disaffected towards a League dominated by the faction of Ismenias.

The Spartan Attack

When the Boiotians invaded Phokis in aid of the Lokrians, the Phokians promptly sent to Sparta for aid, and the Lakedaimonians, apparently urged on by Lysander,[49] provided it. Xenophon (*Hell.* 3.5.5) says that the Spartans were particularly incensed *inter alia* over the treatment of Agesilaus. Lysander was given the job of raising an army from Phokis, Oite, Herakleia, Malis and Ainianis and of attacking from the west, while King Pausanias with the Peloponnesian allies was to invade from the south.[50] The strategy of concentric attacks was not dissimilar to that attempted by the Athenians thirty years earlier, at the time of the battle of

Delion. It may even be that the pro-Spartan factions played the same sort of disloyal rôle now that the pro-democrats had played then.[51]

The Athenian Alliance

The Boiotians, once it was clear that the Lakedaimonians were going to invade, sent envoys to Athens to seek an alliance.[52] Xenophon reports that they pointed out the favours owed them, especially by the democrats; they urged a Grand Alliance against the Spartans; they noted the hatred felt against the harmosts; and they hinted at a revival of the Athenian Empire in all its glory. The Athenian reply, voted unanimously and delivered by one of the prominent democrats, one who had also been a leader of the exiles based in Boiotia, Thrasyboulos, was to accept the Boiotian-Athenian alliance.[53] Probably at the same time a similar alliance was concluded with Lokris. The texts of both the Boiotian and the Lokrian treaties are partially preserved.[54]

Athens was willing to become a Boiotian ally at this time because of the growing suspicion and fear of Sparta; then, too, there were the defection of Rhodes from the Spartan alliance and the promises of financial aid from the Persian envoy. The King was anxious to buy a war and remove the Spartans from Asia Minor.

The Battle of Haliartos

Lysander moved into western Boiotia with his allies in the summer of 395.[55] Orchomenos immediately joined him and "revolted from the Thebans."[56] The eagerness and promptness with which Orchomenos seceded from the Federation has been explained in different ways,[57] but it seems clear that it was disaffected and full of pro-Spartan sentiment. Such feelings, plus dissatisfaction with a Federal Council dominated by Ismenias' group, a Council that went to war with Phokis without weighing the severe hardships that its own army would impose on the Orchomenians at harvest time, would help to explain its swift and enthusiastic adherence to Lysander.[58]

Lysander with the northern forces then advanced on Haliartos. This was a key spot on Lake Copaïs, on the route along the south shore between eastern and western Boiotia. By arrangement he and Pausanias had made this their meeting point, no doubt after the adherence of Orchomenos.[59] On the way Lysander plundered Lebadeia and apparently by-passed Koroneia.[60] Meanwhile Pausanias with the Peloponnesians (except for Corinth) thrust northward around Kithairon to Plataia to meet Lysander at Haliartos.[61] Their co-ordination was off, however, and when a messenger was intercepted, the Thebans were able to intervene effectively.[62] Lysander got to Haliartos several days before Pausanias and perhaps tried to win a victory before Pausanias arrived.[63] There was no love lost between the two.

Xenophon (*Hell.* 3.5.18–20) reports that Lysander tried to enter the town, after abortive attempts to get it to secede; the Haliartans, reinforced by a Theban detachment, held him off. While Lysander was making an assault on the wall, the main Theban force attacked on the rear, with both horse and foot. The battle took place beside the wall, and Lysander fell. His troops broke and fled to rough country, where they rallied and repulsed their pursuers, inflicting some casualties on them. The Phokians and the other allies then retired home after suffering heavy losses; the Thebans had more than 200 dead.

Plutarch (*Lys.* 28.2–6) gives a slightly more circumstantial version. Lysander was making a very swift approach when his message to Pausanias was intercepted. An Athenian hoplite force, which had just arrived at Thebes, was left to guard the city, while the main Theban force made a hasty night march, arriving at Haliartos a little ahead of Lysander. The Thebans left a detachment to reinforce the Haliartans, and the rest of the Theban force got around behind the enemy "at the spring called Kissousa."[64] The texts all refer to "Thebans." The Thespians and Tanagraians may have been guarding their respective towns against Pausanias. The troops of Koroneia, Akraiphnion and Kopai were presumably similarly deployed against Lysander. Or it may be that the speed of the Spartan attack caught the Boiotians behindhand in their preparations.[65] When Lysander's force attacked Haliartos, the defenders opened the gates and counter-attacked. In the fight Lysander was killed along with his *mantis*. One Neochoros of Haliartos was credited with slaying him.[66] His troops were driven back, and then the main Theban force attacked from the rear. This is different from the version in Xenophon, where the sortie occurs *after* the attack by the main force. At any rate, Lysander's men broke and fled into rough country, where they managed to make a stand and rally. They lost over 1000, while the Thebans lost 300 (not Xenophon's "over 200"), mostly in the rough country. Many of the latter were of the faction of Leontiades. Plutarch emphasizes that they were "eager to clear themselves [of the charge of Lakonizing] with the citizens, and as they were reckless of their lives they threw them away."

By the morning of the following day the Phokians and the others had withdrawn, but later during the same day Pausanias and his Peloponnesians appeared, causing, according to Xenophon, some alarm and despondency among the Thebans and the Haliartans. The Spartans did not advance, however. On the day after that the Athenians marched from Thebes and joined the Boiotians in the field.[67] Pausanias did not move against this now large and confident force. Instead, since the morale of *his* army was very low, Pausanias arranged a truce, so as to recover the Lakedaimonian dead, especially Lysander.[68] He retired westward into Phokis, in this way keeping Orchomenos under control. A Spartan garrison secured it.

Orchomenos and the League

The juridical position of Orchomenos in the Boiotian League at this point is unknown. Roesch has made a good suggestion: that the two shares of Orchomenos in the government were exercised by Orchomenian refugees in Thebes, or perhaps by Thebes on their behalf.[69] This would be much the arrangement that the oligarchic Plataians had when they (or Thebes for them) exercised their two shares after they moved to Thebes. The refugees would have been recognized as the *polis*; the political unit would still have been in existence; precisely where the Orchomenian *Demos* resided was a matter of indifference. The movements of the Orchomenians and Plataians are, in a sense, synoecisms. These are precedents for some of the actions of the democratic League in the 370s. On the other hand, it is a possibility that the seceding members' seats remained vacant, as in the U.S. Congress during the Civil War. The idea, however, that the shares continued to be exercised at Thebes does fit with the evidence about Plataia.

Lysander was buried in the territory of Panopeus, "by the road going from Chaironeia to Delphi."[70] Pausanias returned to the Peloponnese to face disgrace and eventual exile for this truce. This season's fighting according to Plutarch (*Lys.* 27.1) was termed the "Boiotian War." It is a reasonable inference that the title derives from a pro-Spartan source.

The Congress and Alliance

The alliance between Boiotia and Athens led to the summoning in the winter of 395 of a congress at Corinth, of the Boiotians, Athenians, Argives and Corinthians. It was decided to form a Grand Alliance against Sparta.[71] The four states then sent envoys to many states, especially to allies of Lakedaimon, asking them to join; many of them defected and did so: all of Euboia, Leukas, Akarnania, Ambrakia, and much of the Chalkidike, but none of the Peloponnesians did, beyond those who already were members. A Council to establish unified strategy and control operations was agreed upon.

The question of why Corinth and the other states joined with Boiotia has been the subject of much discussion.[72] Clearly, hatred and fear of Sparta played the primary part, no doubt aided by economic dislocation resulting from the Peloponnesian War and by Persian promises of financial support. Sparta's brutality and arrogance were all too apparent; the citizens of most states were not accustomed to be treated like helots.

The first military act of the Congress was to send 2000 hoplites to Thessaly to help Medios of Larissa. With their aid he gained Pharsalos from the Lakedaimonians.[73] The alliance with Medios was probably to secure cavalry, and it was of some assistance when Agesilaus returned through Thessaly in the next year. His entry into Boiotia was delayed by a few days.

The next act, in late 395 or early 394, was to send an expedition-
ary force of Boiotians and some Argives under the command of Ismenias against Herakleia. A night assault delivered the town to them. They
restored to their own land the Trachinian refugees previously exiled by
the Spartans.[74] Leaving the Argives to garrison the town, the Boiotians
then persuaded the Ainianes and Athamanes to revolt from Sparta and
provide troops. With a little fewer than 6000 men Ismenias then invaded
Phokis. He encamped near Naryx in Epiknemidian Lokris. Shortly
thereafter he met the Phokians, who were under the command of the
Lakonian Alkisthenes. After a long hard fight the Boiotians were victorious, killing about 1000 for 500 of their own. Then they returned
home.[75]

IV Boiotia in the Corinthian War, 394–387 B.C.

 The Boiotians had an important rôle in the Corinthian War and fought hard and well, suffering many casualties. They provided a major part of the land forces and worked closely and effectively with Athens and the other Allies. Their association lasted until the lack of funds consequent on the King's Peace, as well as some Spartan successes, brought an end to hostilities. The factions of Kephalos and Thrasyboulos in Athens and of Ismenias in Boiotia played an important part in keeping the two neighbours together, though the relationship was sometimes uneasy.

Recall of Agesilaus

The danger presented to Sparta by the formation of the Grand Alliance among Boiotia, Athens, Corinth and Argos was regarded as so grave that in early 394 the government summoned Agesilaus home from Asia Minor. There was much booty to bring back, and with the naval situation becoming increasingly serious, it was perhaps inexpedient to sail to Greece. The Peloponnesian fleet had sufficient difficulties to cope with, and Peisandros, the Spartan naval commander, was outnumbered.[1] Agesilaus returned by land, crossing the Hellespont and following the path of Xerxes, as all the sources are careful to point out.[2] It was a good way to shore up Spartan fortunes in Macedonia, northern Greece, Thessaly and central Greece. The route also led to Boiotia.

43

The Battle of Nemea

Since the second king, Agesipolis, was still a minor, the Spartans appointed Aristodemos to command the home forces, and in early 394 he began to assemble his army. The plan was to pick up various allied contingents as he proceeded north through the Peloponnese to meet the forces of the Grand Alliance.[3] Since most of the hoplites were farmers, this meant that the campaign could not begin until after the harvest was completed, sometime in June.[4]

The Grand Alliance at about the same time began to concentrate its forces at Corinth, under the same constraints, and its contingents, too, were slow to come in.[5] The proposal of Timolaus of Corinth, to catch the Spartans as close to Sparta as possible, just as one kills wasps in their nest before they can get out, was sensible advice.[6] But it was overtaken by events.

After picking up the Tegeans and Mantineans, Aristodemos and the Spartans moved north to the Corinthian Gulf in Sikyonian territory and prepared to move east on Corinth.[7] Meanwhile the forces of the Grand Alliance were advancing from Corinth in a southerly direction towards Lakonia and were nearing the town of Nemea.[8] In other words each force was advancing against its enemy's main base, in what is sometimes called the "revolving door," much as the French and Germans started to do to one another in 1914. But the Spartans were closer to their opponents' base. The latter were forced to return to block the Spartan advance. It is of some interest that specialized troops (Xenophon's γυμνῆτες [*Hell.* 4.2.1]) were able to inflict heavy casualties on the advancing Peloponnesian force in the area of Epieikeia.[9] The Peloponnesians broke through, however, and reached the coastal plain, where they began devastating the country and firing the crops (presumably those not yet harvested). The forces of the Grand Alliance returned and fortified a position with the gully of the Rachiani in front.[10] This put them some 4 km west of Corinth and the site of the battle in the plain between the Rachiani and the River Nemea.[11]

There is much confusion over the numbers of combatants, but Pritchett and Anderson are probably correct in estimating that each side deployed about 23,000 to 24,000 hoplites.

Both sides waited a few days, and after some shifting of Allied contingents (snidely commented on by Xenophon [*Hell.* 4.2.18] who imputes cowardice to all concerned), the Boiotians took over the right wing opposite the enemy left, which consisted of Achaians and Sikyonians; the Athenians held the left wing opposite the Peloponnesian right wing, where the Spartans were. Whether the shifts imply a rotation of command,[12] or a brief and abortive struggle for control of the land forces between Boiotia and Athens,[13] remains unknown. Either is possible, though the former seems preferable, since it was the more usual.

Tactically the battle is of some interest, because the Boiotians tried to mass forces on one wing, as they had apparently done at Delion, in an anticipation of their manoeuvre at Leuktra; and because the Spartans evolved a drill for outflanking and rolling up the opposing left wing. In this case the drill worked, and the Spartans swept the battlefield. The forces of the Grand Alliance fled in disorder and were excluded from Corinth. They eventually returned to their old camp.

It was a victory for the Spartans, but not a decisive one. The Boiotians had demolished the Peloponnesian left wing and apparently withdrew in fairly good order; the Athenians came off with comparatively few casualties. The defeat did not dissolve the Alliance, as the defeat at Mantinea had done in 418. It ensured, however, that the Allies continued to have respect for the fighting qualities of the Spartans, and that no other state from the Peloponnese made any effort to join them. Ismenias' dominant position in Boiotia does not seem to have been impaired, but the Allied forces seem to have spent some time in occupying fortifications in the Corinthia, so as to help block the Spartans in the Peloponnese and to hold Corinth.[14] As a consequence the Allies were slow in moving north to Boiotia to meet Agesilaus. No doubt they had little intelligence on his exact whereabouts, and perhaps they expected the Thessalians to slow him down more than they did. The Battle of Koroneia cannot have been much more than a month after Nemea.[15]

The Battle of Koroneia

Meanwhile Agesilaus was advancing through northern Greece. He had reached Amphipolis when he received the news of the Spartan victory at Nemea.[16] He continued to advance, but he ran into resistance from the Boiotian allies in Thessaly, the people of Larissa, Krannon, Skotousa and Pharsalos, who slowed down his progress. They were, however, defeated in a cavalry battle and consequently were unable to stop him (Xen. *Hell.* 4.3.5–8). According to Xenophon (*Hell.* 4.3.9) on the day after this battle Agesilaus crossed the mountains of Achaia Phthiotis and, apparently by-passing Herakleia, proceeded through friendly territory (Oite, Malis, Doris and Phokis) before turning to attack Boiotia. This should mean, if Xenophon is correct, that he did not pass through Thermopylai, which was in Lokrian territory; Plutarch (*Ages.* 17.2), then, is in error on this point.[17]

The Boiotians, meanwhile, did not move up into Phokis or into the area around Thermopylai to block Agesilaus. The speed of his advance probably caught them by surprise.[18] When he was about to enter Boiotia, there was an eclipse of the sun. This can be dated to August 14, 394 B.C., and gives us one of the very few reasonably secure dates for this period. At the time of the eclipse Agesilaus learnt of the Spartan naval defeat off Knidos, a battle that marked the end of its naval hegemony.[19] The Spartans lost most of the islands and the Greek cities of Asia Minor.

Agesilaus lied to his troops about Knidos, claiming that Peisandros had been killed in the moment of victory, "since his men were the kind of people who were glad enough to share in good fortune, but whom he did not consider the sort to share any difficulties with."[20] By this time the forces of the Grand Alliance had moved up into Boiotia; Agesilaus was reinforced by the Orchomenians, Phokians and other allies from central Greece, half a *mora* of the Lakedaimonian garrison of Orchomenos, and one or two *morai* from the Peloponnese.[21] His original force included *neodamodeis*, a mercenary force under Herippidas, contingents from the cities of Asia Minor and other mercenaries, including Xenophon. The forces of the Grand Alliance were Boiotians,

Athenians, Argives, Corinthians, Euboians, Ainianes and both Opuntian and Ozolian Lokrians.[22] Both sides were about equal, approximately 20,000 to 24,000 each.

A first skirmish, somewhere on the frontiers of Boiotia, was a victory for Agesilaus, and he advanced from the Orchomenian area south to the neighbourhood of Koroneia, while the forces of the Grand Alliance came north from the slopes of Helikon. In the ensuing fight they were defeated but not decisively, falling back on Helikon.

The battle is of interest because the heavy Boiotian phalanx was able to carve its way (after breaking the Orchomenians) through the Spartan forces to join its retreating allies on Helikon. They wounded Agesilaus in the process.[23] Though tactically it was an Allied loss, strategically it was a stand-off, or even a gain for the Grand Alliance: Agesilaus, though ordered to invade Boiotia, found he was too weak to do so;[24] and he even lacked the strength to overcome and hold down Ozolian Lokris.[25] He managed to get the booty back to Sparta, but he did little for the Spartan cause in the North.

There is no record of further fighting on land in 394. The Peloponnesian army crossed the Gulf of Corinth in Peloponnesian ships, and it disbanded as soon as it landed. Presumably most of the forces of the Grand Alliance returned home, too. It was probably now that Athens began to consider rebuilding her naval power, as she continued the rebuilding of her walls. It is to be noted that the islands and the coastal cities of Asia Minor joined "those with Konon" and so were in the way of being more closely associated with Athens than with the Grand Alliance.

The War Continues: 393 B.C.

Although it must have been apparent to all that it was going to be a long war, there is no evidence for any shift in Boiotia towards peace. The year had seen Sparta fight several pitched battles by land and sea in an attempt to crush the Grand Alliance. On land the Spartans had won the battlefields, but not the war. On sea their overconfidence and arrogance had led to their crushing defeat at Knidos and their loss of control of the Aegean. Sparta was losing the war, or at least the balance was shifting against her.

The key area, and recognized as such by both sides, was the Isthmus. Both Sparta and the Allies concentrated their efforts there, the latter basing themselves on Corinth, the former on Sikyon.[26] Since the Aegean was now an Allied lake, and the Isthmus could be forced only by heavy fighting, control of the Corinthian Gulf was vital for the Peloponnesians to maintain communication with the north and west. A naval struggle began, principally between Corinth and the Spartans, one that continued down until 391.[27] The Boiotians seem to have taken little or no part in it.

In the late spring or early summer of 393 there was a *synhedrion* of the Allies at Corinth, to which the Persian satrap Pharnabazos came with his admiral, the Athenian Konon, after a long string of successes against the Spartans. It is instructive to see the difference between how Xenophon and Diodorus report it. Xenophon (*Hell.* 4.8.8–9) says that the Persian Pharnabazos encouraged the Allies to continue fighting Sparta and to show themselves loyal (πιστοὺς) to the King. He felt he could trust them and left them a considerable sum of cash. The implication is that they were little better than hired lackeys of the King. Diodorus (14.84.5), following the Oxyrhynchus Historian (by way of Ephoros), says that Konon and Pharnabazos both attended the *synhedrion* and made an alliance (συμμαχίαν) with the Allies, who received cash. The Oxyrhynchus Historian makes it a partnership, not a clientage. Whichever version is preferred, clearly the Grand Alliance had a new official partner, and more cash was coming in.

Boiotia was willing to go on fighting. An indication of its enthusiasm for the struggle is the fact that when Konon arrived at Athens in the early summer of 393, after the meeting with the *synhedrion*, and the Long Walls began to rise again, among those helping put them up was a contingent of Boiotians. They were volunteers according to Xenophon (*Hell.* 4.8.10), but 500 craftsmen and masons according to the Oxyrhynchus Historian (Diod. 14.85.3). The inscriptional evidence supports the latter by indicating that at least one of them was a mason contractor.[28] Clearly the defence of Athens was regarded by the

Allies as important: it was then in Boiotian interests to have Athens fortified again, since it would provide a strong base and doubtless would release more Athenian troops for field duty. It seems that Ismenias and his friends still dominated Boiotia.

The funding provided by Pharnabazos and Konon was necessary for paying and maintaining the permanent garrisons manning various strong-points, such as Herakleia and the forts in the Corinthia, as well as the mercenary and naval forces. Since the Corinthia was where most of the skirmishing happened, it naturally suffered considerable damage to its rural areas, as Xenophon emphasizes (*Hell.* 4.4.1). There is no detailed record of any fighting, but it is certain that Boiotian contingents were involved. It is not until early in the next year, 392, that things became lively enough to be recorded.

The Coup at Corinth: 392 B.C.

There were signs of increasing disaffection and disloyalty to the Alliance among most of the Corinthian gentry (οἱ πλεῖστοι καὶ βέλτιστοι), the landed class, whose estates were being harried.[29] Their opponents, the democrats (τινὲς ἐπιθυμούντων δημοκρατίας),[30] were loyal to the Alliance. In late February or early March, 392, at the end of the festival of Artemis Eukleia, what might be termed a pre-emptive strike was launched against the gentry. The latter were all unsuspecting, and a great number were massacred while attending or presiding over various festival activities, and even while sitting as suppliants at the altars, about 120 according to Diodorus (14.86.2). Xenophon, probably wrongly,[31] says that the attacks and massacre were planned and carried out together by the Argives, Athenians, Boiotians and the loyal Corinthians ("those in receipt of funds from the King and those who were chiefly responsible for the war," in his impartial prose). The author of the *Hellenica Oxyrhynchia* (Diod. 14.86.1f.), better informed and less biased, says that the massacre was organized by pro-democrats, and that they began the killing. Then they were joined by the Argives, and together they slew 120 citizens and drove 500 into exile. "When the Lakedaimonians were preparing to restore the exiles and were concentrating a force, the Athenians and Boiotians came to the aid of those who carried out the massacre, so as to keep the city firmly on their side." Thus it seems likely that the pro-democrats, who were probably the more radical members of the mercantile and manufacturing class, supported by the craftsmen and workers,[32] planned and carried out the initial stages of the massacre. At this point they were joined by the Argives. Only when the Spartans were thought to be preparing to intervene did the Athenians and Boiotians reinforce the pro-democrats.

Some of the Corinthian exiles returned after a short time and, having made their peace with "the tyrants," began quietly plotting the overthrow of the new government. The democracy seems to have made some special arrangement with Argos, probably some form of sympolity.[33] It had strong enough popular support to drive the gentry to desperate measures to protect their land. In the summer some of them betrayed the city.[34]

The Peace Conference: I

Meanwhile, in late 393 or in the spring of 392, after the rebuilding of the Long Walls at Athens, the Spartans sent a mission headed by Antalkidas to the Persian commander of the land forces, Tiribazos. It must have been dispatched at about the time of the democratic revolution at Corinth, or possibly a little earlier. Antalkidas' purpose was to bring about a bilateral peace between Sparta and Persia. The lever for accomplishing this, according to Xenophon,[35] was the denunciation of Konon's activities in strengthening Athens, which rendered her once again a threat to all. It was therefore necessary for Persia and Sparta to form an alliance to counter this. As part of the deal Sparta would renounce any interest in the Greek states in Asia Minor. In return financial help would be acceptable.

The Athenians somehow heard of this mission[36] and decided to send one as well, probably unofficially,[37] including in it Konon. They invited the other allies to send missions, too, and the Argives, Boiotians and Corinthians did so. They all arrived at Sardis, and there was, according to Xenophon,[38] a full-scale debate. The meeting ended inconclusively, the main results being that Konon was arrested, the Spartans got a subvention, and Tiribazos felt it wise to consult King Artaxerxes in Susa.[39]

Tiribazos went to Susa, and, for whatever reason, was replaced by Strouthas, who was apparently a trouble-shooter sent to problem areas. He was also pro-Athenian, because of the damage that Agesilaus had done to the King's territories.[40] Ultimately this led to a complex situation: the Spartans in 391 sent a punitive force to raid the Asia Minor coast in a manner and for reasons that foreshadowed Sphodrias' raid on Peiraieus thirteen years later. It got itself roughly handled. Such behaviour did not ensure the transmission of more Persian funds.[41]

The Spartans had advanced the old programme from the Peloponnesian War, that all Greek cities should be autonomous. At least they were consistent in their propaganda. The proposal was clearly a hit at the Allies: at Athens and its nascent new island League; at Argos and its association with Corinth; and at the whole idea of the Boiotian League. It was *inter alia* an acknowledgement of Spartan obligations toward Orchomenos.[42]

In Boiotia it did little to strengthen any pro-Spartan sentiments among the ordinary Boiotian hoplite voters. Something else, however, may have weakened the position of Ismenias' faction, a military defeat.

Counter-revolution at Corinth: 392 B.C.

In the summer of 392 disaffected Corinthian gentry of the hoplite class treacherously admitted a Peloponnesian force to the long walls between the harbour of Lechaion and Corinth.[43] This separated a Boiotian garrison of unknown size in Lechaion from the main Allied force garrisoning Corinth. The invaders, two *morai* of Spartans, with Sikyonians and Corinthian exiles, defeated the Allied troops who sallied out from Corinth and wiped out the Boiotians in Lechaion in vicious street-fighting.[44] "The Boiotian garrison in Lechaion perished, some on the walls, others after climbing on the roofs of the ship-sheds." The town was captured, and the Spartans thereby destroyed the Corinthian naval power in the Corinthian Gulf.[45]

The Peace Conference: II

In the fall of 392[46] there was another abortive peace conference, this time at Sparta. This one is *not* reported by Xenophon, but we learn of it principally from Andokides (*de Pace* 27–29) and Philochoros (*FGrH* 328 F 149a). Preliminary articles were presented by the Spartans to the plenipotentiaries from Athens (among whom was Andokides), Boiotia, Corinth and Argos. Apparently these articles tried by some modifications to counter objections raised at Susa: recognition of the Athenian right to their walls and a fleet, as well as possession of various islands in the Aegean; the Boiotian League to be continued, except for Orchomenos; and, in spite of the testimony of Philochoros, the states of Asia Minor were to be free.[47] On the other hand the sympolity between Argos and Corinth was to be dissolved.[48]

These terms were apparently acceptable to the Athenian and Boiotian envoys, but not to the Argive and Corinthian. It seems for this reason, to judge from the tone of Andokides' speech, that the matter was referred back to Athens. Philochoros indicates that the Athenian Assembly was displeased with the ambassadors for their acceptance of the Peace and on the motion of Kallistratos exiled all of them in the archon year 392/1.[49]

It seems that the negotiations that led to the conference at Sparta were undertaken because of a certain war-weariness and the idea that Persian funds would not continue to be forthcoming.[50] This feeling was strengthened by the anti-Athenian policies of Tiribazos. The disappearance of Tiribazos and the coming of Strouthas in late 392 or early 391, with the prospect of more Persian funds, altered the situation and the feelings. The Allies were prepared to carry on the war.

Boiotia 392/1 B.C.

The political situation in Boiotia at this time is unknown, but the fact that the Boiotians, along with the Athenians, were at one point willing to negotiate with Sparta leads to the belief that the League was suffering financial difficulties, and that the faction of Ismenias was no longer commanding as much support. It was losing its clout. The opposing faction or factions doubtless capitalized on the expense of the war and the heavy casualties. But the "hawks" were not finished yet. Since neither Boiotia nor Athens ratified the terms but continued hostilities, and Boiotian contingents were still deployed in the Corinthian area, the Ismenian faction was probably still dominant, at least for the time being. The recovery of Orchomenos and the defeat of Phokis were still tempting prospects.[51]

Hamilton and others[52] have argued that the Boiotian League was not too disturbed at seeing Orchomenos independent. This, however, is a misreading of the political situation in Boiotia. Since the Ismenian faction was anti-Spartan, then the prospect of continued independence for a pro-Spartan Orchomenos on the western frontier, between Boiotia and its allies in the northwest, next to its old enemy Phokis, must have been most unwelcome. If the faction of Leontiades was more inclined to follow the will of the local oligarchy, as apparently it did in regard to Oropos, then the secession of a pro-Spartan Orchomenos could be accepted by them with equanimity. In other words policy towards Orchomenos was to a large extent a reflection of Boiotian factional positions.

Cook's idea that Orchomenos "could easily act as a focus for rebellion for the small cities around Lake Copaïs which were almost powerless in the structure of the Confederacy" probably misreads the situation. The members of those states inclined to separation would be allies of Leontiades, while those content with the League and suspicious of their neighbour Orchomenos would support Ismenias. The history of Orchomenos' relations with nearby towns was not conducive to trust.[53] I suspect that the small cities preferred the League.

The War 392/1 B.C.

The Corinthian War continued. Lechaion was recaptured for the Allies, probably late in 392 or early in 391, by the Athenians in full array (πανδημεί), according to Xenophon; they rebuilt the long walls to block any Spartan approach to the Isthmus that way.[54] Xenophon, however, is not to be relied on to say much about the Boiotians; but the author of the *Hellenica Oxyrhynchia* (in Diod. 14.86.40) notes that the Boiotians were also present with the Athenians in full force (πάσῃ τῇ δυνάμει) at the storming and recapture of Lechaion, as one might expect.

For further military activities by the Boiotians in the Peloponnese the evidence, which comes primarily from Xenophon, is patchy. What little we have indicates that Boiotian troops were on garrison duty in Corinth in 390 (*Hell.* 4.5.9), and that a cavalry force was operating around Argos in 388 (*Hell.* 4.7.6). There were other operations, in 389 in Akarnania and around Kalydon, probably not on a large scale. It is, however, improper to draw the inference, as some authorities have done, that there was a significant decrease in Boiotian military activity, one indicating an unwillingness to participate further in the war.[55] Xenophon is usually not interested in discussing the Boiotians and their military activities except if there is something to be said to their discredit. We may infer that there was little of that sort to report, except for the incident where Agesilaus caught some Boiotian officials, whose mission, whatever it was, was thereby aborted; or the one where the Boiotian cavalry were squeezed "like bats" against the walls of Argos for all of one night.

The reports from Xenophon on activities in the year 391 are brief and obscure. We simply do not know whether there were any Boiotians in the garrison when Lechaion was recaptured from the Allies by the Spartans in a combined operation commanded by the brothers Agesilaus and Teleutias.[56] Clearly control of the Corinthian Gulf was back in Spartan hands. Whether any Boiotian cavalry was used in Argos is unknown, though their presence is not unlikely. Whether any Boiotian units were co-operating with the Athenians in the Aegean is unknown, but again not unlikely.

The War 390 B.C.

In 390 at the time of the Isthmian Games Agesilaus invaded Corinthia and disrupted them. He then feinted at Corinth, where there was a Boiotian contingent. The Corinthians, however, desired reinforcement, since they were afraid of a "fifth column" in the city. This pulled Iphikrates and his Athenian force out of position from near modern Loutraki, where he had been protecting Peiraion (modern Perakhora). He, with the aid of Athenian (and Boiotian?) hoplites, but primarily with his mercenary peltasts, proceeded to destroy a *mora* of Spartiates near Lechaion in a memorable defeat.[57] The fact that the Amyklaians were going home to celebrate the Hyakinthia dates this to early May, 390. The area Iphikrates had been covering was now unprotected, however, and Agesilaus overran it.

The peninsula of Peiraion (Perakhora) was where the Corinthian grain supplies and livestock were being kept, along with some country folk. There was also a route, fast for foot traffic, between Corinth and Boiotia via Pagai and Aigosthena.[58] This is no doubt why some Boiotian and other officials were picked up when Agesilaus and his force occupied the peninsula (Xen. *Hell.* 4.5.6).

Some authorities, relying on Plut. *Ages.* (22.1), suggest that the Boiotians, along with the others noted by Xenophon, were there because of the Spartan successes on the Peiraion peninsula, which opened a direct way north.[59] Since the route north through the peninsula is not particularly good for armies (the going is better farther east on another route to Aigosthena), it seems more likely that these envoys were simply taking a fast route south: it is most likely that they were delegates going to a meeting of the *synhedrion* of the Grand Alliance in Corinth when Agesilaus' attack caught them.[60] The other envoys could be the Euboians and the Lokrians taking the same direct route as the Boiotians. The context of Xenophon's passage (4.5.5) seems to mean that, along with everyone else, the envoys fled into the sanctuary of the Heraion at the cape.

Boiotian Peace Feelers?

When the capitulation occurred, Xenophon says the Boiotians came to Agesilaus, who was at some distance from the temple, over by the lake, to ask him through Pharax, who was the *proxenos* at Sparta for Boiotia, what they might do to get peace. The Greek (4.5.6) reads πρεσβεῖαι δὲ ἄλλοθέν τε πολλαὶ παρῆσαν καὶ ἐκ Βοιωτῶν ἧκον ἐρησόμενοι τί ἂν ποιοῦντες εἰρήνης τύχοιεν. Ἧκον could mean a walk from the Heraion to Agesilaus' headquarters rather than a trip from Boiotia, particularly if, as Xenophon indicates, everything happened very quickly. The attack took no more than a couple of days; then the surrender; this was followed in a very short time by the triumphant (μάλα μεγαλοφρόνων) snubbing and ignoring of the Boiotians, with Pharax (surely Xenophon's informant) standing by; then *immediately* (like the *peripateia* in Greek tragedy) the messenger coming in with the news of the defeat and destruction of the Spartan *mora* by Iphikrates between Lechaion and Sikyon. It seems clear that the time constraints require the envoys to have been on their way to Corinth. If Xenophon's allegation is right, that they were going to ask about peace (they actually did not get a chance to say anything), it must have been an idea on their own initiative, to see if the old terms still applied. Plutarch (*Ages.* 22.1) says that the Boiotians arrived from Thebes for peace (ἀφίκοντο πρέσβεις ἐκ Θηβῶν περὶ φιλίαν), but this is nothing more than a paraphrase of Xenophon.

The next day, when the Boiotians had their interview with Agesilaus, they made no mention of peace (*Hell.* 4.5.9), but requested permission to go into the city to visit their own troops. Agesilaus politely refused and after raiding the Corinthia sent them home by sea from Lechaion. At any rate the Boiotians did not make peace at this time, and there is no good evidence that any alleged request for terms on the first day was anything but a personal initiative.

For the rest of 390 the War went rather satisfactorily for the Allies. They regained control of the Isthmus area and Perakhora, recapturing Krommyon and reoccupying most of the Corinthian territory in general. Communication between the Peloponnesian garrison at Lechaion and the main base at Sikyon had to be by sea.[61]

The War 389 B.C.

Iphikrates, the victorious Athenian commander, was sent home in disgrace. In late 390 or, more likely, in 389 Corinth and Argos changed sympolity for outright union. Somehow he got involved and killed some pro-Argive Corinthians, perhaps in an attempt to hold the town for Athens.[62]

Athenian and Boiotian forces, both land and naval, had been engaged in operations north of the Corinthian Gulf against Achaian possessions, notably Kalydon. There were probably several reasons for military activity here. First, the Akarnanians apparently needed encouragement; second, the Hesperian Lokrians (who were always weak) could be pressured by the Achaians, who were apparently expanding in the area; third, the control of Kalydon would materially advance any project to regain control of the Corinthian Gulf. At any rate the Allies were pressing hard on the Achaians by late summer 390, and the latter were forced to go to the expense of maintaining a permanent garrison in Kalydon. Eventually, probably in 389,[63] the Achaians appealed to Sparta for help, threatening to make peace if it was not forthcoming. In addition to the Athenian and Boiotian army units there was an Athenian squadron based on Oiniadai. There appears to have been a considerable effort being made by the Allies in the area.[64] It was regarded by Sparta as important enough to send out Agesilaus.

Agesilaus led a *mora* of Spartans plus Peloponnesian allies, and the Achaians πανδημεὶ, across to attack Akarnania. The Akarnanian peltasts seem to have done most of the fighting and caused the Peloponnesians severe losses. There is no mention of any Athenian or Boiotian hoplites engaging in combat. Eventually Agesilaus won one pitched battle.[65] The threat to devastate their crops in the next year brought about Akarnanian capitulation in 388, and their adhesion to the Peloponnesian League and the frustration of any Allied attempts in the area.[66]

Whether any Boiotian ships were with the Athenians in the Aegean during the rest of 389 is unknown, but it is not unlikely. Given the bias of our main source, all that can be said is that Boiotian military units did fight in 389, just as in 390 and in 388, in a variety of areas.

The War 388 B.C.

The situation worsened for the Allies in 388. The defection of Akarnania nullified any schemes on the north coast of the Corinthian Gulf;

the capture of Aigina severely hampered Athenian operations. The repercussions in Boiotia are unknown. Boiotian contingents continued to fight in the northeast corner of the Peloponnese, as even Xenophon informs us (*Hell.* 4.7.6). The death of Thrasyboulos was a severe loss to the Alliance and to its determination to carry on the war; Argos and the democrats at Corinth had formed a union that satisfied their war aims.

Agesipolis, the other Spartan King, now of age, led a raid into Argos that was opposed by an ineffective force containing some Boiotians. He was able to do this, because apparently the main Argive force (with Boiotian cavalry assisting?) was away on an expedition into Lakonia.[67] Most of the activities reported in the sources for this year were centred in the Aegean, mainly concerning the Athenians. Late in 388 Antalkidas went on his mission from Sparta to Susa, to get an agreement with Artaxerxes, which, thanks to the influence of Tiribazos, he did.[68]

The Peace of Antalkidas, 387 B.C.

By the spring of 387 the changes from Strouthas to Tiribazos (who had accompanied Antalkidas back to the coast), the attendant change in Persian policy towards financing the Allies and the revival of Spartan aggression led to pressure on Athens to quit the war. The Spartan fleet, led by Antalkidas, who was back from Susa, was reinforced by a Syracusan squadron, and outnumbered the Athenian fleet. Antalkidas outmanoeuvred the Athenians and cut their supply lines from the Black Sea to Athens. The Athenians were soon willing to negotiate for peace.[69] The Argives and Corinthians, having achieved their aims by their union, and being exhausted as well, were willing to sign. The representatives met at Sparta in 387.[70]

The terms were proclaimed in a rescript from the King. Asia Minor and Cyprus were to go to Persia; Athens could keep her three islands in the Aegean; all other Greek states were to be independent. Argos and Corinth, thinking themselves one state, and Athens, under threat of blockade, signed.

There was a difficulty with Boiotia. Xenophon (5.1.32f.) says that "the Thebans had been given the right [to sign] on behalf of all Boiotia." When Agesilaus refused to accept their signature "unless they swore that every city, large or small, should be autonomous," they said they had to refer the matter back to their home government. Agesilaus then gave them an ultimatum. Unless their government agreed, the full Peloponnesian League would invade Boiotia.[71] Since none of the other allies would support them, the Boiotian Federal Council gave way and the Boiotian League collapsed. Later the Spartans forced Corinthians to dissolve their union with Argos. The War was over.

It is clear that Boiotia was still willing to fight until it found itself alone and unsupported. At this point enough of the Councillors changed their vote, and the motion for capitulation passed. The League dissolved into its constituent towns: Orchomenos was no longer alone as a separate state; the resurrection of Plataia was imminent.

V Boiotia Without
the League,
387–379 B.C.

 After the Boiotian League was dissolved under pressure from Sparta, the constituent cities became independent, not only the major cities like Thespiai, but also, so it seems, many of the minor ones. Independence did not mean the dissolution of the amphictyonies regulating the various Boiotian shrines and any festivals that may have existed. It did not mean the dissolution of any cultural or sentimental links, or of any feeling of belonging to one people. It meant the abolition of the Federal Council, the federal magistracies, the federal courts, the treasury and the eleven districts, in other words of any federal organs of defence, finance and common legal and political action. It also meant the crippling of Theban power.

It is claimed that many of the states began to coin their own money in 386 and continued to do so until the late 370s, just as Plataia did after its re-establishment.[1] One must be careful of reading out historical inferences on the evidence of Boiotian coinage, since the coins are organized on the numismatists' interpretation of history, and there is always a danger of a *petitio principii*. Most Boiotian coins (wherever they were minted), used on their obverses the symbol of the Boiotian shield. A reasonable inference is that at the time they were produced there was still a certain sense of ethnicity (the words "nationhood" or "nationalism" should not be used, because of their anachronistic connotations). There is evidence that throughout Boiotia there persisted considerable support for the re-establishment of the

League, and that it became stronger in the late 380s. This support led to a hardening of feelings among the Spartans about the Boiotians and to the Spartan condoning of extra-legal adventures in Boiotia.

Probably all the cities remained at first under their accustomed constitutions, changing their dominant factions. The war had cost many Boiotian lives for much expense and little or no apparent gain; but Sparta was still regarded by many as a threat, and it was allied to such foes as Phokis. There were doubtless mixed feelings about the Peace that were reflected in the factional politics of the time.

Theban Government

At Thebes the archon was now the senior official, the head of state, giving his name to the year, performing state religious ceremonies, wearing a crown and holding a ceremonial spear of state.[2] The actual executive power lay in the hands of a committee of three polemarchs and their secretary.[3] A similar arrangement seems to have been usual in the other Boiotian states.[4] At Thebes the followers of Leontiades made up one of the prominent factions; they still advocated peace and friendship with Sparta. They may have been reinforced by the return of exiles, whom Xenophon (*Ages.* 2.21) claims the Spartans forced the Thebans to accept. Leontiades' group was in uneasy equilibrium with the anti-Spartan faction of Ismenias. It is widely suspected that for the rest of Boiotia most of the governing groups were pro-Spartan, or at least not of a disposition to challenge Spartan pre-eminence.[5]

Losses of Territory

Probably unexpected were some territorial losses that occurred sometime after the Peace. Oropos became independent and rejoined Athens;[6] Plataia was reoccupied by the Plataians, "during the peace which the Spartan Antalkidas made with the Persian king."[7] These changes have usually been set in 386, as immediate results of the Boiotian acceptance of the principle of autonomy for its states, but they could have occurred later, perhaps in 385 or even 384.[8] In either case the loss of Plataia could have contributed to a weakening of the popularity of Leontiades' faction in Thebes. The loss of Oropos probably did not sit well with members of the hoplite class in other cities either, with negative results later for pro-Spartan factions.[9]

Spartan-Theban Alliance?

Isokrates, Plutarch and Pausanias[10] all mention a Spartan-Theban alliance that was ratified after the Peace of Antalkidas. One of its results was supposed to be the despatch of a force to Mantinea, one in which Epaminondas and Pelopidas served as hoplites. In a battle there Epaminondas is alleged to have saved Pelopidas' life. In spite of all this testimony an alliance at this time seems most unlikely. There is no mention of it in Xenophon and Diodorus, while Isokrates, in making a rhetorical case against the Thebans, accuses them of joining the Spartans at some point after the end of the Corinthian War, not very precisely.[11] He makes no mention of any heroic incidents. Plutarch's anecdote, repeated in Pausanias, of how Pelopidas was saved by Epaminondas during a pitched battle at Mantinea, is a doublet of the more famous incident at Delion where Socrates saved Alkibiades.[12] As far as is known there was no pitched battle at the siege of Mantinea, only a siege. The Theban resolution of a couple of years later reported by Xenophon (*Hell.* 5.2.27), which forbade any Theban from going on any expedition against Olynthos, would have been a clear violation of any such alliance.

Theban Politics and Spartan Reactions

By 383,[13] if not earlier, Ismenias was elected as one of the polemarchs. His faction was by then strong enough to get embassies despatched in an attempt to distance Thebes from Sparta, especially by trying to revive the Athenian alliance and to establish co-operation with Olynthos, which was being troublesome to the Spartans. Since, however, no such agreements were ratified, it is clear that Ismenias and his faction were still not quite strong enough in the Theban Council to get all their policies adopted. Nonetheless, the Spartans felt that Ismenias had to be stopped before he got too dangerous.[14]

The Spartans and their Allies were well informed about what was going on in Thebes and in the rest of Boiotia. Xenophon reports a speech by an envoy from Akanthos who warned a meeting of the Peloponnesian League, "Consider this: how is it reasonable for you, who have taken such steps concerning Boiotia, so that it would not be unified (μὴ καθ' ἕν εἴη), to be so careless of the concentration of much more power, one that not only on land but by sea is becoming stronger!"[15] The implications of this are worth considering. First, it is clear that there were Theban efforts at reunification already apparent and regarded as a danger. Second, since efforts were being made to develop sea-power, and the key Boiotian naval posts were Siphai and Anthedon (both independent at this time),[16] some of the impetus for reunion was coming from non-Theban sources. Strong sentiments for unity were affecting many parts of Boiotia, feelings no doubt fostered by pro-League factions, as at Thebes. Third, Sparta was not alone in regarding Boiotian reunion with alarm. Many of her allies were uneasy.

The Spartan Intervention of 382 B.C.

In 382 the Spartans did intervene; the sources, however, all disagree on the exact circumstances. They all say that a Spartan force under the command of Phoibidas on its way to reinforce Eudamidas at Olynthos had obtained permission to cross Theban territory and to camp near the city.[17] They all agree that Phoibidas took advantage of the Thesmophoria, when the Theban men were excluded from the Kadmeia, to march in and seize it. They all have Ismenias arrested, imprisoned and executed. Beyond this the sources differ: over the reasons for Phoibidas' action; over who proposed the seizure; over the reaction at Thebes; over the reaction at Sparta; even where, why and how Ismenias was executed.

According to Diodorus (who here is following Ephoros, not *Hellen-ica Oxyrhynchia*) Phoibidas occupied the Kadmeia in accordance with Spartan policy. The Spartan government by 382 was convinced that the Thebans would try for the leadership of Boiotia again, and they gave orders secretly to their commanders to seize the Kadmeia if the chance presented itself.[18] Plutarch in one passage (*Pel.* 5.1) says much the same thing and gives more detail. "In reality they [the Spartans] were suspicious of the spirit and power of the city, and in particular they hated the faction of Ismenias and Androkleidas, to which Pelopidas belonged." In other words it was all a Spartan plot.

Xenophon, on the other hand, says nothing about any such secret Spartan policy. Phoibidas acted entirely on his own responsibility. In fact the Spartans were enraged at Phoibidas for acting as he did without authorization from the state. In other words Sparta (if not some Spartans) was pure and innocent.

Diodorus (i.e., Ephoros) says that the Thebans became angry, rallied and fought a pitched battle, but were defeated. Three hundred of the most prominent citizens (presumably the followers of Ismenias) were then exiled. After crushing resistance and leaving a strong garrison Phoibidas went on to Olynthos.[19]

In Xenophon and in most places in Plutarch[20] there is no resistance at all. It is a very different picture. At Thebes a resolution had recently been passed that forbade any Theban from taking part in any expedition against the Olynthians. Leontiades went out to meet Phoibidas and made this resolution the main point of a speech by which he persuaded Phoibidas to occupy the Kadmeia. Phoibidas, after camping near Thebes, was to set out as if continuing on to Macedonia. He would be met by Leontiades, who would guide him back at the right time so that he could enter Thebes inconspicuously and with a minimum of risk. The arrangements worked. The result was that the Spartan force entered Thebes at siesta-time, during the Thesmophoria. "After establishing Phoibidas and his troops there [in the Kadmeia] and handing over the key of the gates, he [Leontiades] immediately proceeded to the Council." It was meeting "in the stoa in the agora." The Kadmeia, their normal place of meeting, was reserved for the women during the Thesmophoria. To this session Leontiades announced what he had done, and he ordered the *lochagoi* and their detachments to arrest Ismenias on a charge of war-mongering. The latter was imprisoned in the Kadmeia, in Spartan hands. Clearly Leontiades' supporters in the Council and the Army had been tipped off. The coup was now over, and a new polemarch was chosen (by method unknown) *vice* Ismenias. Xenophon agrees with Diodorus' source that there were 300 opponents of Leontiades, but states that they "withdrew" to Athens along with Androkleidas (ἀπεχώρησαν, not Diodorus' "banished" ἐφυγάδευσε).

In Diodorus and in three citations in Plutarch, as well as in other authors,[21] the Spartans yielded reluctantly to outraged Greek public opinion. They fined Phoibidas, 100,000 drachmas according to Plutarch, but they did not evacuate the garrison. In Plutarch's words, "they punished the doer, but they approved the deed."

In Xenophon,[22] however, the Spartans were as outraged as the other Greeks but were turned around by Leontiades, who, he claims, had even more influence on the Spartans than Agesilaus. Leontiades went to Sparta to calm them, "[since they] were furious with Phoibidas because he had acted in this manner without authorization from the city." Agesilaus, Xenophon is careful to emphasize, also supported Phoibidas saying that "if he [Phoibidas] had carried out any deed harmful to the Lakedaimonians, it was right that he should be punished; but if it was good, it was long-established practice that it was lawful to act on one's own initiative." Phoibidas got off, and there is no mention of any fine. There is a neat implicit denial of any Spartan culpability coupled with praise for Spartan discipline. Xenophon's placing of the responsibility on a Boiotian villain makes a nice contrast with Ephoros' ascription of everything to Spartan machinations.

In Plutarch (*Pel.* 5.3), Ismenias was "seized" (συναρπασθείς) and taken to Sparta, where after a short time he was put to death (ἀνηρέθη). In *de gen. Soc.* (576A) it is implied that he was executed in a very unpleasant way. Plutarch is probably following Ephoros. In Xenophon (*Hell.* 5.2.35), however, it is all different. The Spartans "send" (presumably to Thebes) three Lakedaimonians, and "one from each allied city, large and small. When the *dikasterion* was convoked, then charges were laid against Ismenias: that he 'barbarized'; that he was a *xenos* of the

Persian King, to no good advantage to Greece; that he received some of the monies from the King; and that he and Androkleidas were the ones most responsible for all the disorders in Greece." After a prosecution and a defence, "he was condemned and put to death" (κατεψηφίσθη καὶ ἀποθνῄσκει).[23]

Thus there are two very different versions of what happened at Thebes, one in Diodorus, the other in Xenophon. Plutarch seems to use material from both, and from other sources, as he sees fit. The idea that Plutarch was following here a *third* source, Kallisthenes, is probably wrong. Kallisthenes was certainly *one* source for *Pelopidas* and *Agesilaus* (as well as for *Kimon* and *Camillus*),[24] but to term him the *main* source for the *Pelopidas* is unwarranted.[25]

In Diodorus' source, Ephoros, and in the parts of Plutarch close to or depending on him, we have an anti-Spartan bias. The Spartans, he says, instructed their commanders to attack and occupy Thebes if the opportunity offered. They were quite prepared to act unethically. They were guilty of deliberate aggression with malice aforethought. Only under pressure of Greek public opinion did they fine Phoibidas, although he had been acting in accordance with Spartan policy; but even so they kept the Kadmeia. The Spartans arrested Ismenias and hauled him off to Sparta, where he was, shortly thereafter, brutally executed. Leontiades and his followers played a comparatively minor rôle.

Very different is the story in Xenophon. The Spartans are for the most part innocent; it was *all* Leontiades' fault. He talked the not-too-bright Phoibidas into occupying the Kadmeia; it was he who arrested Ismenias and turned him over to the Spartans for imprisonment; it was he who persuaded the Spartans, who were very upset, to drop charges against Phoibidas and to keep their hold on Thebes; it was he who collaborated enthusiastically with the occupiers and ruled Thebes in their interests. It is true that Ismenias was put to death, but only after a full trial for anti-Hellenic crimes before an international tribunal drawn from all the allies, and the locale was Thebes, not Sparta.

Which is correct, if either? Most modern scholars have, like Plutarch, combined portions of both versions in a manner palatable to their own tastes, and they have either ignored or papered over the inconsistencies and contradictions. Methodologically this is unsound.[26]

Many authorities have argued that well before Phoibidas' march through Boiotia the Spartans had negotiated secretly with Leontiades, and that Agesilaus and his friends were backing him, so as to prevent the Ismenian group from getting control.[27] There is little to support this idea. Diodorus (Ephoros) says only that the Spartans acted on their own initiative, and that Leontiades opportunistically seized power as a result; Xenophon says that Leontiades took advantage of the presence of a Spartan force in the area to talk its commander into seizing an opportunity. Only Plutarch says that accusations were later made that Agesilaus had counselled Phoibidas to seize Thebes.[28] No source says that there were any negotiations with Leontiades prior to the appearance of Phoibidas and his force.

The strong anti-Spartan bias, even in his choice of words, and the inherent improbabilities in his story make for suspicions of the veracity of Ephoros. The idea of a long-standing Spartan policy to seize the Kadmeia at the first opportunity sounds like a rhetorical construct. Sparta was suspicious of the revival of Ismenias' faction, but a feeling of suspicion and dislike is a long way from a planned pre-emptive strike. The story of the battle between Spartans and Thebans after the coup sounds like some self-justificatory fable. It is noteworthy that the Boiotian Plutarch makes no mention of such a fight; since he was aware of both versions, it must mean that he rejected it, as do all modern authorities.

On the other hand, the attempts by Xenophon to show that the Spartans were virtually blameless, and that Leontiades was the villain are often regarded as whitewashing. But Xenophon makes it clear that the Spartans were a pragmatic lot, strongly disliking the Ismenian faction (and disliked by them), and that they had been warned about Theban and Boiotian irredentism by various allies. Leontiades exposed Phoibidas to great temptation. On balance, Xenophon's version is to be preferred here.

If this is so, then the sequence of events should be of this sort: first, that the Spartans had been warned by a variety of people of the resurgence of Boiotian irredentism, and, though suspicious, they were not prepared as yet to take steps. Meanwhile at Thebes Leontiades was in political trouble, in a tight struggle against Ismenias for dominance.

Under Ismenias' guidance the state had already banned any participation in the campaign against Olynthus, and embassies were being despatched to seek alliances with Athens and Olynthus. Opportunistically seizing the moment Leontiades persuaded Phoibidas, the Spartan commander of some reinforcements on their way to Olynthos, to take Thebes. The Spartan commander entered the Kadmeia during the siesta time on a holiday, the Thesmophoria, when the Theban men were excluded from the Kadmeia. Not surprisingly, he had no trouble. Leontiades then carried out a bloodless coup, handing over Ismenias to the Spartans. The arrest must have been supported by a majority of the Council to have been effective, and perhaps some motion authorized a trial by an international tribunal. Leontiades, it may be concluded, had organized his supporters and had lined up the votes. Ismenias was tried and condemned at Thebes by a jury drawn from members of the Peloponnesian League. This was undoubtedly unlawful, but perhaps the precedent of the trial and condemnation of Timagenidas and other Theban leaders at the end of the Persian Wars for Medism could have been adduced. Ismenias, then, was tried before an international tribunal, since the main charge was Medism, at least nominally.[29] Plutarch's phraseology, however, lends credence to the idea that even at the time it was widely regarded as no more than a show trial and judicial murder.

Leontiades defended himself and Phoibidas before the Spartans, who were as upset as the rest of Greece was at the occupation of the Kadmeia.[30] Agesilaus threw his support behind Phoibidas, and the Spartans found themselves, willy-nilly, in the position of having to continue holding Thebes. If they withdrew, the rival faction in Thebes would gain power and make an alliance with Athens; the campaign at Olynthos would be jeopardized, not to say the whole Spartan position in central and northern Greece; and the Boiotian League would be on its way to reconstitution.

The Tyranny 382–379 B.C.

Leontiades and the leadership cadre of his faction governed Thebes for more than three years. He needed no hoplite support for his government: he was kept in power by a Spartan garrison. This was 1500 men according to Ephoros and some passages in Plutarch,[31] though this seems excessive when compared to the 750 who occupied Athens in the time of the Thirty. Ephoros also claims that they were commanded by three harmosts, Lysanoridas, Herippidas and Arkesios.[32] Xenophon does not give a figure for the size of the garrison, though he alleges that they were "few" (ὀλίγοι), and he speaks of only one harmost.[33]

Various attempts have been made to deal with these discrepancies;[34] a common way is to regard the versions as supplementary to one another. One harmost, for example, was the commander, another was his deputy, and the third was for the northern garrisons. Another way is to argue that since the blame for the occupation is regarded as ultimately resting on Sparta, the matter of who was in charge of the occupation of the Kadmeia is really irrelevant. Such attempts raise more questions than they solve. Perhaps Ephoros is more accurate than Xenophon, and the commander had two deputies or two commanders for the *morai*, ignored by Xenophon. But 1500 men are not "few." Perhaps the figure of 1500 was the total for the garrisons in Boiotia,[35] or perhaps it was the size of the garrison plus refugees at the time of the surrender, or perhaps the garrison plus the puppet troops (cf. *de gen. Soc.* 586E). Though the discrepancies may thus be explained away or edited out, it seems more reasonable to reject the testimony of Ephoros as unreliable. Xenophon, in spite of his biases, is to be preferred here.

Xenophon (*Hell.* 5.4.46, 49) makes it clear that very small controlling groups, narrow oligarchies, δυναστεῖαι, were established in all the cities of Boiotia, "just as in Thebes." They are described by both Xenophon and Plutarch as being "tyrannies," and those running them as "tyrants."[36] Plutarch (*Pel.* 6.1) says that the Thebans suffered the subversion of their ancestral constitution; they were enslaved by the faction of Archias and Leontiades; and (in *de gen. Soc.* 576A) Leontiades and Archias ruled unconstitutionally and brutally (ἄρχοντες παρανόμως καὶ βιαίως). Probably the oligarchic system installed in 446, of quadripartite Councils, was no longer in use, or it only existed as a vestigial "rump:"[37] rotation of magistrates may have been obtained by co-option among the "tyrants." Before 382 Thebes and the other Boiotian states were probably using their traditional constitutions, or Ismenias would not have been able to secure a polemarchy, and there would not have been any Spartan fears of Boiotian reunion.[38]

What was established after the Spartan occupation is clearly not one of the customary Boiotian hoplite oligarchies, but something much narrower and more repressive: the direct control of the state by the leaders of a faction and no one else. The Spartans were behind the changeover, but precisely what they did in the other Boiotian towns and how they did it remain obscure. They may have forced small garrisons on the towns as "protection,"[39] or they may have exerted pressure through their *auctoritas*.[40] Plutarch also emphasized the point that as long as the Spartan garrison occupied the Kadmeia, the people of Thebes had no hope of getting rid of the tyranny.

Terror and violence were used to maintain power. Arrests and imprisonments marked by brutality to the prisoners were not uncommon. At the time of the successful conspiracy in 378, there were over 150 political prisoners in the jail in Thebes.[41] They had apparently been beaten and chained, with many kept in stocks.[42]

The Spartans apparently exercised direct control when they desired.[43] At Haliartos, no later than early 379, someone opened up what was thought to be Alkmena's tomb. The finds contained in it were seized by the Spartans on the orders of Agesilaus and removed to Sparta. The subsequent crop failure and the flooding by Lake Copaïs were held by many to be a judgement for the violation of the tomb.[44]

The Theban Exiles

Whether exiles from the other Boiotian cities joined the 300 Thebans of Ismenias' faction in Athens is unknown, but it seems likely, since a fairly large force of exiles deployed in Attica on the Boiotian frontier is implicit in the events of 379/8.

The original leader of the 300 exiles in Athens, Androkleidas, was assassinated by Theban agents some time before 379. His loss was a severe blow to the exiles, and it took them some time to reorganize.[45] The Spartans, at the behest of the Theban government, ordered Athens to expel the exiles, since they were the common enemies of Hellas. The Athenians ignored this command.[46]

The Liberation of Thebes

There was one plot, however, that did succeed in overthrowing the Theban oligarchy and in getting the Spartans out of the Kadmeia. The common version of what happened is melodramatic and bizarre. It is also another of those incidents with so many variants among the sources, Plutarch, Xenophon and Diodorus in particular, that agreement on what actually happened is virtually impossible to obtain.

All sources agree that there were negotiations between the leaders of the exiles and a dissident group within the Theban governing clique, one headed by the Secretary to the Polemarchs, Phillidas. As a result a small band of exiles came from Athens, and, with help from supporters in the city, efficiently assassinated the key leaders of Leontiades' faction. The next morning as soon as it became daylight, the people joined the exiles, and a democracy was established. Later the Spartan garrison of the Kadmeia capitulated and was allowed to depart. The commander and his responsible fellow-officers faced disgrace or death back in the Peloponnese.

There are, however, several important discrepancies between Xenophon and Plutarch. There are also five or so minor differences between Plutarch's versions in *Pelopidas* and *de genio Socratis*, to be explained usually by compression in the former or rhetorical requirements, usually to heighten dramatic effects, in the latter.[47] Diodorus and Nepos give only brief summaries, in which they usually agree with Plutarch (with a disagreement in one important area).[48]

One of the most instructive of the differences between Xenophon and Plutarch is over the costumes that the raiders wore when they slew the oligarchs. Xenophon says (*Hell.* 5.4.5–7) that there were two different versions current in his time: first, that three of the conspirators were dressed as fine ladies of the best class in Thebes (τὰς σεμνοτάτας καὶ καλλίστας τῶν ἐν Θήβαις) and the other four as maidservants; or second, that all seven were dressed as revellers (κωμαστάς).

The version with the conspirators dressed as women resembles a well-known motif first seen in Herodotus (5.20), where the Persians at the Macedonian court (who have been misbehaving) are massacred by young male Macedonians disguised as girls. It is also seen in Plutarch's *Life of Solon* (8.4), where some Megarean sea-raiders receive a rude surprise when what they thought was an Athenian all-female religious procession close to the shore turned out to be a squad of beardless young Athenian hoplites suitably disguised. A similar motif is found in Pausanias (4.4.3), where the Messenians slew a band of Spartan youths who were disguisèd as maidens, and King Teleklos as well, when they tried to overwhelm the Messenians. Because of these parallels this Theban version has been rejected by several authorities as a historical myth. They prefer the revellers.[49] But the disguising of tough young warriors as girls makes a good story, and there is no reason why a Herodotean tale could not have given someone an idea, even a Theban. Catching the enemy at a party all unsuspecting is an aim not unknown even to recent history,[50] and ease of entrance would certainly be facilitated by such a disguise.

Plutarch (*Pel.* 9.2, 11.1) or his source combines both of Xenophon's versions by having the raiders wearing garlands like revellers, with some or all dressed as women, but loose women (γύναια τῶν ὑπάνδρων), though of the highest class (ἐν ἀξιώματι, *de gen. Soc.* 577C). There is no agreement about the disguises between the sources.

A second and perhaps more important discrepancy is in the number of returning exiles: seven in Xenophon (*Hell.* 5.4.1); twelve in Plutarch (*de gen. Soc.* 576C, *Pel.* 8.2) and in Nepos (*Pel.* 2.3). Exiles known by name total only six: Pelopidas, Damokleidas, Theopompos, Melon, Menekleidas and Kephisodoros. Eumolpidas, Samidas and Lysitheos may or may not have been in exile. Plutarch's figure might be the result of later claims for the glory of returning with Pelopidas. On the other hand, Xenophon may have been omitting some of his pet hates from the tally, or he may have got his information from a prejudiced Theban source, or he may have been influenced by story-telling techniques to use a conventional number for an unknown quantity. He apparently did little if any checking of his material.[51] My own view inclines to the idea of omission of pet hates, and that Plutarch's twelve is correct.

Third, Xenophon is biased strongly against Pelopidas and Epaminondas in particular and Thebans in general. He can be shown to omit important items when he deals with Thebes. He gives the major part of the credit for the restoration of freedom to Melon, (*Hell.* 5.4.2). All other sources[52] give Pelopidas the principal rôle, though Melon has a major part in the conspiracy (cf. *Pel.* 8.1). It is certainly possible that Melon originally had a more important part with more authority and power than later tradition recognized,[53] but it is clear that Pelopidas was a key man. His omission by Xenophon means at the least that his narrative must in this regard be supplemented or corrected by other sources. Xenophon credits Phillidas, the secretary of the polemarchs, who had a name vaguely resembling Pelopidas', with many of the deeds that other sources give to the latter.

Fourth, there is a discrepancy over the time that it took the conspirators to get from Athens to Thebes and to prepare for the assault. Xenophon (5.4.3) allows the conspirators to spend a day in the country and then another day in Charon's house. Plutarch's chronology allows for no such time to be spent, but the impression is of quick arrival and almost immediate action. Given the exiles' security problems, the latter at least sounds more sensible,[54] though this does not necessarily mean it is the right choice.

Much more difficult and significant is the fifth, about the nationality of the troops on the frontier and their numbers. Plutarch (*Pel.* 8.1) has a main body of exiles, size unstated, under Pherenikos[55] waiting in the Thriasian Plain; he says nothing about any Athenians, or any official Athenian action, and he emphasizes the importance of these Theban exiles.[56] Xenophon (5.4.9), however, hints at collusion with an Athenian force under the command of two *strategoi*. He says nothing about any force of exiled Thebans, or about any official Athenian action. Diodorus (15.25f.), different again, has the Athenians send help as the consequence of a decree passed by the Assembly, as do Deinarchos (1.39) and other orators.[57]

In spite of Plutarch there is strong evidence for an Athenian contingent aiding in the Theban liberation. Whether it was composed of units operating without official sanction, as Xenophon's silence leads some to believe, or was sent as the result of a resolution of the

Assembly, as Diodorus' source affirms, is much disputed. Many authorities reject the testimony of Diodorus and Deinarchos that at least some
help was sent as the result of a decree of the Assembly. In my view
they are wrong to do so.[58]

The sixth difference is concerned with the mode of the assassination and the number of conspirators. Xenophon (5.4.4–8) has the deed
committed by the one small group of seven exiles, aided only by Phillidas. However they were dressed, they were admitted into the dining
room by Phillidas, who also got rid of some of the servants. They first
killed Archias and the other polemarchs, apparently with no problems.
While *four* remained at the *Polemarcheion*, Phillidas, accompanied by
three of the exiles, went on to the house of Leontiades, who was slain
there in front of his wife. Then Phillidas and *two* (we may infer that
one of the exiles, Kephisodoros, was killed fighting Leontiades) went
on to the prison, killed the jailer, released the prisoners and rallied and
rearmed them at "the Stoa." Nothing is said about the slaying of another high official not at the banquet, Hypates. He is only mentioned
by Xenophon in a much later passage, where it is remarked that he was
killed at this time.[59] Xenophon in Book 5 is clearly somewhat patchy.

A very different version is found in Plutarch and the other sources.
The twelve exiles were joined in Charon's house by 36 residents of
Thebes, for a total of 48 men. After various alarms and excursions (not
to say panic, as when Charon was summoned by Archias, one of the
leading oligarchs), the 48 were divided into two bands. One, under the
command of Melon and Charon, was assigned to kill Archias and Philip, and various other officials at the banquet, while the second band,
under Pelopidas and Damokleidas, was to eliminate Leontiades and Hypates, who "lived near each other." The members of the first band,
costumed as women and revellers, wearing cuirasses under their disguises and armed with swords, were admitted by Phillidas to the ban-
queting room. There they killed their men and some others who resisted, including the unfortunate Archon, Kabeirichos, who was unwise
enough to grab for his spear of state at the wrong time. The second
band, armed with daggers and in normal costume, managed by a ruse
to gain entry to Leontiades' home and to kill him after a struggle, and
then to despatch Hypates after a chase across the roof tops.[60] They lost

Kephisodoros in the process, in a hand-to-hand fight with Leontiades. The two teams then rendezvoused at the Stoa Polystylon. Then they proceeded to the jail to liberate the prisoners.[61] Phillidas did the talking, and was the one who finally killed the jailer. Over 150 men were released. The former prisoners, plus other citizens, armed themselves, as Xenophon also relates.

Xenophon, with his seven liberators, was endeavouring to make the point that with the gods' aid against sinners it took only seven men to free the city. The more circumstantial account in Plutarch does explain how the 48 conspirators in two groups were able to do the deed rapidly and efficiently, with a minimum of casualties to themselves. Cawkwell considers the *Hellenika* as memoirs rather than history, and he argues that Xenophon relied mainly on his memory of what he had seen and of conversations.[62] If this is so, then Xenophon may have used as his source conversations with one of the conspirators in the group attacking Archias, perhaps Menekleidas, who later was bitterly opposed to Pelopidas and Epaminondas.[63]

Though Diodorus followed Ephorus, Plutarch seems to have been more eclectic. His implicit denial of any Athenian presence on the frontier, if it was not his own contribution, must come from some other source than Ephoros.[64] It has been suggested, not unreasonably, that it might be Kallisthenes, but less reasonably that he was Plutarch's main source; he surely used other material, including some ultimately derived from the group of liberators.[65] Xenophon is none too good, but he is closer in time to the events than Plutarch's Kallisthenes, or Diodorus' Ephoros. Equally clearly Xenophon is arbitrary and cranky, and he omits much. He must be supplemented extensively, but cautiously, particularly from Plutarch's Boiotian sources.

My reconstruction of what happened, given with a good deal of diffidence, goes like this. As Xenophon says, some disaffected members of the Theban government, particularly Phillidas, got in touch with the exiles. The negotiations must have started at least some weeks before the actual coup. The exiles had to have time enough to be convinced of the effectiveness and sincerity of Phillidas and his faction; there had to be time to work up arrangements. The date chosen was the Aphrodisia, the festival at the end of the annual magistracies, just before the transfer of powers to the incoming officials on Boukataios 1.[66] The banquet would be an ideal time to cause maximum damage to the "tyrants" and their supporters. Then, too, there was no Spartan field force available for immediate action.[67] It is probable that some considerable time would be needed to reduce the garrison in the Kadmeia, and there would be a chance of success only if the Spartans had to take even more time to mobilize their field force. No doubt these factors were taken into account.

The exiles were probably penetrated by government agents, and so there was a serious risk of leaks; it is clear that the immediate planning was kept in the hands of a trusted and reliable few, including Pelopidas.[68] Careful coordination with Phillidas and his group had to be maintained. The main body of the exiles was to be informed at the last minute and was to stay in Attica close to the frontier, while a small band of young men was to be sent into Thebes to prepare the way. Billeting arrangements at Charon's house were made well in advance, and on short notice a considerable number of disaffected men in Thebes were brought in to help. Not all the members of Ismenias' faction had gone into exile. Even one of the leaders, Galaxidoros, was living quietly at home, apparently undisturbed as long as he kept away from politics.[69]

Word also was passed to at least some members of the Athenian government, notably to the great leader Kephalos, even if there was a risk of further leakage. As a result of arrangements at Athens two of the generals, on a motion by Kephalos in the Assembly, had some forces deployed near the frontier at the right time, along with the main body of exiles. The decree presumably authorized field exercises or the like so that security would not be compromised. Unfortunately the passage of the decree gave the opportunity for the hierophant Archias to send a warning to his namesake, the Theban polemarch Archias, but fortunately it was not opened and read until after the coup.

It was shortly before the date agreed upon that the main body of the exiles (and the Athenian forces) were informed, and the picked band of twelve,[70] including Pelopidas, one of the principal planners, and Melon, perhaps another, crossed the frontier. In dribs and drabs they made their way into Thebes, probably over a couple of days, all arriving on the D-day, the day of the banquet. The raiders, reinforced by the 36 men from Thebes, were divided into two detachments, one to deal with those at the banquet, the other to kill the members of the oligarchy who were not attending the banquet, notably Leontiades and Hypates. The advantage of having a "mole" in the government is apparent, since they had up-to-date information on exactly where their opponents would be.[71] The party told off for the banquet was disguised for easier ingress to the dining room. Some at least were costumed as heavily swathed ladies, clothing reasonable in the bitterly cold weather and concealing their cuirasses and weapons.[72] The polemarchs and their friends were awaiting female companionship of some sort, of those willing to play Aphrodites to their Ares.[73] Apparently at least some of the ladies were supposed to be married.

The attacks were a complete success, all oligarchs slain for only one reported casualty, Kephisodoros, killed in hand-to-hand combat with Leontiades. The two parties, after their successful actions, including a chase over the Theban roofs, met at the Stoa Polystylon. Aeneas Tacticus (34.18) gives a curious detail, how they rallied in the pitch dark night by whistling. They then broke open the jail, killing the jailer and freeing 150 of their political friends. These had been badly treated, as we noted earlier. Then they armed various groups who had joined them. Messages were sent to summon Pherenikos and his body of 300-plus exiles[74] and the Athenian force. Both groups arrived shortly before dawn (they must have been waiting at the ready for the signal). The majority of the Thebans delayed until daylight before joining the revolutionaries, and then they did. Many pro-Spartan Thebans, including a collaborationist force that camped around the Kadmeia, the so-called "Betters" (κρείττους), fled into the acropolis.[75] This built up the total in the besieged force to 1500.

The Installation of Democracy

In the event the careful planning to give enough time to besiege the Kadmeia successfully was not necessary. Panicked by the events of the previous night, the stream of refugees and the absence of the harmost

Lysanoridas (who was in Haliartos),[76] the two commanders of the Spartan contingents capitulated within a couple of days.[77]

An agreement was quickly made whereby the Spartan garrison handed over the Kadmeia and marched out with full honours. Some of the pro-Spartan Thebans who slipped out with them were detected and slaughtered, though it is alleged that the Athenians tried to save some. Most of them, however, escaped to Sparta with the garrison.

The Thebans at a mass meeting before the capitulation had elected Melon, Charon and Pelopidas as Boiotarchs, along with Gorgidas, and by that deed signified their intent of restoring the League.[78] The fact that the Damos, the People, did the voting and electing, not just the hoplites and cavalry, indicates that the commitment of the exiles and their supporters in Thebes was to an Athenian-style democracy; and this was accepted by the populace. Democracy was the sign under which the new Boiotian League would be formed.[79]

The Spartan commanders had managed to send messages to Plataia and Thespiai, the two neighbours closest to Thebes, asking for help. Plataia had a government that was certainly pro-Spartan. There may also have been a small Spartan garrison.[80] The town promptly despatched troops, but they were met on the road by Theban cavalry (it is to be noted that the wealthier Theban classes were supporting the coup in large numbers) and were routed with a loss of over 20. Thespiai, however, did nothing;[81] this despite the fact that its troops were alleged to be waiting a call to action against Thebes.[82] Thespiai seems to have had at this time considerable pro-democratic and pro-League sentiment.[83]

For the rest of the Boiotian cities very little is known. Tanagra was controlled by a faction called "those about Hypatodoros," for some time after the coup in Thebes.[84] The others after 382 became ruled by narrow oligarchies, supporters of Sparta, but there is no information on how precisely it happened, or when each became a *dynasteia*.

This type of regime, no matter how pleasing to the Spartans, seems not to have been very popular with the Boiotians. The support of the Theban upper classes for democracy is perhaps a pointer. A substantial number of citizens of other states made their way to Thebes over the next few years, even if not on the massive scale indicated by Diodorus.[85] If they were not all pro-democratic, they were certainly anti-tyrant. Their numbers were sufficient to give some colour to the idea that the new government in Thebes was federal, not merely something Theban. This idea would be important in helping to gain the allegiance of the rest of Boiotia in the next few years.

VI The Boiotian League Restored, 378–375 B.C.

The years 378 to 375 saw the recapture of the Kadmeia by the Boiotians, the successful defence of Thebes in alliance with the Athenians, the restoration of the Boiotian League, at least in part, and a series of campaigns that culminated in a temporary peace with Sparta.

The Siege of the Kadmeia

How long the siege of the Kadmeia lasted and how much time was available for negotiating with Sparta are questions answered very differently in our sources.

In Diodorus and Plutarch,[1] who mostly followed the same source at this point,[2] Spartan reaction to the coup and the siege was swift and quite efficient. The troops in the Kadmeia got messages out to Sparta informing the government of what had happened and requesting aid. They resisted for a fairly long time, quite successfully. In Diodorus (15.25.4–26.3), but not Plutarch, this was the time when the Thebans sought and obtained an official alliance with the Athenians. Demophon, says Diodorus, was despatched with an advanced force of the levy of 5000 hoplites and 500 horse. Diodorus also claims (15.26.3f.) that there was a concentration of hoplites from other Boiotian cities, and that the total Boiotian and Athenian force available for the siege was 12,000 hoplites and more than 2000 cavalry. The numbers seem highly unlikely. Nothing of this is mentioned in Plutarch. Eventually, Diodorus continues, the food supplies of the besieged began to run low, and the morale of the Peloponnesian allies, who made up a large part of the garrison, dropped so much that a surrender on terms had to be arranged. The siege had, however, lasted long enough for the Spartans to have had time to mobilize a rescue force under Kleombrotos, one that narrowly missed getting to Thebes before the capitulation (βραχὺ τῶν καιρῶν ὑστερήσαντες in Diodorus, meeting the former garrison near Megara in Plutarch). In this version Kleombrotos' force had set out as soon as it could after word had arrived from the Kadmeia. Afterwards in the Peloponnese the *three* commanders of the garrison were tried, and the two who had been left in charge of the Kadmeia were condemned to death. The actual harmost in command, Lysanidoras, who had been absent in Haliartos when the siege started, was fined so heavily that he could not return to Sparta, but he was not put to death.

This is very different from Xenophon's version (5.4.10–17) and what Plutarch says in *Agesilaus* (24.1f.). The siege was short, very short. After the surrender the garrison and the surviving pro-Spartan Thebans arrived at Sparta, apparently before very much had been done there. Then came the trial and execution (not exile) of the *one* harmost (not three). This was followed by the mobilization of a force to go against Thebes. Then there was a dispute over command. Agesilaus refused to serve, for fear of being labelled pro-tyrant. The ephors, after listening to the Theban refugees, decided to send out young King Kleombrotos, "in the middle of winter." He is sent out on a punitive expedition. There is no meeting of the garrison and the rescue force somewhere in the Megarid. A table comparing the sequence of events as laid out in Diodorus and Plutarch and in Xenophon makes the differences clear.

In Diodorus and Plutarch:	In Xenophon:
1) word to Sparta;	1) [word sent to Sparta]
2) long siege while Sparta mobilizes	2) short siege
3) march of the rescue force from Sparta	3) capitulation and evacuation of the Kadmeia

4) capitulation

4) arrival of garrison and exiles at Sparta

5) meeting of rescue force and garrison near Megara

5) trial and condemnation of one harmost

6) trial and condemnation of the three commanders, somewhere outside Sparta

6) Kleombrotos, after a dispute over command, sent out with a punitive force

Clearly the two versions are irreconcilable, but there are several points to notice in deciding which, if either, to prefer. First, Plutarch is inconsistent. In *Agesilaus* (24.1f.) he summarizes the incident told in more detail in Xenophon (5.4.13) of how Agesilaus declined the command of the force, which then was given to Kleombrotos; this all happened *after* the arrival in Sparta from the Kadmeia of the garrison and the Theban refugees, well after the capitulation. In *Pelopidas* the relieving force under Kleombrotos' command met the garrison near Megara; that is, in the first version the command was decided *before* the garrison and the pro-Spartan Thebans arrived in Sparta, and before the capitulation.

Second, if the garrison of the Kadmeia had held out for any length of time, Lysanidoras, the harmost that Plutarch says was in Haliartos, would have had time to organize resistance, or at least to have joined the relief force. Though negligent by being in the wrong place at the wrong time, he was apparently adjudged to have had the opportunity of doing neither, since Plutarch says he was fined, not executed.

Third, Diodorus often gets material out of chronological order, as is well known.[3] The formal Athenian alliance seems out of place at the time he puts it. Furthermore, the idea of help at this juncture from the pro-democrats from other Boiotian cities on such a scale as he claims, that is, about 7000 hoplites and 1500 cavalry (15.26.4), is very unlikely.

Fourth, another set of sources, independent of either Xenophon or Ephoros, should be considered, namely the Athenian orators Isokrates, Deinarchos and Aristeides. In the *Plataikos* (14.29) Isokrates says that right after the Athenians assisted the Thebans to recapture their city, the latter "immediately sent envoys to Lakedaimon and were ready to become slaves and to change nothing of what they had formerly agreed to with the Spartans. Need I say more? If the Spartans had not enjoined them to take back the refugees and to expel the assassins, nothing would have stopped them from marching alongside those who treated them so badly against their benefactors." Stripped of its antitheses and snide embellishments[4] the passage makes it clear that Isokrates believed that there was a considerable time between the expulsion of the garrison (with Athenian aid) and any Spartan reaction; there was enough time for the pro-Spartan Thebans to reach Sparta (presumably accompanying the garrison of the Kadmeia) and to influence the course of negotiations between the Spartans and the embassy from the new government; there was time enough for the new Theban regime to send an embassy to Sparta; and time enough for it to get back to Thebes. All this happened before Kleombrotos and his army were despatched. Therefore Isokrates, like Xenophon, believed in a short siege, or a very slow Spartan reaction and mobilization.

Deinarchos in *Against Demosthenes* (1.38f.) says that Kephalos, Thrason and others, "some of whom are alive even now," [about 325 B.C.] were responsible "at their own risk" (τοῖς ἰδίοις κινδύνοις) for aiding the Theban exiles in liberating their city, and that Kephalos was instrumental in having a decree passed to send forces to help the exiles who had taken Thebes and who were besieging the Kadmeia. The siege had lasted but a short time when "the garrison commander was thrown out." Deinarchos, like Xenophon, has a short siege and one commander. There was also, he claims, official Athenian action taken during the siege.[5] Deinarchos was attacking Demosthenes, but in the presence of some of the elderly participants he could hardly twist chronology too much.

Aristeides (*Panath.* 283D) also emphasizes the importance of official Athenian help in liberating Thebes. Although Isokrates' *Plataikos* is a rhetorical exercise, it must have had to correspond to chronological fact enough to carry some credibility. Since both Isokrates and Deinarchos support Xenophon's chronological sequence and incidents,[6] it should be concluded that Xenophon is preferable here to Ephoros, and that the latter must be used only to supplement Xenophon's narration of events.

The conclusion, then, is that the Spartans, lacking any field army, took time to mobilize their forces. In the short interval between the first news of the revolution at Thebes and the information that the Kadmeia had surrendered very little was done. Probably there was not enough time for the Spartans to do very much. One gets the impression that the siege of the Kadmeia lasted just a couple of days.[7] No doubt preliminary steps toward mobilization had been taken, but even by the time the garrison and the Theban refugees had arrived in Sparta the commander of the force still had not been chosen.

Some scholars suggest that the two Athenian generals were authorized to act as they did by a secret session of the Boule,[8] with more troops despatched later under the command of Demophon and others in accordance with a decree moved by Kephalos. This puts too much reliance on Diodorus: it seems more likely and more in line with Xenophon that the decree of Kephalos nominally did no more than to authorize the two generals to move troops on the frontier.

Many modern authorities doubt all this, however, on the grounds that such behaviour would have been an act of war and too dramatic a step at the time. The generals were acting on their own.[9] But it is difficult to imagine any Athenian general being able to obtain or mobilize troops, to march them through Athens and deploy them on the frontier of Attica without some sort of authorization by the Demos. A decree of the People seems necessary. The phrasing of the decree, however, might simply speak of troop movements near the frontier, with some remarks about acting in the best interests of Athens, or the like. There need have been nothing about the Spartans, except possibly for declarations of friendship.[10] In this way a decree supporting the Theban democrats might not, it was hoped, be construed to be the authorization of a hostile act.

Several scholars also reject the testimony of the Attic orators on the grounds that they are notorious for rewriting history for contemporary purposes and so cannot be trusted. Therefore they cannot be used to bolster Xenophon. Since there were still witnesses alive when Deinarchos delivered his speech, it does not seem that too much rewriting would be acceptable. The parallels with Xenophon, when the rhetoric is stripped away, are striking.

Many also say that the exile or execution of the generals for carrying out officially sanctioned policy ought to have had severe repercussions echoing through the sources, at least for the rest of the century.[11] The repercussions from the executions after Arginousai, however, left few traceable echoes in the sources from the fourth century: there is not that much source material left. It is true that the generals after Naxos took pains to pick up survivors (Diod. 15.35), remembering what happened the last time crews were abandoned. The hint in Deinarchos about some Athenians acting at their own risk could be a similar echo of a considerable controversy surrounding the condemnation of the two generals for doing their duty.

Many historians consider that there was a tacit *de facto* working arrangement between Athens and Thebes.[12] This may also be true, in a way. Deinarchos makes a contrast between two Athenian groups: those who helped the Boiotians at their own risk; and those who helped after the passage of the decree of Kephalos. The former group may, besides the generals, also have included volunteers serving with the force of exiles under Pherenikos, and the Athenian troops on the frontier.

The Athenians, then, and at least two of the Athenian generals played a rôle in supporting the overthrow of the oligarchs and the expulsion of the garrison of the Kadmeia. Xenophon is unequivocal in saying that Athenians were there at the fall of the Kadmeia, and his silence on the despatch of forces officially cannot be significant in the face of the other evidence. A vaguely worded decree, moved by Kephalos, giving implicit approval for the Athenian generals to co-operate with the Thebans, is more in line with the evidence.

It seems most probable that first, there was unofficial aid "at their own risk" given to the Boiotian exiles by a group of pro-Boiotian Athenians. Then, after the exiles had their plans well launched, arrangements were made quietly for Athenian forces to move to help. The two generals were commanded by the Assembly, ostensibly to arrange for movements on the frontier; they found, however, that they too were acting "at their own risk." The coup succeeded. The main force of Boiotian exiles, accompanied by Athenian volunteers and backed by Athenian troops under their two generals, crossed the frontier. The Athenian hoplites returned home as soon as the Kadmeia surrendered, after trying to save some of the pro-Spartan Thebans who were being massacred.

The Athenians continued for a time to support Thebes. Near Eleutherai some of their peltasts, under another general, Chabrias,[13] were posted in a blocking position against any Spartan approach. A small advance force of Theban hoplites, the 150 ex-prisoners, was in touch with them in the hills overlooking Plataia, probably up in the Dryoskephalai Pass.[14]

Xenophon, Plutarch and Diodorus make no mention of any negotiations between the new Theban government and Sparta, though Diodorus (15.28.1) implies that there was some sort of communication between them. Only Isokrates (14.29) says specifically that there were dealings. *A priori* it would be reasonable for the new Theban government to try an approach to Sparta, and it seems not unlikely that it did. The interference of the pro-Spartan Theban exiles and the Spartan demands that they be restored and that the assassins be exiled have, even in Isokrates, the ring of truth. The majority of modern scholars accept the incident as genuine, rightly.[15]

Probably the Thebans offered peace and friendship, rather than re-entry into the Peloponnesian League,[16] but their overtures were rejected. Xenophon indicates that there was pressure on the Spartans from the Theban exiles for the appointment of a royal commander, but most modern authorities look to Spartan politics and the schemes of Agesilaus to explain why the Spartans acted as they did.[17]

A force under the young King Kleombrotos, his first command, moved north in the middle of winter, some time in late January or early February, 378,[18] well after the capitulation of the garrison and after abortive negotiations with the new Theban regime. A new stage in Boiotian-Spartan relations was opening.

The First Spartan Assault

Kleombrotos dodged the Athenian force of peltasts under Chabrias by taking "the Plataia road." This seems to be the fairly steep route over the Dryoskephalai Pass.[19] Here he caught and destroyed the Theban force of 150 ex-prisoners. He then advanced through Plataia, which was still friendly,[20] and went on to Thespiai. From there he advanced into Theban territory as far as Kynoskephalai, a locality not too distant from the town. Most recent studies place it at Rakhi Kendani, about 3.5 km from Thebes, near modern Loutoupi.[21] He stayed there for sixteen days, and then retired to Thespiai. There he left one-third of each of the Peloponnesian contingents under the command of Sphodrias with enough money to hire mercenaries. After this he withdrew by way of Kreusis, disbanding his force near Aigosthena.[22]

Xenophon (*Hell.* 5.4.16) comments that Kleombrotos was extraordinarily inactive while at Kynoskephalai, doing "the least possible damage" and thereby confusing his troops and leaving them wondering whether they were at war with Thebes or not. Modern historians have been equally confused. Some[23] have surmised that Kleombrotos was demonstrating his pacific intentions and waiting for negotiators from Thebes. He was in hopes of reviving his father's and brother's policies. If he devastated Theban territory, he would be doing something insupportable, namely carrying out his arch-rival Agesilaus' policy and ruining his own. If this is so, he failed in his intentions. Others[24] suggest that the Theban refugees in Sparta misled him into expecting a Theban collapse or counter-revolt in the face of a large Spartan army. Still others[25] point to the weather, which at that time of year can be particularly vile and tiresome in Boiotia, as an inhibitor of operations.

The idea that Kleombrotos was pursuing his pacific policies at the head of a large army in the middle of Boiotia is one lacking cogency. That the refugees who had so recently fled in such harrowing circumstances would expect the opposition to collapse argues for an optimism more fatuous than is reasonable to expect even in exiles. Probably the weather was the main factor. It was bitterly cold that winter, with snow and snowstorms, as we learn from the story of the coup at Thebes, and undoubtedly it continued to be unpleasant. It is quite possible that Kleombrotos was waiting for a break in the weather or a thaw, and he waited in vain. On the return trip his force suffered a blizzard, which caused some losses to his transport from the high winds, and "many shields, snatched away by the wind, fell into the sea."[26]

His invasion had two important effects. One was that it terrified the Athenians. There was a great fear of invasion, and it led to a revulsion of feeling against Kephalos and his pro-Theban policies, with Kallistratos' group gaining the advantage. Xenophon (*Hell.* 5.4.19) says that the two generals who had "been involved" (συνεπιστάσθην)[27] in the plans of Melon for the rebellion against the faction of Leontiades were brought to trial. One was executed; the other fled to exile. Xenophon is followed in this by Plutarch (*Pel.* 14.1), who is inconsistent here, since elsewhere he makes no mention of any Athenian military activities at this time. The Athenian Assembly reversed itself, and Athens pulled back from close ties with Boiotia, to the great indignation of the Theban democrats. There were even overtures by Athens to Sparta.

Three Spartan envoys, Etymokles, Aristolochos and Okyllos,[28] were sent to Athens at some time before March, 378, presumably to carry on the negotiations and perhaps to dissuade the Athenians from further close ties with Thebes. It was probably not at this time that Athens started making diplomatic forays among Spartan allies, but later.

The second result of Kleombrotos' invasion was the preparation of new defences by Thebes, the palisades. They may also have taken some desperate undercover measures, at least so it seems. With Thespiai, Orchomenos, Haliartos, Plataia and Tanagra occupied by Spartan garrisons or controlled by hostile oligarchic factions,[29] the city was isolated, and with Athens growing increasingly timid, there was little hope of outside aid. It was not surprising that the Thebans became very angry at the Athenians (χαλεπῶς ἔχοντας καὶ προδότας νομίζοντας in Plutarch's phrase). At some point in the first few months of 378 pro-democrats from the other states began to filter through to Thebes (cf. Xen. *Hell.* 5.4.49). But by March, 378 there was an abrupt change in Theban fortunes.

The Athenian Alliance

There are, however, difficulties in the sources with the sequence of events explaining the change. Diodorus (15.28.1–29.8) gives one version, while Xenophon (*Hell.* 5.4.20–34) and Plutarch (*Pel.* 14.1–3; *Ages.* 24.3–26.4) have another, though they are slightly different among themselves. Plutarch is *not* following Diodorus' source here.

In Diodorus the sequence is:

In Xenophon and Plutarch the sequence is:

1) The Boiotians (still allies of Athens) in the wake of Spartan discomfiture start organizing a large army against an expected Spartan invasion (5.28.1).

1) In fear of Sparta Athens tries two generals; Thebans very angry at Athenian cowardice (*Pel.* 14.3; Xen. *Hell.* 5.4.19).

2) Athens sends high-calibre diplomatic missions to states ruled by Sparta, preaching the cause of common freedom. Many turned to Athens, especially island states. Start of Second Athenian League (28.2–3).

2) Sphodrias, bribed by some Thebans (Xen. *Hell.* 5.4.20f.), by Pelopidas and Gorgidas (*Pel.* 14.1–3) or Pelopidas and Melon (*Ages.* 24.3–6) raids Attica. Failure (5.4.22–33).

3) Spartans tried to stop the rot, but in vain. Made preparations for war with Athens and Boiotia (28.4–5).

3) Sphodrias tried and acquitted at Sparta. Rupture with Athens (5.4.34).

4) Sphodrias, as commanded by Kleombrotos, invades Attica. Failure (25.29.5f.).

4) In Plut. *Pel.* 15.1 at this point the Athenians start a flurry of diplomatic activity, usually seen as the first steps in forming the Second Athenian League. Nothing said in Xenophon, but cf. *Hell.* 5.4.63.

5) Sphodrias tried and acquitted. Rupture of Athenian-Spartan relations. Election at Athens of Kallistratos, Chabrias and Timotheos. Mobilization of 20,000 hoplites, 500 horse and 200 ships (25.29.7).

5) Failure of Spartan attempts to to stop the rot in the system of alliances. (Plut. *Pel.* 15.1, *Ages.* 26.1; nothing in Xenophon).

6) Thebes joins the Second
   Athenian League (15.29.7).

6) Theban alliance with Athens
   (Xen. Hell. 4.34; Plut. *Pel.*
   15.1).

There are two intertwined problems here: 1) the reason for the formation of the Second Athenian Confederacy; and 2) the reason for the
raid by Sphodrias.

In Diodorus the raid is the *result* of the formation of the Second
Athenian Confederacy by way of the machinations of the Spartan King,
Kleombrotos. The Second Athenian Confederacy was formed as the
result of the success of the Athenian missions in the Aegean and the
Spartan failure to stop the falling away of its allies. The Athenian missions were the result of the alliance of Athens and Thebes. This was
the result of the Theban request after the coup. These form an interlocked unit, with the Second Athenian Confederacy as the *cause* of
Sphodrias' raid.

In Plutarch (and a source close in other respects to Xenophon: Kallisthenes?) there is the converse. The Second Athenian Confederacy is
the result of Sphodrias' raid by way of the machinations of some Theban leaders. The machinations were the result of Athenian fears and
the consequent Theban frustration over the lack of an alliance. The
Athenian fears were the result of the Spartan foray into Boiotia under
Kleombrotos. The foray was the result of the Theban coup and the reduction of the Kadmeia with Athenian aid. These form an interlocked
unit, with Sphodrias' raid as the *cause* of the Second Athenian Confederacy.

It is methodologically unsound to pick and choose segments from
one or the other to make a reasonable picture. Especially this should
not be done with such tightly interwoven material.

Scholarly opinion on the worth of each of these sequences is split,
with the general view[30] preferring Xenophon and Plutarch, with others, including many of the more recent researchers,[31] preferring Diodorus. Cawkwell[32] has tried to supplement Xenophon by filling in from
the Diodoran sequence, with the formation of the Second Athenian Confederacy set just *before* Sphodrias' raid, not after. Kallet-Marx has gone
even further, arguing that Athens had begun to take steps against Sparta

by laying the foundation of the Second Athenian Confederacy as early as the autumn of 379; the aid to the Theban dissidents is seen as part of the same policy. The idea was to undermine the Spartan domination of Greece, especially since Persia was otherwise occupied.[33] Both Cawkwell and Kallet-Marx implicitly reject the testimony of Plutarch, who places the formation just *after* the raid, not before. It is possible that Plutarch is filling in gaps in Xenophon by his own invention of a *post hoc propter hoc*, but it seems more likely that he has used a source that gives details omitted by Xenophon, perhaps the one he is commonly believed to follow here, Kallisthenes. If this is so, then it is clear that the chronology followed by Xenophon and Plutarch is the one to be preferred, and that Diodorus is to be rejected.

Although the Athenians had been making some alliances among the islands much earlier, as with Chios, clearly the big push for forming the Confederacy came after the raid by Sphodrias.[34]

The story in Xenophon (*Hell.* 5.4.20) and Plutarch (*Pel.* 14.2, *Ages.* 24.3–4) of how Pelopidas and/or other Theban officials through an intermediary bribed and cajoled Sphodrias into making the raid has generally been rejected as incredible. As Grote argued, if the raid had succeeded, the Thebans would have been in greater trouble than before, and Agesilaus would never have supported Sphodrias if he had taken Theban bribes.[35] A few, however, do accept it, usually with some reservations.[36] Even Xenophon inserts ὡς ὑπωπτεύετο after the allegation of Theban bribery; while Plutarch in *Pelopidas* says that they sent money *and* advice, with the latter acceptable to Sphodrias and the former not; in *Agesilaus* that it was the advice devised by Pelopidas and Melon and planted by men pretending to be Spartan sympathizers that did the job.

On the other hand, it could be argued that the Theban situation was desperate. Facing inevitable defeat if they did nothing, they had nothing to lose by taking a chance on a provocation. Presumably the Boiotians had time and opportunity to size up Sphodrias for what he was. Perhaps they had a shrewd idea that he had little chance of success. From Thespiai to the Peiraieus is about 65 miles, a distance impossible for an overnight march.[37] A foray intended to go as far as the edges of Eleusinian territory seems more reasonable. Kallet-Marx suggests that

Sphodrias was intending to make a raid into Attica to terrify the Athenians into good behaviour again, much as Kleombrotos had done.

A possibility more in consonance with what we know of the virtuous and honourable Pelopidas, is that the original Theban idea was to assault Thespiai in the absence of most of its garrison. At the urging of Theban agents Sphodrias would have despatched his force on a mad chase into Attica, out of the way. It would have been suggested by the agents that this was a tried-and-true way of terrifying the Athenians into good behaviour, just as Kleombrotos had done, not as an assault on the Peiraieus. The primary purpose of the Boiotian effort, then, would have been the capture of Thespiai. On a secondary level, if the Athenians were cowed, Thebes was no worse off than she already was; but if the Athenians reacted as they actually did, the situation would be highly satisfactory. Plutarch (*Pel.* 14.2) reports that Pelopidas and Gorgidas sent in an agent, one Emporos,[38] to play a double game and persuade Sphodrias to "embark on large-scale enterprises." They must have felt they had a good chance of clearing the Spartans from their main base in eastern Boiotia. A similar strategy was later aimed against Orchomenos, at the time of the battle of Tegyra, when it was thought that the garrison was out in Phokis on a raid.[39] In the event Sphodrias and his force returned to Thespiai before the Thebans succeeded in taking it. The siege mentioned by Diodorus (15.27.4) may be referring to this incident. The main result was that Thebes soon had a new ally.[40]

In the Xenophon-Plutarch version the treaty signed *after* the abortive raid is the only full and formal alliance. Any earlier Athenian aid under the decree of Kephalos was unofficial. There is a much battered and mutilated inscription (*IG*² 2.40) that may or may not refer to a preliminary stage of the alliance.[41] The full alliance, by which Thebes (though probably not the Boiotian League) joined the Second Athenian Confederacy (*IG*² 2.43) has been the subject of a careful study recently.[42]

Attacks on Thebes: The Palisades

Thebes, by mid-378, had done quite well: the city was free and democratic; to judge by the fact that numerous refugees were coming into

Thebes, there was support in Boiotia for the new democratic League; it had Athens as an ally. On the other hand, the Spartans were determined to crush it; the governments of the other Boiotian cities were oligarchic and supported Sparta; and at least the key ones, Orchomenos, Thespiai and Plataia, had Spartan garrisons. A Spartan invasion was more than likely. Against this threat Thebes had erected some field defences.

At some point early in 378, probably as soon as they could, the Thebans, perhaps with official or unofficial Athenian help, began to construct a ditch with a palisade to protect the main Theban plain. It ran, according to the latest study,[43] not in a "circle," as Xenophon puts it (*Hell.* 5.4.38), but in a curving line from near Kynoskephalai, southwest of Thebes, to near Skolos on the Asopos. Since Sparta normally timed its invasions to arrive about harvest time, when the ripened grain could be fired, we may assume that the invasion came in late June.[44] This gave Thebes some five months to construct its Maginot Line. It was about as useful as that fortification, too.

Agesilaus moved against Thebes in late June, sending mercenaries lent him by Kleitor ahead into Kithairon as a vanguard (5.4.36f.).[45] He had more than 18,000 hoplites, including five *morai* of Spartans, each of 500 men, as well as 1500 cavalry.[46] The Athenians sent 5000 infantry and 200 horse to Thebes as reinforcements.[47] These probably arrived just after the Spartans reached Thespiai. Agesilaus moved the camps of his troops into Theban territory outside the Line and though the soldiers were not eager to do so, they damaged the crops when Agesilaus shifted their camps around.

Meanwhile the Theban and Athenian troops moved up to a long ridge some twenty stades (about 3.5 km) from Thebes, probably Kynoskephalai.[48] Agesilaus was held up by the Lines and the troops behind them who matched his moves. There were some skirmishes and unsuccessful assaults, in which the Thebans did quite well, and the Spartans sustained some casualties.[49] After several days Agesilaus by a stratagem pierced the line at an unmanned point.[50] Possibly at the Line or more likely during a fighting retreat towards Thebes the Athenian mercenaries under Chabrias gained a considerable reputation by a stratagem. After the Spartan light-armed troops had harassed the

Theban hoplites, Agesilaus deployed to advance; but the snappy and precise drill of the Athenian mercenaries and their obvious readiness to receive an attack caused Agesilaus to hold off and to withdraw his main force.[51] The Spartan light-armed troops did considerable damage to Theban territory,[52] but the Theban and Athenian forces were able to retire and were preserved to fight again.

Agesilaus returned to Thespiai, where he, too, constructed fortifications. Then he marched back to the Peloponnese, leaving the experienced Phoibidas as harmost.[53] He was criticized for not bringing the Thebans and Athenians to a decisive battle.

Phoibidas proceeded to carry out a series of raids, and in retaliation the Thebans made a counter-raid on Thespian territory. They wiped out a *prophylax* of 200 men, but failed in assaults on the town.[54] After some skirmishes they withdrew with Phoibidas' peltasts hanging on their flanks. In pressing the pursuit Phoibidas was killed. The Thebans stopped retreating and turned; there was a panic that involved both Spartan mercenaries and Thespian hoplites in a complete rout.[55]

"Then," says Xenophon (*Hell.* 5.4.46), "after this the Thebans' affairs caught fire again." By this he probably means that support for the League throughout Boiotia was materially strengthened, and its prospects were once again taken seriously elsewhere.[56]

The Thebans, along with pro-democrats who had joined them from other cities, sent out forces in another foray against Thespiai "and other neighbouring cities (Xen. *Hell.* 5.4.46)." Plutarch in the same context as the death of Phoibidas mentions Spartan defeats at Plataia and at Tanagra, where the harmost Panthoidas was killed (*Pel.* 15.3). The Boiotians apparently were not able to exploit these victories, and the Spartans replaced Phoibidas by another harmost and reinforced the garrison at Thespiai. Still the year 378 was remarkably successful for Thebes and the infant Boiotian League.

The Fighting: 377 B.C.

In June, 377, Agesilaus led another force from the Peloponnese, after troops from the garrison of Thespiai occupied Kithairon to forestall the

Thebans and Athenians.[57] He planted all sorts of false and misleading information that implied he was heading for Thespiai; this was rapidly picked up by the Thebans (their Intelligence was quick and efficient, doubtless through pro-democratic and pro-League Boiotians). They made their dispositions around Kynoskephalai accordingly. He then marched all day through Kithairon to Plataia, then after a short night's rest he continued rapidly to Skolos, where he turned or pierced the left edge of the unoccupied Lines,[58] anticipating the German tactics in outflanking the Maginot Line in 1940. Agesilaus' forces then devastated eastern Theban territory as far as the border of Tanagra.[59] Diodorus (15.34.1) in a confused passage claims that the Thebans arrived in time to prevent any devastation, a version universally rejected.

The Spartans began to withdraw, "keeping the wall on the left." This must refer to the Lines (not the city wall of Tanagra, the territory of which was not invaded)[60] and mean that the Spartans were heading west towards Thespiai.

The Thebans and their Athenian allies had regrouped and occupied a position from which they could challenge the Spartans to battle, on a hill called Graos Stethos,[61] a very strong tactical position for forcing a fight. The hill is set in various places, but Munn is probably right in identifying it with Golemi, some 5 km southeast of Thebes.[62] Here the Thebans would have the Lines to their rear as they faced the Spartans, with both forces inside the Lines.

Agesilaus was not prepared to fight a pitched battle on such disadvantageous terms as those here, and he neatly out-manoeuvred the Thebans. He turned northwest along a fairly rough track, so as to feint an attack on Thebes. The Thebans and Athenians were forced to dance to his tune: they had to evacuate their position so as to get back to Thebes in a hurry by way of the easier route via Potniai (Xen. *Hell.* 5.4.50f.)

The two armies skirmished briefly near the city, according to Xenophon, and then Agesilaus swung back to camp on Graos Stethos, from which the way was clear to Thespiai. The Thebans claimed a victory on very flimsy grounds. Diodorus (15.34.2), however, speaks of heavy fighting before Thebes, broken off by the Spartans when reinforcements arrived from Thebes. This version is generally rejected, but the fighting was probably heavier than one might gather from Xenophon's acerbic description.

In some skirmishing on the way to Thespiai the Theban mercenary peltasts sustained casualties when they got beyond the protection of the main forces, which were apparently under the command of Chabrias.[63] The Thebans and their allies regarded the withdrawal of Agesilaus as a victory and erected a trophy. The fact that they could face the Spartans was a great boost to morale, since they "realized they were not inferior to the Spartans."

On his arrival at Thespiai Agesilaus found the city in *stasis*. One faction wanted to destroy its opponents; both presumably were pro-Spartan, since Agesilaus refused to permit this, but made them come to a sworn agreement. This seems to have settled matters in Thespiai temporarily. He then returned to the Peloponnese. On his way back he fell ill at Megara and was unable to return to duty for more than a year.[64]

The Thebans, with their land devastated for two years, were now short of grain and other food. Xenophon and Frontinus[65] report a Hollywood-style incident: the Thebans sent out two triremes to buy some supplies from Thessaly. Spartan Intelligence was good, too, and the harmost in Oreos in Euboia sent out three triremes which captured the two Boiotians on their way back, taking at least 300 prisoners. They were imprisoned on the Acropolis of Oreos, but observing some slackness in the security arrangements they made a mass breakout, "whereupon the city revolted," and in the confusion of the popular revolution the prisoners got themselves out of town and their cargo back to Thebes.

The year 377 ended with Thebes still unsubdued and the Spartans gradually weakening financially. Since they had to rely on troops from their garrisons to protect Kithairon, it is clear that they were short of resources for hiring mercenaries. Support for the Boiotian League was steadily strengthening, as Thebes fought off Spartan attacks. The Boiotian cities were kept under control, mainly by the Spartan garrisons.

The Fighting: 376 B.C.

In early spring 376 the Spartans prepared to make their usual attack on Boiotia. They seemed not, however, to have had the necessary resources to occupy Kithairon early enough, and this time the Athenians and the Boiotians got there first. By the time that Kleombrotos, who was in command in the absence of Agesilaus, sent up his peltasts to occupy the heights, they were met and defeated by the Athenians and Boiotians. Kleombrotos thereupon abandoned the invasion.[66]

The Peloponnesian allies, moreover, were becoming discontented and began pressing for more action against the arch-enemy, Athens. They thought that Athens could be starved into submission by imposing a blockade and cutting off the grain supplies. This would require an effort by sea, and so it was resolved to man a fleet of some 60 ships, with Pollis in command.[67]

Athens found itself blockaded by the fleet and mobilized a larger one, of 83 ships, under the command of Chabrias. It soon cleared a way for the grain ships, and off Naxos the two fleets met. The Spartans were defeated, with 24 ships sunk and eight captured against the Athenian losses of 18 ships. The generals, remembering the aftermath of Arginousai, were careful to pick the survivors. The result was that much of the Spartan fleet got away. Nevertheless it was a decisive battle, the first Athenian victory since the Peloponnesian War.[68] It happened about September, 376 and marks the end of fighting for the year.

The Fighting: 375 B.C.

The year 375 saw a string of Boiotian and Athenian successes, with the balance tilting increasingly against Sparta. It had fewer and fewer resources available, so much so that it found that it was not able to offer any assistance to its *proxenos* Polydamas of Pharsalos against Jason of Pherai.[69] The government still planned an assault against Boiotia, but, since it was now prohibitively costly in losses to negotiate Kithairon in the teeth of the Athenian and Boiotian forces, a seaborne invasion was planned. The Boiotians, whose Intelligence was a good as ever, asked the Athenians for aid. The latter sent a fleet of 60 ships under the command of Timotheos around the Peloponnese to control the Corinthian Gulf.[70] This stopped any attempt at a seaborne attack, and, as Xenophon says, "the Thebans consequently marched boldly on the neighbouring cities and took them over again (5.4.63)."

Since Thespiai, Orchomenos and Plataia were still occupied by Spartan garrisons, he probably means cities like Tanagra, Haliartos, Lebadeia, Akraiphnion, Kopai, Koroneia and Chaironeia.[71] The Boiotian League was once again something more than Thebes plus exiles. This was probably in the late spring and early summer, early June to July, 375.

During this period the Boiotians handed the Spartans a smart reverse in the Battle of Tegyra.[72] Intelligence reported that the garrison of Orchomenos had moved out on an expedition into Lokris, and Pelopidas with the Sacred Band moved against the town, presumably from Chaironeia. He found, however, that the town had received other troops from Sparta, and it was impossible to attack. He decided to withdraw north and east, around Lake Copaïs. He got as far as the shrine of Tegyra,[73] when he met the Spartans returning from Lokris. He charged with his cavalry spearheading the Sacred Band and broke the Spartan line. It was on a small scale, but significant in that a Spartan force was defeated in a pitched battle, and that the Sacred Band was used as a tactical unit for the first time. Tegyra left a deep impression on Greece and gave a boost to Boiotian morale.[74] The Spartan expedition into Lokris was probably in response to trouble in a former Boiotian ally and enemy of Phokis. The Thebans retaliated later by marching against the Spartan ally Phokis.

Meanwhile Timotheos and the Athenian fleet had sailed up to Kerkyra, which they apparently conquered.[75] Other states in the area of the Straits of Otranto were enroled in the Second Athenian Confederacy. The Spartan fleet was sent out under the command of Nikolochos and was defeated off Alyzia, sometime in July.[76] The remnants withdrew to the Peloponnese. All this meant, however, that Timotheos was far away from the Corinthian Gulf when the Spartans made another move.

The Thebans and their new League colleagues had marched into Phokis, and the Phokians appealed to Sparta for help. It was decided to send a force across under the command of Kleombrotos, while Timotheos was still absent in the Ionian Sea. It arrived sometime in late August, and the Thebans retreated to protect their passes.

The Athenians had gone to a great deal of expense in sending out the fleet, and the returns from the expedition were probably not commensurate. The Thebans had not contributed much, either. At any rate the fleet was withdrawn in the autumn, when the Athenians' finances, more than their weariness with the war and their suspicions of Boiotia, led them to send envoys to Sparta to seek peace.[77]

VII   The League to Leuktra, 375–371 B.C.

The temporary peace of 375 soon gave way to war, and the Boiotians again fought against Sparta. The Athenians, however, grew increasingly disenchanted with their allies, as Thebes captured Plataia and tightened the control of the League over the other Boiotian towns. The democratic League became in the minds of many within and without Boiotia another device to make all Boiotia Theban. By 371 everyone was ready for peace again, but the negotiations broke down over the question of the autonomy of individual states, and the Battle of Leuktra settled the matter.

The Peace of 375 B.C.

The peace treaty of late 375,[1] between Sparta and her allies and Athens and hers (including Boiotia), differs considerably as reported by Xenophon or by Diodorus.[2] In Xenophon its adoption stems from an Athenian initiative; in Diodorus it is primarily due to the efforts of the Persian King. Nothing is said about the terms in Xenophon, except that the withdrawal of Timotheos from the western areas was an important item; Diodorus gives a long and involved account, but one omitting anything about the withdrawal of Timotheos.

The Persian King, says Diodorus, was planning to fight in Egypt and wanted to hire a mercenary force of suitable Greek veterans. He therefore sent envoys to Greece to invite the various states to conclude a common peace. Most of the states accepted the terms he proposed: all states were to be autonomous and all garrisons were to be evacuated; the Greeks were to establish disarmament commissioners (ἐξαγωγεῖς) to inspect each city and get rid of any foreign garrisons they found. Philochoros (*FGrH* 328 F 151) as cited in a passage of Didymus is said to mention a peace promulgated by the King that has much the same terms as that of Antalkidas. Consequently many authorities accept the idea of Persian influence on the Peace and use Philochoros to supplement Xenophon.[3]

In doing this they usually ignore as a cause Xenophon's point that the Athenians were discontented because of the lack of financial support from Thebes; and his other point that the result of this discontent was the Athenian mission to Sparta (not to Susa) to arrange peace. The testimony of Philochoros when examined closely is not very cogent. He says only that the Athenians made a peace at some time, one very close in its terms to that of Antalkidas. The King's influence is an inference of Didymus', and it is not in Philochoros' statement.

In Diodorus the Thebans refused to agree to the terms, since each of the Boiotian cities would have to sign on its own behalf. Thebes, said Diodorus, wanted to "set all Boiotia under the federation of the Thebans" (Θηβαίων ... τὴν Βοιωτίαν ἅπασαν ὑπὸ τὴν τῶν Θηβαίων συντέλειαν ταττόντων). The Athenians opposed this vigorously. Epaminondas led the Boiotian negotiating party. The upshot was that Thebes refused to sign. Consequently, according to Diodorus, its hostilities with Sparta were not terminated.

All this in Diodorus seems most improbable.[4] The desire of the Persian King for peace, so as to obtain mercenaries, sounds like a recooking of the story of Cyrus, and his sending of a rescript sounds like a rehash of the events of 387, garbled. The idea of a squad of Persian envoys distributing a rescript, one eagerly seized upon because everyone was bankrupt, lacks persuasiveness, as does the idea of a disarmament commission.

Furthermore, the exclusion of Thebes from the Peace is incredible for five reasons. First, there were Spartan forces in Phokis; these did not make any effort to attack Boiotia, as they were ready to do before the peace negotiations. Second, all the Spartan garrisons in Boiotia *were* evacuated, as we learn from sources other than Diodorus.[5] Third, Thebes could hardly sign a treaty on behalf of Boiotian cities that at the time of the treaty were garrisoned by Sparta or continued to be hostile to Thebes. Fourth, the Boiotians continued to take an active part in the Second Athenian Confederacy, *inter alia* sending ships to join the Athenian fleet after hostilities were resumed, hardly the acts of a state that had crossed its senior partner. Fifth, Diodorus' source here, Ephoros, is well known for his habit of doubling incidents.[6] The set here on the peace conference is strikingly similar to the series connected with the Peace of 371. Although a few authorities argue for Theban exclusion from the Peace of 375,[7] the majority hold, I think rightly (even if several accept Persian diplomatic intervention), that Xenophon is to be preferred and that Diodorus is anticipating here, with slight artistic variations, what really happened in 371.

The Peace was made in 375, then, on the initiative of Athens, which was suffering considerable financial hardship, partly because of the lack of financial help from Boiotia. Presumably Thebes was a party to the peace as an Athenian ally, not as the head of the Boiotian League. Persia had nothing to do with it.

From the *events* recorded in the sources (not from terms in Diodorus) one may conclude that the terms were basically no more than those of a cease-fire. The Athenians withdrew their forces from the western area and presumably from other parts of Greece; the Spartans withdrew theirs from areas outside the Peloponnese. For Boiotia this meant that the Spartans evacuated any garrisons in the area, including those of Plataia, Thespiai and Orchomenos. What the Thebans as allies of Athens were to do, presumably, was to refrain from hostilities against Sparta and her allies. The implication is that the oligarchic Boiotian cities were still Spartan allies, even if no longer garrisoned. The Boiotian oligarchs were now on their own and open to attack if hostilities should be resumed.

The Union of All Boiotia

The Peace of 375 did not last long. It was a rest between rounds, so to speak, while the parties built up their funds. Sometime in 374 or 373 the activities of Timotheos led to Spartan counter-action, and once again Athens and her allies were at war with Sparta and hers.[8]

Boiotia played a not inconsiderable part in the activities of the Second Athenian Confederacy,[9] and the renewal of the war may have opened the door for the Theban treatment of Plataia and Thespiai. Pausanias says that two years before the battle of Leuktra, in the archonship of Astios at Athens (373), Plataia was taken by the Thebans. Thebes and Plataia were technically at peace, but the Plataians watched the Thebans with some suspicion and went out to their fields only when they were satisfied that the latter were holding their public assemblies, "knowing that the deliberations were long." The Boiotarch Neokles became aware of this and decided to take advantage of it. He ordered all the citizens to assemble as if for an assembly but fully armed. Then he took them to Plataia by a circuitous route. They arrived and cut off those in the fields from the town and forced its surrender. As a result all the Plataians were expelled and went as refugees to Athens, and the townsite was razed except for the temples.[10]

Shortly after the reduction of Plataia, there was some fighting between the Boiotian League and Thespiai and Orchomenos.[11] It might have been started by the two at the behest of Sparta, or have been a pre-emptive strike by Thebes against Spartan allies. Clearly the Thespians and Orchomenians came off second best. Unlike the Plataians the Thespians were not expelled. Thespiai "was compelled to 'syntely' into Thebes" (συντελεῖν μόνον εἰς Θήβας ἀναγκάζειν), as was Tanagra.[12] Presumably the complete reduction of Orchomenos at this point would require more resources than the League had available as yet. It has been argued, not very convincingly, that Thespiai may have at this point suffered a *dioikismos*, that is, a dissolution into villages.[13] More likely the walls erected by the Spartans after 378 were demolished, and the Thespian adult males had to walk or ride to Thebes if they wanted to take part in the Federal Assembly, where all the important decisions were made.

It was probably after the fighting with Thespiai and Orchomenos that the Thespians (along with the Plataians) besought the Athenians "not to stand idly by while they [the Thespians] became cityless," ἀπολίδες.[14] This has often been taken to mean that the Thespians were afraid of receiving the same treatment that the Plataians had suffered. The term ἀπολίδες, however, has other significations besides exile after the physical dissolution of one's *polis*. It could mean "not having a state," as Herodotus (8.61) uses it, or the disappearance of one's citizenship by a sympolity, or, as in Plato (*Legg.* 576D) the absence of a real constitution. According to Pausanias a Thespian contingent was part of the Boiotian force concentrating before the battle of Leuktra. It was apparently not a happy or trustworthy force, but it was there, even though Epaminondas did not use it.[15]

Between 374 and 371, then, the states that were not part of the League were constrained to capitulate. Orchomenos, the last, yielded after Leuktra, probably late in 371. Diodorus puts it this way: εἰς τὴν τῶν συμμάχων χώραν κατέταξαν (to be translated as "they assigned it to the category of allies").[16] The phraseology would indicate that Orchomenos was not admitted to the League but was treated as an ally. The Orchomenians, then, would not attend the Assembly of the League, any more than the Lokrians would. In effect they were, as Boiotians, no more than *perioikoi*, second-class citizens.

Distance might possibly explain the special status of Orchomenos after its reduction. It was quite a long way around the west end of Lake Copaïs, and it might be just a little too far for convenience in attending the Assembly. On the other hand, it may well be, and I think it more likely, that the rest of Boiotia, i.e., the democrats, simply did not trust the Orchomenians. The best attested evidence of discontent within the democracy comes from the conspiracy of 364 and the activities of the 300 Orchomenian *hippeis*. This was clearly part of an oligarchic attempt at a coup, with the Orchomenians providing the core.[17] There is no evidence at this time of democrats who were anti-League (though there were in the Peloponnesian War), and one may infer that opposition to the Boiotian federal system was largely a matter of factional politics, although the idea that there was always a strong sense of separatism must not be ignored.

Boiotian Federalism and Democracy

At this point it seems reasonable to ask just what sort of government the Boiotian League had by 372. All sources and authorities agree that Thebes was a democracy, and that the League was democratic but dominated by Thebes. This is more than a little ambiguous: it is true that a democracy can control and dominate a hegemonal league, just as Athens did the Delian League. But if the Boiotian League was in itself democratic, then it was nothing like the Delian League and nothing like the old oligarchic League. The latter had been a federation, a federal league, with rights and privileges belonging to its constituent members. The federal powers had been exercised through a Council and other bodies *representing* the various states and districts and named by their respective oligarchies. With the rejection of oligarchy and the implementation of a direct democracy all the old apparatus and infrastructures so intimately associated with oligarchy could not be revived and were not revived.

In their stead was a democratic system modelled on the Athenian: an assembly of all adult male Boiotians;[18] a boule chosen by the lot with probouleutic powers and limited authority;[19] an executive, the Boiotarchs, analogous to the Athenian *strategoi*, elected by the assembly; and no doubt numerous other committees and officials to carry out the dictates and desires of the assembly; perhaps there were even nomothetes, to temper zeal with constitutional checks. It may be that the majority of the minor officials, as well as the jurors in the courts, were chosen by lot, with only those offices requiring special expertise elected by vote, but there is no evidence on this point.[20]

Athenian-style democracy, however, evolved in a unitary state, not in a federation. Such a type of democracy, if it was to have the citizens of all the Boiotian cities participate, could not be structured so as to reflect the constituent parts of a federation: all available citizens would attend the Assembly as citizens of Boiotia, that is, as Boiotians, not as Tanagraians or Koroneians. The essence of a democracy was direct participation of all voters in the assembly and equitable selection for service in all other parts of the government. No delegation or representation was possible. For various committees a selection was made on tribal or other such basis, but the citizens so chosen were not delegates of or representatives of their units. Representative democracy was virtually nonexistent in fourth century Greece, and the few examples extant, such as Mantinea, were usually regarded as rather strange oligarchies.[21]

Diodorus describes this new and democratic Boiotia as a *synteleia* (συντέλεια) in three places,[22] all in the context of the Thebans setting or arranging (τάττω or ἄγω) Boiotia into one *synteleia*, one association or union. The corresponding verb (συντελέω εἰς) is used to describe how a given state is "syntelied" to Thebes, apparently with the connotation of some subordination to or union with Thebes.[23] *Synteleia* is a term used by Polybius and others for a league,[24] but one where local units are strictly subordinated to a central government, to some sort of union, one with organs of state in common.[25] In the oligarchic League the states sent *representatives* to run the federal government; in the democracy *everybody* ran the federal government. Very different philosophies of government are implicit here: in place of a federal government representing constituent *poleis* there is a supreme democratic government with the states as subordinate creatures to it. The states in a directly democratic *synteleia* simply cannot have had any rights and powers beyond those granted by the federation, that is, any sovereignty.[26] The Boiotian cities would be subordinate parts of the state, rather than the components of an association of states.

Under the democracy there would still be a place for the cities, but they would be no more than local conveniences, much as the demes, tribes or other local units were in a unitary state.[27] In effect the Boiotian democrats envisaged Boiotia as an Attica, with all Boiotians enjoying one citizenship and one Assembly. By legal fiction everyone was, so to speak, "moved" to the capital in a kind of sympolity. Just as there were no Atticans, but only Athenians, so there would only be Boiotians, in one big citizenship. The urban centres could no longer be independent cities: they could be only subordinate units, administrative conveniences like Athenian demes or tribes.

Many Boiotians did not see it quite this way: for them this League democracy was a device to give Thebes control, and it was an infringement on their states' liberties. Xenophon[28] and other authors mention the bitterness of many Boiotians towards the union forced on them, a union that they felt unjust and stifling. Even though the Thespians or Tanagrans were not physically transported to Thebes or exiled, it is understandable that many of them could describe themselves under such a dispensation as being "cityless," in spite of the fact that the towns were, with the exception of their walls, untouched.[29] In other words all Boiotia became for practical purposes as much a part of the *polis* of Thebes as Attica was of Athens.[30]

The fact that the ethnic Βοιωτός is never used in inscriptions between 378 and 338 (except at Delphi), but only the names of towns,[31] makes it plain that the local ethnic was used in Boiotia in the same way as the demotic was used at Athens, to identify the individual by his local designation as a member of the whole state.

The Boiotians (except for Orchomenians, Plataians and Oropans) were all citizens of Boiotia (i.e., the democratic state centred on Thebes) politically, not simply of the local state. The national Boiotian army had Tanagraians and Thespians in the ranks at the time of the Battle of Leuktra, but it was brigaded by towns, much as the Athenians were brigaded by tribes.[32]

The importance of Thebes, or at least of the use of "Thebes" rather than "Boiotia" was played down by the Boiotians themselves, even if the effort did not impress Xenophon or other Greeks: the officials of the state were still Boiotarchs; the Boiotian federal coinage, which from 447 to 386 was always labelled "Thebes" (ΘΕ),[33] was now labelled with the name of the responsible Boiotarch or of some high official, like Ismenias.[34] The Assembly is always "the People (Damos) of the Boiotians."

The Assembly, the Damos, legislated in all fields. It set foreign policy, military policy, monetary policy; it named commanders, and ruled the state. It could and did amend motions put before it and could be quite as arbitrary as the Athenian Assembly. It met on the Kadmeia, apparently at set intervals between meetings. It elected the Boiotarchs and other key officials.[35]

The Boiotarchs, at least in 372 when we have inscriptional evidence, were only seven in number.[36] They were elected and dismissed by the Assembly, not by any constituent cities or districts.[37] Considerable discussion has centred around the number of seven, many scholars trying to associate it with the old districts of the earlier League: four from the two districts of Thebes; one from Tanagra; one from Haliartos-Koroneia-Lebadeia; and one from Akraphnion-Kopai-Chaironeia. The double districts of Thespiai and Orchomenos were not represented, it is claimed, the former because it had just been captured and its loyalty to the democratic League was suspect; the latter because it was still independent, and after it was captured it was placed in a special status.[38]

There is, however, no evidence that the number of Boiotarchs was constant at seven, or that they represented districts, or that they were linked in any way to the districts, or, for that matter, that the districts were still in use for any purpose.[39] Any Boiotian was eligible for election as Boiotarch, and several non-Thebans were elected, though we have no indication of how many of them there were.[40] The Boiotarchs could be re-elected. They entered office on 1 Boukataios, the first day of the Boiotian year. At the end of the year they underwent audits, and failure to lay down authority at the end of the year was a capital offence.[41] Their authority was analogous to that of the Athenian *strategoi*. Judicial and financial officials and other offices seem to have been copied from the Athenian model. There is also a federal Archon, noted in inscriptions from the 370s on, whose sole function apparently was to lend his name to the year, rather like the Athenian eponymous Archon.[42]

In all cases there is no indication of any selection by constituent states, or the choosing of representatives for or by constituent states. In a direct democracy there is no need and no way. Most modern authorities have been quick to point out that the democratic constitution readily lent itself to the domination of Boiotia by its most populous city, Thebes. There were nearly as many Thebans as the total of all the other Boiotians; it was much easier for the Thebans to attend meetings of the Damos on the Kadmeia than, say for the Tanagraians, Haliartans, or Lebadeans.[43] The same arguments apply, of course, to the residents of Athens *vis-à-vis* those of Eleusis, Marathon or Sounion, and one would hesitate to decry Athenian democracy on that score. The vigour of the old farmer in Aristophanes, going to Athens before dawn, shows that even distant citizens made their way to the Assembly.[44] One must conclude that distance was not an insuperable barrier for the non-Theban Boiotian citizens to take part in Boiotian democracy. But it was observed by such outsiders as Xenophon that many of the non-Thebans were resentful of Thebes and reluctant to attend meetings. The Boiotians were proverbial for their mutual dislike. Perikles is supposed to have said that the Boiotians were like the ilex trees, always knocking one another down.[45]

The Boiotian Army

The Boiotian army remained, if the evidence from Leuktra is acceptable, brigaded by its local contingents. If any use were to be made of the old eleven districts, it would be for manning and supplying the army; but these activities were apparently carried out by the localities themselves. This may be inferred from the aftermath of Leuktra. The Thespians only (not including the other inhabitants of their district) abandoned the town and fled to Keressos, where Epaminondas had to reduce them.[46]

The major striking force of the Theban section of the Boiotian army after the Battle of Tegyra was the Sacred Band (ἱερὸς λόχος), a permanent force of 300, maintained at public expense and stationed on the Kadmeia.[47] Whatever its origin (and this may lie in some Dark Age or Archaic chariot group, if its nomenclature has any significance),[48] it was probably reconstituted and remodelled as a regular, professional force by Gorgidas shortly after the coup of 378, just as Plutarch (*Pel.* 18.1) says. Gorgidas apparently used the band as a stiffener for the rest of the Theban army, as it is claimed that it was used at Delion.[49] Pelopidas is given the credit for first employing the band as a separate tactical unit, after he was named its commander.[50] It formed the most formidable unit of the Theban army. The members were all "picked men" (ἐπίλεκτοι), though it is not stated who did the picking and how it was done. With some uncertainty Plutarch goes on to claim (ἔνιοι δέ φασιν) that the unit was composed of sworn lovers. It is difficult to see how this was accomplished among 300, 150 pairs, without undue turbulence. More likely there is a misunderstanding of the two-man teams, the ἡνίοχοι καὶ παραβάται, the charioteers and crewmen,[51] into which the *lochos* was divided. Undoubtedly, however, many young men of the better families would hold to aristocratic traditions of homosexuality.[52]

Boiotian Politics 378–371 B.C.

Next to nothing is known about internal Boiotian politics during this period. The oligarchs were in full retreat if not routed, and the democrats had opportunity to air their quarrels. The only one of which we know anything involves Menekleidas. He had been one of the leading conspirators, one of the twelve (or seven) young exiles who returned to Thebes. He split with Pelopidas and Epaminondas for reasons unclear to us. Jealousy is alleged. He spoke against them in the Damos.[53] He tried to promote a rift between Pelopidas and Charon and had some success in keeping Epaminondas out of office. Eventually, about 372 or so, he was defeated by Pelopidas. Possibly Charon and Pelopidas were leaders of rival democratic factions, as some suspect, but in the absence of any evidence it must remain just a conjecture.

The Peace of 371 B.C.

By 371 Athens and Sparta were growing tired of the war. Athens was unable to pay the fleet and, in spite of many advantages gained, was going bankrupt. The Assembly voted to negotiate peace.[54] Sparta was losing and most anxious not to continue on this road to defeat. It had had to deploy a large force in Phokis to secure it against the Boiotian ally Jason of Pherai, but there were also revolts in the Peloponnese that needed to be quelled. No doubt it, too, was running out of money. The two powers agreed to a peace conference at Sparta. The Athenians invited their chief land allies, the Boiotians, to accompany them to the negotiations at Sparta. Epaminondas was their leader.[55] The Athenians also invited the maritime members of the Second Athenian Confederacy, though it is not stated what proportion of them went.

The Athenian mission seems to reflect the indecision at Athens about the sort of peace terms desirable and what the post-war arrangements should be.[56] According to Xenophon one of the Athenian envoys, Kallias, pointed out the mutuality of interest between Athens and Sparta, especially against Thebes, mentioning the "destruction" (ἀναίρεσιν) of Plataia and Thespiai.[57] Another, Autokles, was more truculent and pro-Theban, making the point that the Spartan dissolution of the Boiotian League and occupation of Thebes had been self-defeating (6.3.7–10). A third Athenian, Kallistratos, smoothed things out and made the point that as a result of the wrongs done to the Thebans, all the cities that the Spartans had wanted to be independent "were once again under them (ἐπ' ἐκείνοις γεγένηται)," but that everyone wanted peace and now was a good time to secure it. It was not just for Athens and Sparta (6.3.10–17).

As a result a treaty was drawn up. Whether it was under the King's auspices or not, it reflected much the same sentiments as the King's Peace and later treaties: autonomy for all; harmosts and garrisons to be withdrawn; general disarmament; and, slightly inconsistently, that violators would be punished by voluntary action of other states. This last was to allow Sparta to go after a state like Thebes, while Athens could stand apart.[58] In spite of all this Sparta signed for herself and for her allies. Whether or not this really implied their lack of freedom, if not of nominal autonomy, is debated.[59] Athens signed on her own behalf, as did each of the allies of the Second Athenian Confederacy. Presumably Thebes signed in this capacity only.

On the next day Epaminondas requested that the Theban envoys' signature should be changed to be on behalf not of "the Thebans" but of "the Boiotians."[60] According to Plutarch, Agesilaus asked Epaminondas whether he thought it right for Boiotia to be autonomous. Epaminondas asked Agesilaus in reply whether *he* thought it right for Lakonia to be autonomous. Agesilaus turned nasty and seized the opportunity to strike Thebes from the treaty. Xenophon's version is different. Agesilaus merely said that if they had signed one way in the first place, he saw no reason to change anything. But if they wanted to get out of the treaty, he would strike out their names. In both versions, less explicitly in Xenophon, the Thebans did not sign.[61] According to Plutarch the treaty was concluded on 14 Skirophorion, and Leuktra was fought on 5 Hekatombaion, three weeks later.[62]

The Campaign to Leuktra

The intervening three weeks were filled with activity. Kleombrotos had been asking the home government for instructions about what to do with his force in Phokis.[63] The Spartans apparently thought that this was an ideal opportunity to invoke the enforcement clause of the treaty and break up the Boiotian League. Kleombrotos' force would march through Boiotia to see whether the treaty had been implemented and the Boiotian cities were autonomous.[64] It was clear that the Athenians, though they would not join the fight against Boiotia, would not oppose any punitive measures against it.[65] When Kleombrotos learned that the Boiotians were not only not giving the cities independence, but were mobilizing their reserves, he led his army into Boiotia.[66]

Meanwhile, the Boiotian government was ready, with Epaminondas and a blocking force occupying a position "above the Cephisian [Copaïc] Lake."[67] It was near Koroneia, in the defile between Mt. Helikon and the Lake. Another force, under Chaireas, principally Thebans, was posted to guard against any Spartan attempt to use the passes through Helikon to the south.[68] A third force, under the Boiotarch Bakchylides, was deployed to guard Kithairon, presumably against any incursion from the Peloponnese.[69]

The sources[70] are not in agreement about the events leading up to Leuktra and the course of the battle. They all say that Kleombrotos, after learning of the dispositions of the Boiotians and demonstrating at Chaironeia[71] swung south through Phokis "in the direction of Ambrosos." Precisely where he went is unclear: the route through Helikon by way of the plain of Koukoura is the strongest possibility.[72] Less likely is the way along the seacoast by way of Bulis and above Chorsiai that Diodorus indicates.[73] Pausanias reports that he fell on and destroyed Chaireas' detachment before he captured Thisbe. He then went on to occupy the naval harbour of Siphai, where he seized ten (Diod.) or twelve (Xen.) triremes. He then proceeded up the heights towards

Thebes, stopping to rest his troops at Leuktra, where he met the Boiotians coming up under Epaminondas.

The Boiotian decision to stand and fight was made by majority vote of the Boiotarchs, after Bakchylides brought his forces down from Kithairon to join the others. The battle has been fully described and various problems explored by many modern authorities.[74] Clearly the massive Theban phalanx deployed on the left wing and centred on Pelopidas' crack force, the Sacred Band, was the principal instrument of the Spartan defeat. The Spartans withdrew under an armistice arranged by Jason of Pherai, and the Boiotians under Epaminondas started on their career of military victory and diplomatic mischance for the next thirty-odd years.

VIII Boiotia, 432–371 B.C.

Boiotia between 432 and 371 saw a reorganization and professionalization of elements of the Boiotian army and the creation of the Boiotian navy. It saw the erection of large-scale field fortifications, in scale and usefulness an anticipation of the Maginot Line, and many innovations in tactics. The Boiotian army defeated the Athenians in several battles in the Peloponnesian War, and it was instrumental in the eventual defeat and eclipse of Sparta. To judge by the archaeological remains Boiotia was prosperous during this time: no doubt the wealth accruing from the booty of Attica during the Dekeleian War was a lucrative windfall, but the natural wealth of this fertile area was a more important factor. There were also two transmutations of the Boiotian League, as well as an interval when there was no League at all.

The oligarchic League lasted under the guidance of different factions from 446 until 387.[1] It gave representation to the various member states in proportion to their size, or to the size of their hoplite contribution to the army, in what seems a roughly equitable manner. There was considerable loyalty to the League and support for it, not to say enthusiasm, as the story of the attempt on Plataia in 432 makes clear. The League was a careful ally of Sparta during the Peloponnesian War, though not nearly as loyal as is sometimes stated. It changed governing factions shortly after the end of the War from one largely pro-Spartan to another one, strongly anti-Spartan. By the time of the Corinthian

115

War the League had become Sparta's enemy, and one city, Orchomenos, had seceded.

During the Corinthian War Boiotia fought long, hard and well against Sparta. Sparta forced the dissolution of the League in 387; the threat of invasion and the prospect of great destruction and irremediable defeat in the face of a complete lack of any support from anywhere else in Greece led the Boiotians, a practical people, to give way.

Throughout the period of the oligarchic League there was some opposition to the existing regime observable. There were two varieties. First, opposition more to the governing faction than to the League, but willingness to sacrifice the League for the sake of political advantage and local power. This was the position of the old democratic faction of Ptoiodoros in the days of the rule of Leontiades' faction, and apparently of Leontiades' faction in the days of the rule of Ismenias' faction.

This variety of opposition sometimes tied in with the second type, the strong particularism for which the Boiotians were infamous. This particularism was there as a kind of sullen undertow to the tides of Boiotian unity. It was a feeling to be played on by politicians out of office or out of sympathy with existing conditions, sometimes democrats under an oligarchy, sometimes oligarchs under a democracy.

Thebes is usually thought to have run Boiotia on a tight rein, but control seems not to have been exercised by Thebes as rigidly as has sometimes been thought: in the days of the hoplite oligarchy it seems usually to have been exercised with the agreement of the oligarchic rulers of each constituent city. If the hoplites and cavalry wanted out, there was little inclination to stop them. The fact that the oligarchic League lasted nearly sixty years shows that it was reasonably satisfactory to the majority of the hoplites and cavalry classes that controlled the various states.

The Boiotians did not at this time develop those intense feelings of unity, one might almost say nationhood, that made the inhabitants of Attica think of themselves as Athenians, feelings of a sort that might have made them place the concept of Boiotia before that of, say, Kopai. No doubt some of the Boiotians felt that way, but many, if not most, certainly did not. To be sure, there was some feeling of ethnic kinship, as the coin types indicate. They show the Boiotian shield. It would, however, be a mistake to talk of a feeling of nationhood and anachronistic to talk of nationalism.

For about eight years, from 387 to 379, the League was dissolved. There is some evidence from around 383 of attempts to re-form the League. The Spartans were alert for any signs of such activities, and the takeover of the Kadmeia by Phoibidas in 382 was for this reason condoned. Narrow oligarchic regimes were installed in all the Boiotian cities, remembered as "tyrannies" in the Boiotian historical traditions. The brutal puppet regime of Leontiades at Thebes was overthrown in a coup led by pro-democrats in 379/8 and the democratic League was symbolically re-established. It was not until 375 that many of the other states were able to join, though many democrats from all over made their way to Thebes.

The new League had a desperate fight for its life from 379 to 375, Fortunately, by some gross blunder the Spartans managed to get Athens, which had been wavering between ideological solidarity with the Theban democrats and deep fear of a Spartan invasion of Attica and the expense of another war, firmly on the Boiotian side. The two democracies were strong enough to carry on a successful struggle against Sparta, but only just.

Each year down to 375 the Spartans invaded Boiotia, and it remained an important theatre of operations. The Boiotians tried fortified defensive lines with mixed success, while the Spartans were unable to reduce Theban fighting ability. They seem to have educated the Thebans in devising ways to deal with the formidable Spartan phalanx. The Thebans won over many of the minor cities of Boiotia. The improved Theban forces eventually handed the Spartans a smart defeat at the Battle of Tegyra. They were good pupils. By 375 everyone wanted peace. In effect the Spartans had lost a war of attrition.

The war broke out again in 374/3, but with little threat to Boiotia. The Thebans improved the opportunity by reducing the last Boiotian towns and annexing them to the League. The last one, Orchomenos, was taken over shortly after the Battle of Leuktra. At the price of alienating Athens the Boiotian League gained all the Boiotian cities, including Oropos and Eleutherai. Democracy was the sign under which victory was gained.

The democratic League was very different from the old oligarchic League. To the Greek mind the mark of a democracy was direct rule by the people exercised through a sovereign Assembly of all adult male citizens. Such an Assembly had authority in all areas of government and acted forcibly in them. In such a system there is no place for and no need for the formal division of the sovereign powers among various levels of government that is the mark of modern federal constitutions. In no way could the member states be sovereign *poleis* under a democracy. They were merely local units of administration, analogous to the demes or perhaps *phylai* of Attica. Some sources, especially Diodorus, describe Boiotia as a *synteleia*. This term is used for a league by Polybius and others,[2] but one where the units are subordinated to the general government. This seems to be the type of government established under the democracy.

The Boiotarchs, at least in 372, where we have inscriptional evidence, were only seven in number. There is, however, no evidence that their number was constant at seven or that they represented any districts.

The Boiotian army remained, if the evidence from Leuktra is acceptable, brigaded by its local contingents. If any use were to be made of the old eleven districts, it would be for manning and supplying the army; but these activities were apparently carried out by the individual localities themselves.

Though undoubtedly the long-standing mutual antipathies among the Boiotians remained, the democratic League was successful and reasonably popular, Boiotia having gained under its aegis the leadership of Greece for a few years and remaining a major power for many more. The democratic Boiotian League lasted for forty years until the defeat at Chaironeia in 338 and the consequent harsh terms laid on by Philip.[3] The democracy was abolished, many democrats were killed or exiled, and oligarchies were once again established in the Boiotian cities. A Macedonian garrison was stationed on the Kadmeia. The Boiotian League remained in being, but apparently with a much looser organization than before. Any feeling of synoecism or democratic unity was discountenanced, and the Boiotian cities were regarded as distinct and separate oligarchic units.[4] Even after the restoration of Thebes in 316 the League remained loosely integrated, and was able to conciliate the rugged individualism of the constituent states.

One constant that runs through the part of Boiotian history included in this work is the vigour and fertility of the attempts, under all regimes, both democratic and oligarchic, to grapple with the difficulties implicit in a confederation: how to balance, if possible with fairness and justice, the rights of the constituent parts against the rights of the whole; how to maintain simultaneously unity and diversity; how to ensure an effective state that can defend itself without the risk of oppressing its parts; how to overcome mutual hatred and distrust. Matters were complicated because one of the constituent states, Thebes, was considerably larger than the others and so had a certain preponderance. Various ways were tried, some successful for a time, others not.

One of these was to base the federal organs and army on equal units of population, or at least on the provision of equal units of cavalry and hoplites for the Boiotian army. This was tried in the League between 446 and 387 under the hoplite oligarchy. In recognizing equality of units of population, the principle of equality of representation by the states was ignored. This was a principle not unfamiliar in Greece, as the synods of the Peloponnesian League and the Second Athenian Confederacy were both organized on this basis, but no trace of such a principle is observable in the oligarchic Boiotian Federation. Functionally the units were for raising equal numbers of troops and equal amounts of funds, and for selecting various officials from across Boiotia on the basis of equal representation for equal population. It meant, however, that the other states had few formal devices for keeping Thebes from what may be considered as undue dominance.

This representative system was not well suited to democracy, as the Greeks understood the term. Representative organs of government were normally associated with oligarchies, usually fairly broad hoplite oligarchies, though not all members of the hoplite class were necessarily voters. The concept of representative democracy was virtually unknown at the time.

A second solution, one practised by both oligarchs and democrats, was the physical moving of people to the *polis*, in what is usually termed συνοικισμός, synoecism. In the early 420s the oligarchs moved the acceptable elements from Plataia, the Platais and unwalled towns in Theban territory into Thebes, doubling the Theban population; the Plataian elements were still nominally the Demos of Plataia. The democrats encouraged or permitted the members of the democratic factions in other cities to move to Thebes in the 370s. In this way the Boiotian population could be integrated and controlled. The other cities, however, were not pleased at the loss of population and of power. Many of their citizens felt themselves "stateless."

A third solution, one experimented with by the democrats, was the granting by legal fiction of the rights of a citizen (one dwelling in the city) to those actually not residing in the city. There seems to be no standard term for this in the Greek texts, but συνοικισμός and συμπολιτεία both occur. For convenience it might be well to use *sympolity* for this and *synoecism* for physical moving.[5] This process of sympolity was not uncommon: it had been used to extend Athenian citizenship to virtually all the inhabitants of Attica, so that there were no Atticans as contrasted to Athenians. This process was used with the residents of Thespiai and the other Boiotian cities (except Plataia), when they were freed of their oligarchic rulers and were able to exercise the right of attending the Assembly which was held in the capital, Thebes. In effect they were all made Thebans, though the term used was "Boiotian." Orchomenos was not granted this right after 371; instead it was given the status of an ally or of a perioecic city.

As Thebes was the largest city in Boiotia at the time, there was undoubtedly dislike of it in other parts of Boiotia, a feeling stemming from fear of being overwhelmed by its sheer size, jealousy, suspicion that it would get all the advantages, and considerable envy. This solution, which had worked so well in Attica, apparently was not enough to overcome the particularism of Boiotia.

A fourth solution was the forcible repression or elimination of a dissenting minority by the majority. Both the democrats and the oligarchs used armed force against opposition factions and against Thespiai, Plataia and Orchomenos at different times. This culminated under the democracy in the destruction of Orchomenos. Though force stifled dissent, the difficulty was that the hatreds and bitterness engendered were counter-productive to fostering unity. When the Thebans rebelled after the false rumour of the death of Alexander, in 336, there were in the besieging forces that utterly destroyed the city Orchomenians, Thespians and Plataians.

The difficulties faced by the oligarchic and democratic Boiotian federations may well have had some influence on the organization of the reconstituted League of Hellenistic times, as far as it can be ascertained.[6] Thebes was resettled in 316 under Kassandros, but its prestige and authority were diminished. The capital had been moved to a neutral site, in what had been variously Haliartan or Theban territory, the sanctuary of Poseidon at Onchestos.[7] There it remained, so that the federal Archon is often referred to in inscriptions as the "Archon at Onchestos." This relocation of the capital helped to restrict Thebes from exercising undue influence.

The Assembly of all adult Boiotian males remained as the sovereign body, but, if the current view is correct, the vote was not of the majority of individuals, but of the majority of the constituent towns. The Boiotians had a system of unit voting, like that in the Roman *comitia tributa*.[8] In a way this gave some recognition to the principle of equality of representation by states, though not of equality of individual votes. Though most authorities say that it was democratic, this is arguable.

There was also a federal body called the Synedrion.[9] It was composed of members elected by their respective cities. It seems to have had the same sort of responsibilities as the Athenian Boule. Thespiai returned three representatives each year. If the other cities regardless of size did the same, it would form a Council of 60 or so. This synedrion could be considered an example of the principle of representative democracy in use in Hellenistic Greece, but it bears all the earmarks of oligarchy.

The Assembly seems to have elected most of the federal officials, including the Boiotarchs,[10] but they were apparently chosen by rules that assured equality among the towns. The precise method is unknown.[11] Other federal officials, the aphedriateuontes (ἀφεδριατεύοντες), of unknown duties, were elected by and represented their respective towns.[12] These were also representative officials.

The federation was much more loosely controlled than the previous Leagues. The cities were permitted on occasion to have direct relations with foreign states, sending and receiving embassies.[13] Nonetheless, the federal state still had considerable and wide-ranging powers, powers that could be used when required, as the story of Nikareta makes clear. The Hellenistic League bears all the earmarks of being the product of a deliberate effort to overcome many of the shortcomings of the previous Leagues. Since it lasted down into Roman times, it seems to have been successful in its aim.

Throughout Boiotian history there was considerable loyalty to the concept of the Boiotian League, even when the League was in limbo. Though there was a feeling of ethnic kinship, as the shield coins make clear, it was not a "nationalism" in the nineteenth-century sense, of the type that informs so much of recent history, the type seen in the U.S.A., Germany or Italy and today raising its head all over the world. In Boiotia there was a very different view of things, a practical and pragmatic one: a feeling of tribal solidarity that was colliding with the ideals of the autonomous *polis*. If things worked, well and good; if it did not, try something else.

Appendix
Oropos

Oropos has been the subject of some recent studies, notably by Bearzot,[1] Camp,[2] and Rocchi.[3] They all agree that it was disputed between Boiotia and Athens and switched between them with some frequency. It was for both nations usually a perioecic community, as Thucydides (2.23.3) indicates, when it was not independent.

It was originally Boiotian, as Pausanias (1.34.1) says, presumably after being Ionic or Eretrian, but it came under Athenian dominance before 500.[4] It stayed by and large under Athenian control (except perhaps during the Persian Wars in 480 and 479) until the Dekeleian War in the winter of 412/11.

At that time it was captured from its Athenian garrison by the Boiotians through treachery (προδοσίᾳ). They had the co-operation of some Eretrians who were plotting the revolt of Euboia as well as of the Oropans themselves.[5] Thucydides (8.60.2) says that the Eretrians controlled Oropos shortly after its capture; but this should mean simply that it was available for Eretrian purposes.

An Athenian named Philon moved to Oropos before the overthrow of the Thirty at Athens (Lys. 31.9). He became a metic in a foreign land (εἰς τὴν ὑπερορίαν). Most scholars hold that this means that Oropos was independent by 403, but a few[6] argue that it was then part of Boiotia. Which is chosen depends on one's view of the worth of Diodoros.

Diodoros (14.17.1–3) claims that in 402/1 the Oropans got into *stasis* and expelled some of its citizens. After some time (μέχρι μέν τινος) the Thebans helped these citizens regain power. The Thebans also moved the city seven stades inland. They permitted self-government for some time (χρόνους μέν τινος), but then "they established a system of government (πολιτείαν) and made the land Boiotian." The sequence is *stasis*, Boiotian occupation, independence, Boiotian annexation, the lengths of time appreciable but uncertain.

Many authorities from Wilamowitz[7] on have been suspicious of both the sequence and the chronology here, and have accused Diodoros of various crimes: telescoping the events of several years under one; mixing the sequence; omitting and/or doubling various happenings. The majority of authorities agree that what Diodoros credits to one year might be better spread over a few, but that more than doubts are required to reject the actual events. Diodoros is ultimately based here on the source of Pausanias, which cannot be rejected on mere suspicion.

If the events described by Pausanias are to be spread over several years, then they should either begin in 402/1 or they should end there. The date should mean something. If the events start in the year 402/1 with the *stasis*, then this *stasis* and the eventual appeal to Thebes imply a previous period of no Theban rule, of independence, starting somewhere between 411 and 402, as most scholars believe.[8] It is likely that the civil dispute was between the full citizens, the πολῖται, those of hoplite census, and the Demos, the ordinary people, but we cannot be sure. Diodoros (14.17.3) says, "For some time they [the Thebans] let [the Oropans] govern themselves."

The Oropans are not mentioned by Pausanias in his discussion of the Boiotian constitution. It is therefore inferred by some authorities that Oropos was independent in 396. This has been used to reject the idea of any Boiotian rule until much later, usually just before or in the early stages of the Corinthian War, when Boiotia and Athens were allies![9] Even the Boiotians were not that stupid. One may with equal validity argue that Oropos presumably had by 396 lost its status as a perioecic community (or perhaps as a constituent state like Kopai) and had received that of a Mykalessos or an Aulis. It would seem more likely that the union with Boiotia should be put before the rapprochement with Athens, say before 399.

The idea of *stasis* in 402/1 poses difficulties for some; they assume that the indication of Theban support for one faction of citizens in Theopompos (*FGrH* 115 F 12) implies that the other faction had Athenian support. This is an unwarranted inference, since we have no information on the cause or nature of the civil discord.[10] Nonetheless it has been used to support a date earlier than 402/1 for the *stasis*.

If the events conclude in 402/1 with a Boiotian annexation, then the Theban occupation in 411 must be followed by a period of independence, so that there could be the conditions for a civil discord in which Thebes would not immediately intervene; then the *stasis*, the appeal to Thebes, the restoration of the exiles, the period of self-government and the takeover by Boiotia finally in 402/1.

One must posit a period of independence before the *stasis* to make sense of this sequence. Bearzot has tried to avoid this by equating the seizure of Oropos by the Boiotians in Thucydides with the *stasis* of Diodorus.[11] This eliminates the posited early period of independence and simplifies the sequence: *stasis* in 411, between the supporters of Boiotia and Eretria on the one hand and those of Athens on the other; capture by Boiotians with the support of the pro-Boiotian Oropan exiles and discontented Eretrians; removal of Oropos from the sea; self-government down to 402/1; annexation by Boiotia in that year.

Chronologically this idea has great attraction, but the incidents as related by Thucydides and Diodoros are so dissimilar that it is difficult to believe they refer to the same events. A Boiotian seizure by treachery from an Athenian garrison and a Theban invasion to restore citizens of a pro-Boiotian faction after they were kicked out are different in almost every respect. There is no fit. The removal of the Oropans seven stades inland immediately after the Boiotian annexation and the visit of the Peloponnesian fleet to the town of Oropos later in 411, as reported by Thucydides (8.95.1–4) also cannot be made to fit with any conviction. Therefore the idea of Bearzot should be rejected, and the usual reconstruction remains: capture in the winter of 412/11 by the Boiotians; independence supported by Eretria sometime after late 411, but before the time of the Thirty; a state of civil discord in Diodorus' year, 402/1, with full citizens, that is, members of the hoplite and cavalry classes, being expelled. Then a call on Thebes (sc. the Boiotian League) some time later, but before 400 (possibly in the same 402/1); the removal from the sea; self-government (as a perioecic community for a brief time); then the takeover by the League into the subordinate status of an Aulis or an Anthedon well before the outbreak of the Corinthian War, perhaps even before 400. The inscription *IG* 7.235[12] is dated to a period of independence, but which one is uncertain. Either the one set between 411 and 402/1 or the one after 387 would do.

However it is argued, it is clear that a period of independence must be placed in the period between 411 and 402/1. The shift between independence and annexation to Boiotia is most simply explained as based on the desires of the hoplite and cavalry classes of Oropos, rather than those of Thebes. Thebes was the leader of the League, but it was not a dictator; it reacted to opportunities, rather than initiating them.

Notes

Introduction

1. G.L. Cawkwell, Preface to Xenophon, *A History of My Times*, tr. by R. Warner (Harmondsworth, 1979), 43.
2. Cf. V.J. Gray, "Two Different Approaches to the Battle of Sardis in 395 B.C.," *CSCA* 12 (1979): 183–200, and P.R. McKechnie and S.J. Kern, *Hellenica Oxyrhynchia* (Warminster, 1988), 14–16.
3. J. deVoto, "Agesilaos in Boiotia in 378 and 377 B.C.," *AHB* 1 (1987): 75.
4. B.V. Head, "On the Chronological Sequence of the Coins of Boeotia," *NC* 1 (1881): 177–275. Reprint (Chicago, 1974) paginated 1–99. This remains the standard work.
5. P. Roesch, *Thespies et la confédération béotienne* (Paris, 1965); *Études béotiennes* (Paris, 1982).
6. A. Schachter, *The Cults of Boiotia*, Vol. 4 (London, 1981).
7. J.M. Fossey, *The Topography and Population of Ancient Boiotia* (two vols. in one) (Chicago, 1988).
8. R.J. Buck, *A History of Boeotia* (Edmonton, 1979), 5–21, 33. This lists some 140 sites, of which about a half-dozen had been systematically excavated, and only two had been properly published. Fossey, *Topography and Population of Ancient Boiotia*, gives the most up-to-date list of sites. The situation of excavation and publication is little better than it was in 1979.
9. J. Bintliff and A. Snodgrass, "Mediterranean Survey and the City," *Antiquity* 62 (1988): 57–71; "From Polis to Chorion in South-west Boeotia," in *Boiotika*, H. Beister and J. Buckler, eds., (Munich, 1989): 285–99; A.M. Snodgrass and J.L. Bintliff, "Surveying Ancient Cities," *Scientific American* 264 (1991): 88–93. See also Fossey, *Topography*, vol. 2.

10. A. Schachter, *Cults of Boiotia* (Vols. 1–).

11. Fossey, *Topography*, 271–73, with bibliography of both sites, especially J. Ducat, *les Kouroi du Ptoion* (Paris, 1971); S. Lauffer, *RE* 23.2 (1959), *s.v.* "Ptoion," 1505–78; Schachter, *Cults,* 1.52–73.

12. Fossey, *Topography*, 308–12; Schachter, *Cults.* 2.207–21, with bibliography 207–9.

13. Fossey, *Topography*, 211f.; Schachter, *Cults*, 2.66–110.

14. S. Symeonoglou, *The Topography of Thebes* (Princeton, 1985), gives full bibliographies and the best description of the site and the excavations. Fossey, *Topography*, 1.199–208.

15. For a depressing description of the excavations, Fossey, *Topography*, 1.135–40.

16. Set at Mamoura by, e.g., Fossey, *Topography,* 1.330f. and Buck, *History of Boeotia*, 6. Set just to the north of Koroneia by, e.g., Schachter, *Cults,* 1.119.

17. Set at Solinari by many since Leake: Fossey, *Topography,* 1.332f. Set at Agoriani by others: Schachter, *Cults,* 1.111.

18. P. Salmon, *Étude sur la confédération béotienne (447/6–386)* (Brussels, 1976).

19. N. Demand, *Thebes in the Fifth Century* (London, 1982).

20. P. Cloché, *Thèbes de Béotie* (Namur, 1952); see also "La politique Thébaine de 404 à 396 av. J.-C.," *REG* 31 (1918): 315–43.

21. L. Prandi, *Platea: momenti e problemi della storia di una polis (Serie di antichità e tradizione classica*, 11) (Padua, 1988).

22. E. von Stern, *Geschichte der spartanische und thebanischen Hegemonie vom Königsfrieden bis zur Schlacht bei Mantinea* (Dorpat, 1884); *Xenophons Hellenika und die böotische Geschichtsüberlieferung* (Dorpat, 1887).

23. J. Buckler, *The Theban Hegemony* (Cambridge, Mass., 1980).

24. M.L. Cook, "Boeotia in the Corinthian War: Foreign Policy and Domestic Politics." Ph.D. diss., U. of Washington, 1981; H.M. Hack, "The Rise of Thebes: A Study of Theban Politics." Ph.D. diss., Yale, 1978; C.J. Dull, "A Study of the Leadership of the Boeotian League from the Invasion of the Boiotoi to the King's Peace." Ph.D. diss., Wisconsin, 1975; G. Clarke, "A History of Boeotia, 405–395 B.C." M.A. thesis, Alberta, 1986.

25. C.D. Hamilton, *Sparta's Bitter Victories* (Ithaca, 1979); *Agesilaus and the Failure of Spartan Hegemony* (Ithaca, 1991); P. Cartledge, *Agesilaos and the Crisis of Sparta* (Baltimore, 1987); I.A.F. Bruce, *An Historical Commentary on the* Hellenica Oxyrhynchia (Cambridge, 1970); McKechnie and Kern, eds., *Hellenica Oxyrhynchia* with translation and commentary; S. Accame, *La lega ateniese del secolo IV a. C.* (Rome, 1941); *Ricerche intorno alla guerra*

corinzia (*Collana di studi greci* 20), (Milan, 1957); T.T.B. Ryder, *Koine Eirene* (Oxford, 1965); J.A.O. Larsen, *Greek Federal States: Their Institutions and History* (Oxford, 1968); *Representative Government in Greek and Roman History* (Berkeley, 1955); J.L. Cargill, *The Second Athenian League: Empire or Free Alliance* (Berkeley, 1981); W.P. Henry, *Greek Historical Writing: An Historiographical Essay Based on Xenophon's* Hellenica (Chicago, 1966); D.G. Rice, "Why Sparta Failed: A Study of Politics and Policy from the Peace of Antalcidas to the Battle of Leuctra, 386–371 B.C." Ph.D. diss., Yale, 1971; D. Kagan, "Politics and Policy in Corinth (421–336 B.C.)" Ph.D. diss., Ohio State, 1958.

26. M.L. Cook, "Ancient Political Factions: Boiotia 404–395," *TAPA* 118 (1988): 57–85; "Ismenias' Goals in the Corinthian War," in *Teiresias*, Supp. 3, A. Schachter, ed. (1990): 57–63.

27. G.L. Cawkwell, "Notes on the Peace of 375/4," *Historia* 12 (1963): 84–95; "The Foundation of the Second Athenian Confederacy," *CQ* 67 (1973): 47–60; "Epaminondas and Thebes," *CQ* 66 (1972): 254–78; "Agesilaus and Sparta," *CQ* 70 (1976): 62–84; "The Imperialism of Thrasybulus," *CQ* 70 (1976): 270–77; Preface and Commentary to the Penguin Classics Xenophon, *A History of My Times*, tr. R. Warner (Harmondsworth, 1979).

28. J. Buckler, "Dating the Peace of 375/4 B.C.," *GRBS* 12 (1971): 353–62; "The Thespians at Leuktra," *WS* 90 (1977): 46–49; "The Re-establishment of the *Boiotarchia*," *AJAH* 4 (1979): 50–64; "The Alleged Theban-Spartan Alliance of 386 BC," *Eranos* 78 (1980): 179–83; "Plutarch on Leuktra," *Symb Oslo* 55 (1980): 75–93; "Plutarch and Autopsy," *ANRW II*, 33, no. 6 (1992): 4788–4830.

29. C.J. Tuplin, "Pausanias' and Plutarch's Epaminondas," *CQ* 78 (1984): 346–58; "The Fate of Thespiae during the Theban Hegemony," *Athenaeum* 64 (1986): 321–41; A.P. Burnett, "Thebes and the Expansion of the Second Athenian Confederacy," *Historia* 11 (1962): 1–17; R.M. Kallet-Marx, "Athens, Thebes and the Foundation of the Second Athenian League," *ClasAnt* 4 (1985): 127–51; M. Sordi, "La restaurazione della lega beotica nel 379–8 a.C.," *Athenaeum* 51 (1973): 79–91; S. Lauffer, "Die Diodordublette XV 38–50 über die Friedenschlusse zu Sparta 374 und 371," *Historia* 8 (1959): 315–48.

30. W. Judeich, "Athen und Theben vom Königsfrieden bis zur Schlacht bei Leuktra," *RhM* 76 (1927): 171–97; J.H. Thiel, "De synoecismo Boeotiae post annum 379 peracta," *Mnemosyne* 54 (1926): 19–28; G.M. Bersanetti, "Pelopida," *Athenaeum* 27 (1949): 43–101.

31. W.K. Pritchett, *Studies in Ancient Greek Topography*, Vols. 1– (Berkeley, 1965–); M.H. Munn, "Agesilaos' Boiotian Campaigns and the Theban Stock-

ade of 378–377 B.C.," *ClasAnt* 6 (1987): 106–38; V.D. Hanson, *Warfare and Agriculture in Classical Greece* (Pisa, 1983); J.K. Anderson, *Military Theory and Practice in the Age of Xenophon* (Berkeley, 1970).

I Boiotia and the Boiotian League, 432–371 B.C.

1. P. Garnsey, *Famine and Food Supply in the Graeco-Roman World* (Cambridge, 1988), 112.
2. See e.g., A. Schachter, *The Cults of Boiotia*, vol. 2, *s.v.* "Kabiroi."
3. The Boiotians, probably mainly from Thebes and Tanagra, shared with Megara in the foundation of Herakleia Pontike; see S.M. Burstein, *Outpost of Hellenism: The Emergence of Heraclea Pontica on the Black Sea* (Berkeley, 1976), 16f.; J. Ducat, "La confédération Béotienne et l'expansion Thébain à l'époque archaïque,"*BCH* 97 (1973): 65. Individuals may have had a minor share in a few other colonies in the Propontis and Black Sea areas, such as Byzantion, Chalkedon and Astakos; Burstein, 17 and n. 61 on 108.
4. Bintliff and Snodgrass, "From Polis to Chorion," 287f.
5. Garnsey, *Famine and Food*, 91.
6. Bintliff and Snodgrass, "From Polis to Chorion," 288.
7. Plut. *Arist.* 13.
8. There is no evidence for the Pamboiotia or the games at Onchestos before the third century B.C., but both have all the earmarks of being established much earlier. W.G. Forrest, "Central Greece and Thessaly." Chap. 41 in *CAH*[2] vol. 3, part 3, 292.
9. Buck, *History of Boeotia*, 107–20. Whether Thessaly can be considered a league or a loose-knit defensive arrangement is arguable.
10. Hdt. 6.108; Thuc. 3.68.5.
11. *Hell. Oxy.* 11.1; B.V. Head, "On the Chronological Sequence of the Coins of Boeotia," 185–88. Head's chronology need not be taken seriously.

II Boiotians in the Peloponnesian War, 432–404 B.C.

1. For recent studies see Demand, *Thebes*, 40–44; Salmon, *Étude,* 111–21; Cook, "Ancient Political Factions," 57–85; Dull, "Leadership of the Boeotian League," *passim*, esp. 82; Buck, *History*, 155; P. Roesch, *Thespies et la confédération béotienne* (Paris, 1965), 42; Clarke, "History of Boeotia," 39; M.L. Cook, "Boeotia in the Corinthian War," 1–4.
2. Hamilton, *Sparta's Bitter Victories*, 147; Cook, "Boeotia in the Corinthian War," 1, 3; Clarke, 48f.
3. P. Cartledge, *Agesilaos and the Crisis of Sparta* (Baltimore, 1987), 276f.

4. See, e.g., Salmon, *Étude*, 112; Demand, *Thebes*, 40–44; Cook, "Boeotia in the Corinthian War," 3.

5. Buck, *History*, 150–53; Salmon, *Étude*, 34–43.

6. McKechnie and Kern, eds., *Hellenica Oxyrhynchia* 16.2–4 and comm. *ad loc.*, 154–60. Demand, *Thebes*, 35–40; Hamilton, 138f.; Salmon, *Étude*, 49, 55–58; Cartledge, *Agesilaos*, 278, thinks that the other citizenry had the vote as well, in my view wrongly. C.J. Dull, "A Reassessment of the Boeotian Districts," in *Proceedings of the Third International Conference on Boiotian Antiquities*, J.M. Fossey and H. Giroux, eds. (Amsterdam, 1985), 33–39, regards the districts of the League as a device for preserving Theban control, but he is wrong in this. The status of the hoplites from the districts attached to Thespiai, Thebes and Orchomenos as voters is uncertain.

7. *Hell. Oxy.* 16.4.

8. *Hell Oxy.* 16.2.

9. E.g., Roesch, *Thespies*, 40f.; R.J. Buck, "Boeotian Oligarchies and Greek Oligarchic Theory," in *Proceedings of the Third International Conference on Boiotian Antiquities*, J.M. Fossey and H. Giroux, eds. (Amsterdam, 1985), 25f.

10. Aristotle, *Ath. Pol.* 30. Buck, "Boeotian Oligarchies," 29.

11. Thuc. 2.2.2ff.; A.W. Gomme, A. Andrewes and K.J. Dover, *A Historical Commentary on Thucydides*, 5 vols. (Oxford, 1945–1981, henceforth *HCT*) *ad loc.*, vol. 2, p. 3; Salmon, *Étude*, 80f., 112; E. Badian, "Plataea Between Athens and Sparta: In Search of Lost History," in *Boiotika*, H. Beister and J. Buckler, eds., 95–112.

12. Plut. *Arist.* 13; Buck, *History*, 143 and n. 17.

13. Buck, *History*, 161f.

14. Thuc. 3.65.2; Buck, *History*, 161f., Salmon, *Étude*, 81. Thucydides sometimes uses Thebans where the League is really meant. Cf. Thuc. 1.27.2; 3.57.2; 3.59.2,3,4; 3.68.3; 5.17.2; 7.30.1,2,3; 8.100.3.

15. Buck, *History*, 161f.; Demand, *Thebes*, 40; Prandi, *Platea*, 97–101, esp. 99.

16. *Hell. Oxy.* 17.3; McKechnie and Kern, Comm. *ad loc.*, 164; Buck, *History*, 160; Prandi, *Platea*, 108; Salmon, *Étude*, 82; for date see also Salmon, 85f. with citations.

17. Thuc. 2.2f.; Aen. Tact. 2.3–6, for details; cf. Prandi, *Platea*, 101.

18. Hdt., 7.205.2, 7.233; Buck, *History*, 131ff., 152, 160; *HCT* 2.3f.

19. Cook, "Ancient Political Factions," 57–86, esp. 65–70, with citations; B.S. Strauss, *Athens After the Peloponnesian War: Class, Faction and Policy 403–386 B.C.* (London and Sydney, 1986), 15–31. G. Herman, *Ritualised Friendship and the Greek City* (Cambridge, 1987), esp. 142–56.

20. Strauss, *Athens*, 2; the "Family Compact" of Canadian history is in many ways similar to a Greek faction, as are the groupings in the Long Parliament of the English Civil War.

21. Strauss, *Athens*, 18.

22. Herman, *Ritualised Friendship*, 150, 155.

23. E.g., Cook, "Ancient Political Factions," 76f., 79; Strauss, *Athens*, 18, 24–27.

24. Xen. *Hell.* 5.2.31; Diod. 15.20.2.

25. Plut. *de gen. Soc.* 596F, 598C.

26. Plut. *Lys.* 29.6.

27. So also Cook, "Ancient Political Factions," 59.

28. Ibid., 65–68; Strauss, 28–31.

29. Cf . Cook, "Ancient Political Factions," 60, n. 12.

30. A locality in the deme Athmoneis, northeast of Athens. *HCT* 2.77; it is at or near the modern suburb of Amarousion (Marousi). J.G. Frazer, *Pausanias's Description of Greece,* 6 vols. (London, 1898), 2.413f.

31. Thuc. 2.47; cf. Salmon, *Étude*, 112; Cloché, *Thèbes de Béotie*, 77; Demand, *Thebes*, 41; Cartledge, *Agesilaos*, 279.

32. Thuc. 3.52–68.

33. Cf. Roesch, *Thespies*, 42, in reference to Orchomenian refugees acting as the People during the Corinthian War; 96f. for Plataia. M. Moggi, *I sinecismi interstatali Greci* (Pisa, 1976), 197–204, argues for a political synoecism in 424 after a physical one in 426. He looks to attempts to suppress democracy as the basis for the Theban actions. N. Demand, *Urban Relocation in Archaic and Classical Greece* (Norman, Okla., 1990), 83f., indicates that he overstates his case, I think rightly.

34. Thuc. 3.91 and *HCT ad loc.*

35. For the foundation of Trachis and its results, Thuc. 3.92–93 is clear and concise.

36. Thuc. 8.3.1; cf. *HCT* 5.369; Cartledge, *Agesilaos*, 279. Cook, "Ismenias' Goals," 57–59.

37. Thuc. 4.76; Salmon, *Étude*, 114f.; L. Moretti, *Ricerche sulle leghe greche* (Rome, 1961), 157–62; W.K. Pritchett, *Studies in Ancient Greek Topography* (Berkeley, 1969), 2.24–36; *HCT* 3.568–72.

38. *IG* I^3 73; *IG* I^3 72 may also refer to happenings connected with this time, though Lewis dates it to 414/3.

39. Diod. 12.70; Demand, 42, 115; Schachter, *Cults, s.v.* "Apollo," 1.46f., has doubts on when the festival was founded, in spite of Diodorus' testimony.

40. If he is the descendant of the Olympic winner of 680 B.C. (Paus. 5.8.7), he is clearly an aristocrat, and doubtless a leader in the faction of the equally aristocratic Leontiades. Cf. Forrest, "Central Greece and Thessaly," 191.

41. Thuc. 4.91; Pagondas had the supreme command at this time, even though all the other Boiotarchs were opposed; no doubt he had the right to make executive decisions. Moretti, *Leghe greche*, 142, is wrong in considering his appeal to the army illegal. Cf. R.J. Buck, "Group Voting in Boiotia," *AHB* 4 (1990): 61–64; Cook, "Ancient Political Factions," 69 and n. 39.

42. Pritchett, *Studies in Ancient Greek Topography*, 2.24–36.

43. Demand, 41f., e.g., following Roesch, *Thespies*, 41, and Moretti, 165, sees this as an example of Theban tyranny. Most authorities assume that the victory redounded to Theban credit: Salmon, *Étude*, 116; Cloché, *Thèbes*, 84f.; M. Sordi, "Aspetti del federalismo greco arcaico: autonomia e egemonia nel koinón beotico," *A&R* 13 (1966): 55. This is, however, not necessarily the case. All Boiotia voted to fight and fought well.

44. Buck, *History*, 160, and J.A.O. Larsen, "The Boeotian Confederacy and Fifth-century Oligarchic Theory," *TAPA* 86 (1955): 47–50, for this other point of view.

45. If the population had been moved to Thebes in 425, along with Aulis and other towns (*Hell. Oxy.* 17.3 mentions Aulis and Schoinos, but not Mykalessos), presumably they moved back after the Peace of 421.

46. *Hell. Oxy.* 17.3 mentions only Aulis and Schoinos, not Mykalessos.

47. Diod. 14.17.1–3; Theopompos, *FGrH* 115 F12; for full discussion see Appendix: Oropos.

48. See Chapter VII. Cook, "Boeotia in the Corinthian War," 56–61. Diodorus reports that the town was resettled seven stades from the sea, but kept its own government even when becoming part of Boiotia. The move inland was temporary, since when the Athenians regained Oropos after 385, they probably shifted the settlement back to the coast. Frazer 2.466 *ad* Paus. 1.34f.

49. Thuc. 5.26.2, 5.32.5.

50. Thuc 5.39 and *HCT ad loc.*

51. *HCT* 4.40f., *ad* 5.36.2.

52. Ibid.

53. Cf. D. Kagan, *The Peace of Nikias and the Sicilian Expedition* (Ithaca, 1981), 60–62.

54. Thuc. 5.37.2. Thucydides seems to be indicating by ἐπετήρουν that there had been some pre-arrangement between the ephors and the Argives for the meeting with the Boiotian envoys.

55. As noted by Cook, "Ancient Political Factions," 67f.; T. Kelly, "Cleobulus, Xenares, and Thucydides' Account of the Demolition of Panactum," *Historia* 21 (1972): 163, argues that the Boiotarchs were completely deterred "from even proposing such an alliance." Thucydides says explicitly that the Boiotarchs tried and were turned down.

56. Thuc. 5.39.3, 5.42.1.

57. Cook, "Boeotia in the Corinthian War," 53 and n. 14 on 82f.; Cartledge, *Agesilaos*, 279.

58. The Boiotian forces were absent from the Battle of Mantinea, not, as Cartledge, *Agesilaos*, 279, states, because of any hostility, but, as Thuc. 5.64.4 makes plain, because they were posted elsewhere.

59. Andok. *de myst.* 45.

60. Thuc. 7.19.1–2, 7.27.8; Diod. 13.9.2; *Hell. Oxy.* 17.3–5; cf. Demand, *Thebes*, 43; Hamilton, *Sparta's Bitter Victories*, 147; W.G. Hardy, "The Hellenica Oxyrhynchia and the Devastation of Attica," *CP* 21 (1926): 346–55; Cartledge, *Agesilaos*, 279f.

61. Thuc. 8.98; Xen. *Hell.* 1.7.28.

62. Xen. *Hell.* 1.3.15, 1.3.17, 1.3.21–22; Koiratadas as factional leader, *Hell. Oxy.* 17.1. He made an escape from Athens to Dekeleia, Xen. *Hell.* 1.3.20. After the War Koiratadas was apparently a mercenary leader for a time. Xen. *Anab.* 7.1.33–35.

63. Diod. 13.72.3–9.

64. Diod. 13.98.4, 13.99.5–6.

65. Paus. 10.9.9; *SIG*³, 115. His name is variously spelt, Erianthos, Erianthes, Arianthios. He was apparently the son of Lysimachidas, and may be a kinsman or be identified with the Boiotarch Arianthides, son of Lysimachides, from Thebes at Delion (Thuc. 4.91). Cf. Salmon, *Étude*, 194. He certainly should have been a member of the governing faction.

66. Cf. *Hell. Oxy.* 7.2, which refers to frictions in times πάλαι; Salmon, *Étude*, 120; Cloché, 96.

67. *Hell. Oxy.* 17.1,2. Cook, "Ancient Political Factions," 62f. For chronology see Clarke, "History of Boeotia," 43, and Hamilton, *Sparta's Bitter Victories*, 145–47.

68. *Hell. Oxy.* 17.1, cf. 7.2.

69. *Hell. Oxy.* 18.1.

70. Plut. *Pel.* 5.1–3.

71. *Pace* R.J. Bonner, "The Boeotian Federal Constitution," *CP* 5 (1910): 410, who sees continuity.

72. Plato *Meno* 90a; *Rep.* 336a; J.S. Morrison, "Meno of Pharsalos, Polycrates and Ismenias," *CQ* 36 (1942): 57–78; Cook, "Ancient Political Factions," 81, n. 83.

73. Xen. *Hell.* 2.2.19.; Isok. 14.31; Andok. 3.21; Plut. *Lys.* 15; Salmon, *Étude*, 119f.; Hamilton, 146–50; Cook, "Ancient Political Factions," 74; G.W. Botsford, "The Constitution and Politics of the Boeotian League," *PSQ* 25 (1910): 288; Cartledge, *Agesilaos*, 275.

74. Xen. *Hell.* 2.2.19–20 and 3.5.8.

75. Cook, "Ancient Political Factions," 83, argues this point, but she also argues that the defeat of Leontiades' group does not mean that Ismenias was in control. Surely the reversal of policy implies just that: that most voters had started to abandon long-established positions. It seems clear that a discreetly anti-Spartan, but still basically oligarchic set of tactics matched the aspirations and aims of the Boiotian ruling classes at the time. Precisely that seems to have been the policy of the Ismenian faction: to stay on top, keep the voters on their side, and move to a more anti-Spartan stance.

76. Xen. *Hell.* 3.5.5. The *hybris* of Agis and others may have helped to harden Boiotian attitudes, Henry, *Greek Historical Writing*, 207.

77. For the enormity of the insult, G.E. Underhill, *A Commentary on the Hellenica of Xenophon* (Oxford, 1900), xxviii.

78. Xen. *Hell.* 3.5.5.

79. Xen. *Hell.* 2.4.1; Diod. 14.32.1; Clarke, 131f.; Cook, "Boeotia in the Corinthian War," 7f.

80. *Hell. Oxy.* 17.1 and McKechnie and Kern, Comm. *ad loc.* Justin 5.9.8 says that Ismenias aided the Athenians at his own expense, *privatis viribus.*

81. Plut. *Lys.* 27.3; *Pelop.* 6.4; Lysias 12.95; Cook, *Boeotia in the Corinthian War*, 8; Cartledge, *Agesilaos*, 282f., 349f.

82. *Hell. Oxy.* 7.2, 18.1; McKechnie and Kern, 135f.; J.C. Lendon, "The Oxyrhynchus Historian and the Outbreak of the Corinthian War," *Historia* 38 (1988): 300–313, esp. 301f.

III Boiotia Between the Wars, 404–395 B.C.

1. Hamilton, *Sparta's Bitter Victories*, 182–208; Cartledge, *Agesilaos*, 289.

2. Salmon, *Étude*, 112; Cook, "Boeotia in the Corinthian War," 47–77.

3. Plut. *Pel.* 5.1; *Hell. Oxy.* 7.2.

4. Xen. *Hell.* 2.4.30, 3.5.5; Diod. 14.6.3.; Cook, "Boeotia in the Corinthian War," 50 and n. 12.

5. Xen *Hell.* 2.4.24–43 for Xenophon's summary of what transpired. Diod.

14.33.; Cook, "Boeotia in the Corinthian War," 51, 54; T.C. Loening, *The Reconciliation Agreement of 403/2 B.C. in Athens* (*Hermes* Einzelschriften 53, Stuttgart, 1987): 13–16. The Boiotians cited their behaviour during the time of the Thirty as grounds for a favour from the Athenians in 395 as well. Xen. *Hell.* 3.5.8, 3.5.16. For their seizure of goods, Lysias 30.21–22.

6. Or 402, as Cartledge, *Agesilaos*, 285f., suggests. See Appendix I; Diod. 14.17.1; Theopompos, *FGrH* 115 F13. The Athenians may also have had other matters of higher priority to deal with, such as the Thirty at Eleusis.

7. As noted by Cook, "Boeotia in the Corinthian War," 58 and J. Ober, *Fortress Attica* (Leiden, 1985), 112–15.

8. Cook, "Boeotia in the Corinthian War," 59f., gives Leontiades and his faction the credit for the annexation of Oropos.

9. J.M. Camp, "Notes on the Towers and Borders of Classical Boiotia," *AJA* 95 (1991): 193–202, esp. 200.

10. Diod. 14.9.8.

11. Diod. 14.19.4–5. Cook, "Boeotia in the Corinthian War," 62f.

12. Xen. *Hell.* 3.2.21–25; Diod. 14.17.4–7. Cook, "Boeotia in the Corinthian War," 52f., 65–68. The Boiotians may have had the right to refuse, if there was a reciprocal alliance, as suggested in the previous chapter. The dates of the Elean campaigns are uncertain. Cf. Cook, "Boeotia in the Corinthian War," App. I, 530–53; Cartledge, *Agesilaos*, 248–53, prefers 402–400. Lendon, 300–313, esp. 302f.

13. Diod. 14.38.4f.; Cook, "Boeotia in the Corinthian War," 69f.

14. Cf. Diod. 14.82.6. For the date 395/4 see M. Cary, "Heraclea Trachinia," *CQ* 16 (1922): 98f.

15. The incident is reported by Plutarch, *Lys.* 22.2 and *Mor.* 229c. It is attributed by H.D. Westlake, "The Sources for the Spartan Debacle at Haliartus," *Phoenix* 39 (1985): 126, and by Cook, "Boeotia in the Corinthian War," 71, to the invasion of Boiotia in 395. Clarke, 93, argues that it fits better the comparatively peaceful transit of Herippidas in 399, in my view rightly, since Lysander may well have accompanied Herippidas to Herakleia. The "double game" could be the Spartan view of the Boiotian behaviour before the open break, allies but unco-operative.

16. Cook, "Boeotia in the Corinthian War," 73f.; Cartledge, *Agesilaos*, 354.

17. Cloché, "La politique thébaine," 333; Hamilton, 154; Lendon, 303.

18. Cook, "Ismenias' Goals," 59f. and Cartledge, *Agesilaos*, 287f., 354, argue that the Spartans were outflanking Boiotia, and this was one of the principal causes of the war.

19. Paus. 3.9.3. Hamilton, *Sparta's Bitter Victories*, 153; Cook, "Boeotia in the

Corinthian War," 199. One cannot infer from his visit that the faction of Leontiades was predominant. The Spartans may have hoped by the visit to bring over enough support to Leontiades' faction to get the troops despatched.

20. Agesilaus' forces were concentrating at Geraistos on Euboia (Xen, *Hell.* 3.4.4), and Plutarch (*Ages.* 6.4) reports that he was going from there to Aulis with friends for the night. Xenophon refers to one trireme, and it has been inferred that the King was attempting to avoid irritating the Boiotians.

21. Plut. *Ages.* 6.4 reports that Agesilaus was told in a dream to sacrifice what Agamemnon had sacrificed; luckily his daughter was not available. This is obviously an unhistorical anecdote, *pace* Hamilton, *Agesilaus and the Failure of Spartan Hegemony*, 31, n. 106.

22. Xen. *Hell.* 3.4.4; Plut. *Ages.* 6.4–6. This is an interpretation of the factional politics somewhat different from that of Cloché, 95–100, Salmon, *Étude* 121f., and Cook, "Ismenias' Goals," 57–60, but it is more economical with the evidence. Cf. Cartledge, *Agesilaos*, 357. Hamilton, *Agesilaus*, 30–32, 95, suggests that the Boiotarchs may have hoped to provoke Spartan aggression, but I suspect it was more a rejection of Spartan claims to pre-eminence at this juncture.

23. Hamilton, *Sparta's Bitter Victories*, 157 and *Agesilaus*, 95; Cook, "Boeotia in the Corinthian War," 203; S. Perlman, "The Causes and the Outbreak of the Corinthian War," *CQ* 14 (1964): 65. Cook, "Ismenias' Goals," 57–60; Cartledge, *Agesilaos*, 291.

24. Plut. *Lys.* 27.1. The possibility of action against Boiotia by the other king, Pausanias, as suggested by Hamilton, 159f., remains just that, a possibility; just as does the possibility of contacts by the Ismenian faction with the Athenian faction of Epikrates and Kephalos suggested by Cook, "Boeotia in the Corinthian War," 212–17.

25. Cook, "Ismenias' Goals," 58, Map 1.

26. Cartledge, *Agesilaos*, 289.

27. Xen. *Hell.* 3.5.1; Paus. 3.9.8. *Hell. Oxy.* 7.5, gives a slightly different version from that in Xenophon, making the author of the mission Pharnabazos instead of Tithraustes. The latter is the author in the version usually accepted. Cook, "Boeotia in the Corinthian War," 99. *Contra*, Clarke, 62 and n. 70. The precise time of Timokrates' mission is uncertain. Cook, 99 and n. 16 on 122–27, argues for late 397, though this seems early. Lendon, 310f.

28. Bruce, "Internal Politics," 75–86; S. Accame, *Ricerche*, 24.

29. Cook, "Ismenias' Goals," 60, conjectures expansionist aims against Phokis to explain the motivation for the version in the *Hellenica Oxyrhynchia.*

30. L. Lerat, *Les Locriens de l'Ouest* (Paris, 1952), 2.43.

31. For the location and disputes Strabo, 9.3.1 (416), Thuc. 5.32.2, Diod. 12.80.4–5, Gomme, *HCT* 2.11. Lerat, *Les Locriens de l'Ouest*, 2.43 and Clarke, 60 and n. 61 on 95–97.

32. Cook, "Ismenias' Goals," 59f., argues that the "emotional lever" used by Ismenias to stir the Boiotians to war was their expansionist hopes toward Phokis.

33. K.L. McKay, "The Oxyrhynchus Historian and the Outbreak of the Corinthian War," *CR* 3 (1953): 6f.

34. Cook, "Boeotia in the Corinthian War," 242–48.

35. E. Meyer, *Theopomps Hellenika* (Halle, 1909), 88f.; G. Busolt, "Die Neue Historiker und Xenophon," *Hermes* 43 (1908): 278.

36. As Cook, "Boeotia in the Corinthian War," 236, has pointed out.

37. For Xenophon's anti-Theban bias see, e.g., J. Buckler, *The Theban Hegemony*, 263–68, esp. 264f.; Clarke, 6–8; G. Cawkwell in the Preface to the Penguin Classics Xenophon, *A History of My Times*, 36f.

38. Cook, "Boeotia in the Corinthian War," 102–15. Cartledge, *Agesilaos*, 358. In 19.2 the author of the *Hellenica Oxyrhynchia* points out in another context that the Persians were notorious for paying badly and late. Cf. McKechnie and Kern, 171; R. Urban, *Der Königsfrieden von 387/86 v. Chr. (Historia,* Einzelschr. 68, Stuttgart, 1991): 48; Lendon, 311.

39. So Bruce, "Internal Politics," 75–86, esp. 80f.; cf. Cook, "Ancient Political Factions," 64f.

40. Xen. *Hell.* 5.3.35f. He implies the trial was in Thebes before an international tribunal, as does *de gen. Soc.* 576A. Plut. *Pel.* 5.3 and *de gen. Soc.* 576A states he was tried at Sparta, and the latter says he was executed in an unpleasant way.

41. So Cartledge, *Agesilaos*, 292.

42. See also Xen. *Hell.* 3.5.3,4; Paus. 3.9.10. For a detailed analysis and map of the campaign, see Cook, "Boeotia in the Corinthian War," 250–66, map on 256.

43. Busolt, 279f. Cf. Meyer, 90; Hamilton, *Sparta's Bitter Victories*, 197; Clarke, 61f. Busolt argues that the coincidence of 80 casualties suffered at Hyampolis in this campaign and (in Diodorus) in 347 should indicate that this was borrowed from the latter. With Diodorus, however, it may well be the other way around.

44. As suggested by Cawkwell, "Agesilaus and Sparta," 81.

45. As suggested by Bruce, *Comm. Hell. Oxy.*, 121. He seems to have transposed Ozolian and Opuntian Lokris. Cook, "Boeotia in the Corinthian War," 255, and "Ismenias' Goals," 59f., argues that the dispute was a pretext for the

invasion of Phokis. McKechnie and Kern, *Hell. Oxy.*, 170, argue that the raid was premeditated, and that the plan was not to capture towns but to produce a Spartan reaction.

46. Bonner, 410, long ago argued for a "states' rights" party in Boiotia, but thought it was the one led by Ismenias. It may be that each faction, when it was in opposition, appealed to the separatist feelings that are always latent in a federation and seem to have been especially so in Boiotia.

47. Diod. 15.79.3–6. Buckler, *Theban Hegemony*, 182–84, gives a clear picture.

48. Cartledge, *Agesilaos*, 292.

49. Plut. *Lys.* 27.1, 28.1.

50. Plut. *Lys.* 28.2; Diod. 14.81.1; Xen. *Hell.* 3.5.6. Xenophon says that they were to meet on an appointed day at Haliartos, but he seems to be compressing here, since this could not have been agreed on until after Orchomenos fell.

51. Cf. *Hell. Oxy* 18.1, where the author indicates the extent of the intrigues of the pro-Spartan faction of Leontiades.

52. Xen. *Hell.* 3.5.7–17; Diod. 14.81.2. The idea held by many that Orchomenos had revolted before the Athenian alliance is ably refuted by Cook, "Boeotia in the Corinthian War," 257 and n. 41 on 271–73. I cannot agree with her that Xenophon could not have had "reliable information as to what was said" in the speeches. He did have Athenian informants. Westlake, 125, points out that the Spartan plan of attack was a secret; but it was obvious that there would be some attack. It was, *pace* Cartledge, *Agesilaos*, 358, hardly a pre-emptive strike.

53. R. Seager, "Thrasybulus, Conon, and Athenian Imperialism," *JHS* 87 (1967): 96; Hamilton, 206; Cartledge, *Agesilaos*, 292.

54. *IG* II² 14 and 15; Tod, 101 and 102.

55. For a critical examination of the sources and the campaign, Westlake, 119–33.

56. Xen. *Hell.* 3.5.6; Plut., *Lys.* 28.2, says that Orchomenos came over *willingly* (ἑκουσίως); Plut., *Pelop.* 16.1, says Orchomenos *chose* the Spartan cause (ἑλομένη).

57. For a summary of views see Clarke, 45f. and Cook, "Boeotia in the Corinthian War," 643–45. See also Cartledge, *Agesilaos*, 292.

58. Salmon, *Étude* 92; Clarke, 45.

59. Xen. *Hell.* 3.5.6. Xenophon unduly compresses events, because the time and place of the meeting-place could not be fixed until after the adherence of Orchomenos.

60. Larsen, *Greek Federal States*, 159, seems to think that Koroneia was taken, but if so, it was back in Boiotian hands rapidly.

61. Xen. *Hell.* 3.5.17; Plut. *Lys.* 28.2.

62. The story of the intercepted message in Plutarch, *Lys.* 28.2, is sometimes rejected, as by Accame, *Ricerche,* 39, for no good reason.

63. G. Proietti, *Xenophon's Sparta* (*Mnemosyne* Supp. 98, Leiden, 1987), 104. The question of whether Lysander was early or Pausanias was late cannot be answered on present evidence. Cf. Westlake, 124, n. 16; Cartledge, *Agesilaos,* 359.

64. For the location of Kissousa, Frazer, *Paus.* 5.165 on 9.32.5; he places it at a spring on the north foot of Palaiokastro cliff, southwest of Haliartos. Cf. Westlake, 127, n. 31.

65. Cf. Plut. *Lys.* 28.3–5 and Westlake, 125.

66. Plut. *Lys.* 29.6.

67. Pausanias 3.5.3–4 gives the Athenians an exaggerated rôle, putting some of them into Haliartos and having a main force under Thrasyboulos preparing to catch King Pausanias' army from the rear. It sounds as if the Theban move on the left rear of Lysander was transferred to the following day in Pausanias' source.

68. Xen. *Hell.* 3.5.21–25; Plut. *Lys.* 29.1–3.

69. Roesch, *Thespies,* 41f. *Pace* Cook, Orchomenian exiles *a priori* may be assumed; cf. Thuc. 4.76 about democratic exiles from Orchomenos.

70. Plut. *Lys.* 29.3.

71. Diod. 14.82.1–4.

72. Cook, "Boeotia in the Corinthian War," 141–82; D. Kagan, "The Economic Origins of the Corinthian War (395–387 B.C.)," *PdP* 80 (1961): 321–41; "Politics and Policy in Corinth (421–336 B.C.)" (Ph.D. diss., Ohio State, 1958), 69f.

73. Diod. 14.82.5–6.

74. Diod. 14.82.6.

75. Diod. 14.82.7–10. For the site of Naryx, Pritchett, *Studies in Ancient Greek Topography,* 4.155f. and 5.167–71.

IV Boiotia in the Corinthian War, 394–387 B.C.

1. Xen. *Hell.* 4.3.12, but it must have been apparent long before the Battle of Knidos.

2. Plut. *Ages.* 15; Xen. *Hell.* 4.2.1–8; Diod. 14.83.1, 3.

3. Xen. *Hell.* 4.2.9–10.

4. This is a point missed by several of the commentators on this campaign, e.g., Cook, "Boeotia in the Corinthian War," 314f.

5. *Pace* Cook, "Boeotia in the Corinthian War," 314f., who infers from Xen.

Hell. 4.2.13 that a debate in the Congress over tactics delayed the departure of the forces. There was considerable discussion over the arrangements to be employed, but Xenophon does not say it delayed matters; he says that *while* matters were being discussed, the Spartans began moving, and in fact both armies were on the march.

6. Xen. *Hell.* 4.2.12. Cook, "Boeotia in the Corinthian War," 313, rightly rejects Accame's arguments that Timolaus' proposal is an anachronism, a bit of late composition (cf. Cawkwell in the Penguin translation of Xen. *Hell.*, 196 ad loc.). It was sound strategy, and Spartan territory was not as sacrosanct as is often believed.

7. Xen. *Hell.* 4.2.13–14. It is unlikely that they proceeded along the Argolic Gulf, as Brownson suggested in the Loeb translation, 286, if they were on their way to Sikyonian territory, especially as they also picked up a contingent from Pellene (4.2.20). Pritchett, *Studies in Ancient Greek Topography* 2 (Berkeley, 1969), 79–81, suggests that they took the direct Mantinea-Sikyon route via Alea. He emends Xenophon's obscure ἀμφίαλον to ἀμφὶ ᾿Αλέαν, following Herbst.

8. Pritchett, *Studies in Ancient Greek Topography*, 2.76f.

9. For the location of Epieikeia, Pritchett, *Studies in Ancient Greek Topography*, 2.80f.

10. Xen. *Hell.* 4.2.14. Pritchett, *Studies in Ancient Greek Topography*, 2.78f.

11. For the actual battle see Pritchett, *Studies in Ancient Greek Topography*, 2.73–84; Anderson, 141–50; Cartledge, *Agesilaos*, 220f.

12. As suggested by, e.g., Pritchett, *Studies in Ancient Greek Topography*, 2.84 and Anderson, 143.

13. Cook, "Boeotia in the Corinthian War," 323f.

14. Lysias 16.16; Cook, "Boeotia in the Corinthian War," 332f.

15. Cook, "Boeotia in the Corinthian War," 333. K.J. Maidment, *Minor Attic Orators,* Vol. I (Loeb, London, 1941), 486, says there were sixteen days between Nemea and Koroneia.

16. Xen. *Hell.* 4.3.1. Cook, "Boeotia in the Corinthian War," 328.

17. Diodoros 14.83.4 has a textual problem here. The arguments of E. Harrison, "A Problem in the Corinthian War," *CQ* 7 (1913): 132, to explain the omission of Herakleia by changing the chronology of the campaign of Ismenias are not acceptable. They fail to explain why Pharsalos, the adherence of which to the Boiotian cause must be linked to the occupation of Herakleia, is in the forefront of the fight against Agesilaus. Cary, 98f., gives a relative sequence that is correct, though Cook, "Boeotia in the Corinthian War," 330f., is probably wrong in thinking that his dating is late.

18. Cary, 98f.

19. Xen. *Hell.* 4.3.10–13. The Battle of Knidos, therefore, must have taken place near the end of July or in early August, 394.

20. Xen. *Hell.* 4.3.15; Plut. *Ages.* 17.3. Cf. A. Powell, "Mendacity and Sparta's Use of the Visual," in *Classical Sparta: Techniques Behind Her Success,* (Norman, Okla., 1989), A. Powell, ed.,173–92.

21. Xen. *Hell.* 4.3.15 says one from the Corinth area, but Plut. *Ages.* 17.1 says two. Xenophon is more likely to be right about this.

22. Xen. ibid.

23. For the battle itself see Pritchett, *Studies in Ancient Greek Topography*, 2.85–95; Anderson, 150–53; Cook, "Boeotia in the Corinthian War," 337–39; Cartledge, *Agesilaos*, 221f.; Hamilton, *Agesilaus*, 106–8.

24. Plut. *Ages.* 17.1; cf. Xen. *Hell.* 4.3.1.

25. For the effort against Ozolian Lokris, Xen. *Hell.* 4.3.21–23; Anderson, 120.

26. Xen. *Hell.* 4.4.1.

27. Xen. *Hell.* 4.8.10–11.

28. *IG* II² 1657; Tod, 107.

29. Xen. *Hell.* 4.4.1.

30. Diod. 14.86.1, with Wurm's emendation.

31. Xen. *Hell.* 4.4.2; cf. Cawkwell in the Penguin translation, note to 4.4.6, but also see Cook, "Boeotia in the Corinthian War," 366f.

32. D. Kagan, "Corinthian Politics and the Revolution of 392," *Historia* 11 (1962): 447–57; "Economic Origins of the Corinthian War," 321–41; G.T. Griffith, "The Economic Union of Corinth and Argos (392–386 B.C.)," *Historia* 1 (1950): 236–56, esp. 240; C.D. Hamilton, "The Politics of Revolution at Corinth, 395–386 B.C.," *Historia* 21 (1972): 21–37; Cook, "Boeotia in the Corinthian War," 366–69; Cartledge, *Agesilaos*, 364.

33. Xen. *Hell.* 4.4.6 talks of a political union, but Andokides, *De Pace* 26f. and other passages in *Hell.* rebut this, as Griffith, 236–56, has demonstrated. Most modern authorities follow him. Cf. Cook, "Boeotia in the Corinthian War," 367 and n. 5 on. 417f., and Cawkwell in the Penguin Classics *A History of my Times*, 209 n.

34. On the ubiquity of traitors in Classical Greece, C.G. Starr, *Political Intelligence in Classical Greece* (Leiden, 1974), 16f.

35. Xen. *Hell.* 4.8.12. Plut. *Ages.* 23.1 combines this with the later mission of Antalkidas that resulted in the King's Peace in 387/6. For latest discussion see Urban, 59–78.

36. Xen. *Hell.* 4.8.13. One would like to know how the Athenians learnt of the mission. Could a supporter of Agesilaus have passed the word to defeat his

bitter enemy Antalkidas and preserve Spartan claims in Asia Minor? Cf. Plut. *Ages.* 23.1. Cf. Starr, Ch. 4, 29–38. Cartledge, *Agesilaos*, 195, doubts the enmity between them.

37. Urban, *Königsfrieden*, 62 and n. 206.

38. Xen. *Hell.* 4.8.14f.; Diod. 14.85.4 says nothing about such a debate.

39. Xen. *Hell.* 4.8.16.

40. Xen. *Hell.* 4.8.17.

41. Xen. *Hell.* 4.8.18f.

42. Cf. Urban, 68.

43. Xen. *Hell.* 4.4.7–13; Diod. 14.86.3–4; Andokides, *De Pace* 18; Cook, "Boeotia in the Corinthian War," 386–90; Anderson, 154–57. D. Kagan, *Politics and Policy in Corinth,* 96f. For the date, probably August, see Cook, "Boeotia in the Corinthian War," 387 and n. 32 on 425.

44. Xen. *Hell.* 4.4.12; Anderson, 156f.

45. There has been a considerable controversy from the time of Grote as to whether the town of Lechaion was captured at this time along with the harbour. Xenophon himself, *Hell.* 4.4.17, has the Spartans set out from Lechaion and make various expeditions around Corinth after the battle; it is more economical to have Lechaion theirs at this time to set out from. Cf. Hamilton, *Sparta's Bitter Victories*, 251 and n. 52; Beloch, 3.2.219f.; Cook, "Boeotia in the Corinthian War," 388–90. For the naval advantage to Sparta, Xen. *Hell.* 4.8.11.

46. There is some dispute over the date, for which see Cook, "Boeotia in the Corinthian War," 396–401; Cawkwell, "The Imperialism of Thrasybulus," 272 and n. 13; Ryder, *Koine Eirene*, App. 12, 165–67.; Hamilton, *Sparta's Bitter Victories*, 249f.; *Agesilaus*, 112; Urban, 71–78.

47. Philochoros, *FGrH* 328 F 149a; Cook, "Boeotia in the Corinthian War," 402–4; Hamilton, *Sparta's Bitter Victories*, 255.

48. Hamilton, *Sparta's Bitter Victories*, 255.

49. The attempt to attribute this exiling to 387/6 seems unwise and should be abandoned. Cf. Cook, "Boeotia in the Corinthian War," 410.

50. Hamilton, *Sparta's Bitter Victories*, 253f. There is a suggestion based on Andokides, *De Pace* 3.20, that there were separate Boiotian negotiations at this time. Cf. Cook, "Boeotia in the Corinthian War," 409f. It is clear that Andokides is exaggerating the effect of the signing by the Boiotian plenipotentiaries. Since it, too, had to be ratified by the home government, it had the same effect as the agreement of the Athenian envoys: none at all.

51. *Pace* Hamilton, *Sparta's Bitter Victories*, 257 and Cook, "Boeotia in the Corinthian War," 409.

52. Hamilton, *Sparta's Bitter Victories*, 257f.; *Agesilaus*, 113; Cook, "Boeotia in the Corinthian War," 408f.

53. Cf. Buck, *History*, 97f.

54. Xen. *Hell.* 4.4.18; Cook, "Boeotia in the Corinthian War," 390 and n. 35 on 426.

55. Hamilton, *Sparta's Bitter Victories*, 257; Cook, "Boeotia in the Corinthian War," 409f.; cf. Urban, 80 and n. 291.

56. Xen. *Hell.* 4.4.19; before the end of May or early June, if he is to be believed, but cf. Cook, "Boeotia in the Corinthian War," 435 and n. 3. Anderson, 123; Cartledge, *Agesilaos*, 223.

57. Xen. *Hell.* 4.5.11–17; Plut. *Ages.* 22.2. For the details see Anderson, 123–26.

58. N.G.L. Hammond, "The Main Road from Boeotia to the Peloponnese," *BSA* 49 (1954): 103–22. C.A. Robinson, "Topographical Notes on Perachora," *AJA* 31 (1927): 96, stresses the rapidity of the route for foot traffic. A.W. Gomme, "The Topography of Boeotia," *BSA* 18 (1911–12): 189–210, gives a good description of the tracks here.

59. J.B. Bury, History of Greece[3], (London, 1959): 548; Cartledge, *Agesilaos*, 294; Hamilton, *Agesilaus*, 114.

60. As Cook, "Boeotia in the Corinthian War," 440–42, suggests.

61. Xen. *Hell.* 4.5.19; Cook, "Boeotia in the Corinthian War," 444 and Hamilton, *Sparta's Bitter Victories*, 389f., both underestimate the aggressiveness of the Allies at this time.

62. Xen. *Hell.* 4.8.34; Diod. 14.92; Hamilton, *Sparta's Bitter Victories*, 275–82; Cook, "Boeotia in the Corinthian War," 450, 452.

63. Hamilton, *Sparta's Bitter Victories*, 287; Anderson, 140, dates it to 390.

64. Xen. *Hell.* 4.6.1–3.

65. Xen. *Hell.* 4.6.4–14; Plut. *Ages.* 22.5; Xen. *Agesilaus* 2.20; Paus. 3.10.2; Polyainos 2.1.1, 10. For the campaign see Anderson, 126, 140. Cook, "Boeotia in the Corinthian War," 451f.; Larsen, *Greek Federal States*, 168; Hamilton, *Sparta's Bitter Victories*, 287; *Agesilaus*, 116f.; Cartledge, *Agesilaos*, 225.

66. Xen. *Hell.* 4.7.1; Plut. *Ages.* 22.5; Cook, "Boeotia in the Corinthian War," 454; Hamilton, *Sparta's Bitter Victories*, 288; Cartledge, *Agesilaos*, 225f.

67. Xen. *Hell.* 4.7.6. Cawkwell, in the Penguin Classics translation of Xenophon, *A History of My Times*, 227, argues that "the Lakonian" was the name of a location somewhere near Argos, "since it is inconceivable that the Argives had gone so far from their city."

68. Xen. *Hell.* 5.1.25. See, e.g., R. Seager, "The King's Peace and the Balance of Power in Greece, 386–362 B.C.," *Athenaeum* 52 (1974): 36–63, esp. 37f.

69. Xen. *Hell.* 5.1.25–29; Cook, "Boeotia in the Corinthian War," 484–86.

70. Xen. *Hell.* 5.1.29–30; Cook, "Boeotia in the Corinthian War," 486f.; Urban, 109–25.

71. Seager, "The King's Peace," 38f.; Cartledge, *Agesilaos*, 296; Hamilton, *Agesilaus*, 117f.; Urban, 111f.

V Boiotia Without the League, 387–379 B.C.

1. See Head, "On the Chronological Sequence of the Coins of Boeotia," 219–26; *Historia Nummorum* (London, 1910), 346f.; P. Gardner, *A History of Ancient Coinage* (Oxford, 1918), 357f.; for Plataia Prandi, *Platea*, 125.

2. Plut. *de gen. Soc.* 597 ABC. Cf. Roesch, *Thespies*, 158 and n. 5.

3. Xen. *Hell.* 5.2.25, 5.2.32, 5.4.2, 5.4.6–8; Plut. *Pel.* 7.3, 11.4. Roesch, *Thespies*, 162f.; J. Buckler, "The Re-establishment of the *Boiotarchia* (378 BC)," *AJAH* 4 (1979): 50f. It is sometimes argued that Plutarch's "archon chosen by lot" (κυαμευτὸς ἄρχων, *de gen. Soc.* 597A) is the third polemarch; but since Plutarch uses the term "polemarch" regularly, it seems an unnecessary hypothesis.

4. For archons, Roesch, *Thespies*, 158; for polemarchs, ibid., 167; Buckler, "Re-establishment of the *Boiotarchia*," 51, n. 14, gives inscriptional evidence for polemarchs at various Boiotian towns over a wide variety of dates.

5. Hack, "The Rise of Thebes," 6–8.

6. Isok. *Plat.* 14.20 implies that Oropos joined Athens voluntarily. Buckler, *The Theban Hegemony,* 14; Frazer, *Paus.* 2.463.

7. Paus. 9.1.4; Prandi, *Platea*, 123.

8. Cartledge, *Agesilaos*, 374, suggests the refounding of Plataia should be placed after 382, but this is too late for fitting Pausanias.

9. Cf. Cartledge, *Agesilaos*, 296.

10. Isok. *Plat.* 14.27,28; Plut. *Pel.* 4.4,5; Paus. 9.13.1

11. As Grote pointed out, 10.34, n. 1; Buckler, "The Alleged Theban-Spartan Alliance," 179–83; Urban, 113 and n. 439; 136 and n. 524. But cf. H.M. Hack, "Thebes and the Spartan Hegemony, 386–382 B.C.," *AJP* 99 (1978): 217; *The Rise of Thebes*, 11, 16; D.G. Rice, "Xenophon, Diodorus and the Year 379/78 B.C.," *YCS* 24 (1975): 103–5; Hamilton, *Agesilaus*, 142; Isokrates could even be referring to the time of the Spartan occupation.

12. For Socrates and Alkibiades Plato *Symp.* 220e–221b.

13. von Stern, *Geschichte der spartanische und thebanische Hegemonie,* 35. Hack, *The Rise of Thebes*, 11, 16, following E. Meyer, says 382.

14. Xen. *Hell.* 5.2.25.

15. Xen. *Hell.* 5.2.16.

16. Xen. *Hell.* 6.4.3; Diod. 15.53.1. The inscription *SEG* 24 (1969) 361 (= *BCH* 62 [1938] 149/66 and pl. 28), usually dated to 386/380 (R.A. Tomlinson, "Two Notes on Possible *Hestiatoria*," *BSA* 75 [1980]: 221–28) deals with the sacred property of the Thespian People at Siphai, Kreusis and Chorsiai and is associated with the enforced separation of the three towns from Thespiai. But it is odd that the inscription was set up at Chorsiai for listing Thespian property at Siphai and Kreusis, unless there was still some feeling of association or unity amongst the three. The date is by no means certain.

17. Xen. *Hell.* 5.2.27; Diod. 15.20.2.

18. Diod. 15.19.3 and 15.20.2. Ephoros seems to be following a pro-Boiotian source.

19. Diod. 15.20.2.

20. Xen. *Hell.* 5.2.23–31; Plut. *Pel.* 5.2–3; Plut. *Ages.* 23.6–7. Plutarch also used Ephoros, as noted above. Plutarch does not, *pace* J. deVoto, "The Liberation of Thebes in 379/8 B.C.," in *Daidalikon: Studies in Memory of Raymond V. Schoder, S.J.,* R.F. Sutton, ed. (Wauconda, IL, 1989), 103, say that Agesilaus and his partisans were behind the raid, but only that they endorsed it. There is little to support the idea that Leontiades' faction was planning a coup anyway, Hamilton, *Agesilaus*, 143.

21. Diod. 15.20.2–3; Plut. *Pel.* 6.1, *Ages.* 23.3–4; *de gen. Soc.* 576A; Nepos *Pel.* 1.3; Isok. *Paneg.* 4.126; Polyb. 4.27.4.

22. Xen. *Hell.* 5.2.32–36.

23. deVoto, "The Liberation of Thebes," 108, ignores the possibility of a trial at Thebes.

24. Cf. *FGrH* 124 where Kallisthenes is cited by Plutarch in *Camillus* (F10[b]), *Kimon* (F15, F16), *Pelopidas* (F18) and *Agesilaus* (F26).

25. Diod. 14.117.8 [= Jacoby *FGrH* 124 T27(a)] reports under 387/6 that Kallisthenes wrote a history from the "year of the peace of the Greeks with Artaxerxes," covering the next thirty years in ten books and ending with the seizure of Delphi by Philomelas of Phokis. Unfortunately the citations extant are principally from 378 onward. Von Stern, *Geschichte der spartanische und thebanische Hegemonie*, 47 and 145, put forth the idea of its being Plutarch's main source here, developed in his *Xenophons Hellenika und die Böotische Geschichtsüberlieferung,* 51f., and by K. Ziegler, *Plutarchos von Chaironeia* (Munich, 1964), 842 and S. Fuscagni, "Callisthene di Olinto e la 'Vita di Pelopida' di Plutarco," in *Storiografia e propaganda,* M. Sordi, ed. (Milan, 1975), 31–55. This is accepted by J. Hani in the Budé edition of Plutarch, *Moralia* 8 (Paris, 1980), 41–43, and J. Buckler, *The Theban Hege-*

mony, 270–72 and n. 36 on 321. Kallisthenes was certainly one of the sources, but not the one used at this point. For Kallisthenes as the source for military affairs from 378 on, Buckler, "Plutarch on Leuktra," 76.

26. Kallet-Marx, 128f., is right in saying "The historian of the fourth century can neither flatly reject nor uncritically accept Diodorus' testimony: his information varies in value and must be analyzed and judged on its own merits and on the criterion of its consistency with other evidence of higher authority." Beloch, *GG* 3.1.104f. and Cloché, *Thèbes,* 113, are among the minority who have not combined the versions. They prefer to follow Xenophon exclusively here.

27. Cf. Grote, 10.58f.; Meyer, *GdA* 5.293; von Stern, *Geschichte der spartanische und thebanische Hegemonie,* 36; D.G. Rice, "Agesilaus, Agesipolis and Spartan Politics," *Historia* 23 (1974): 180f.; Hack, *The Rise of Thebes,* 20f.; Cartledge, *Agesilaos,* 296f.

28. Plut. *Ages.* 24.1; Xen. *Hell.* 5.2.28 is taken by Cawkwell, Comm. in Penguin *History of My Times,* p. 266, as a contradiction of this idea.

29. Cawkwell, "Foundation of the Second Athenian Confederacy," 53, n. 3; Hack, *The Rise of Thebes,* 26, n. 74; Cartledge, *Agesilaos,* 296; Hamilton, *Agesilaus,* 144f.

30. For the importance of such a violation of international law, G. Ténékidès, *La notion juridique d'independance et la tradition hellénique* (Athens, 1954), 19–24, 170–72.

31. Diod. 15.25.3; Plut. *Pelop.* 12.3, 13.2; Plut. *de gen. Soc.* 598F.

32. Diod. 15.27.3; Plut. *de gen. Soc.* 576A, 598F.

33. Xen. *Hell.* 5.4.10, 13 for the single harmost. Xen. *Hell.* 5.4.11 for the garrison being ὀλίγοι. Xenophon seldom names errant Spartans.

34. Hack, *The Rise of Thebes,* 29–31; H.W. Parke, "Herippidas, Harmost at Thebes," *CQ* 21 (1927): 158, n. 3; Rice, *Why Sparta Failed,* 73f.

35. Hack, *The Rise of Thebes,* 235–40, argues that there were no garrisons in Boiotia, except for the one at Thebes, until after 379. He ignores the existence of the garrison at Orchomenos, stationed there from 395 and with no indication of its evacuation after 386.

36. Xen. *Hell.* 5.4.1, 5.4.2; Plut. *Ages.* 24.1.

37. Cf. Xen. *Hell.* 5.2.32 concerning the election by the (rump) Council of a replacement for Ismenias. I cannot follow Buckler, "The Re-establishment of the *Boiotarchia,*" 51, where he says that the constitution was not changed, in spite of Plutarch's and Xenophon's remarks about tyranny.

38. *Pace* Grote 10.28f.; E. Meyer, *GdA* 5.292, Rice, *Why Sparta Failed,* 50.

39. Grote 10.80f.; Rice, *Why Sparta Failed,* 14f.; "Agesilaus, Agesipolis and Spartan Politics," *Historia* 23 (1974): 165; P. Roesch, *Thespies,* 44; Cloché, *Thèbes de Béotie,* 112, 119.

40. Hack, *The Rise of Thebes,* 235–40, Parke, 71–74; Ryder, 50, 53.

41. Xen. *Hell.* 5.4.8, 5.4.14; Plut. *de gen. Soc.* 575F–576A, 598AC.

42. The body of the jailer was consequently maltreated by the womenfolk of the prisoners next day. Plut. *de gen. Soc.* 598C.

43. It is curious that the custom of incising votive potsherds came to an abrupt end at the Kabirion in the second decade of the fourth century. It is probably to be associated with the Spartan occupation of the Kadmeia. Schachter, *Cults,* 2.77f.

44. Plut. *de gen. Soc.* 577 EF. The finds included a stone, a bronze bracelet, two amphorai containing hard-packed earth, and a large bronze tablet bearing an indecipherable script. It sounds like a Late Helladic III burial with the skeleton dissolved in acid soil and a long Linear B inscription, or a Geometric cremation burial with a very archaic alphabetic inscription. My guess would be the latter.

45. Hack, *The Rise of Thebes,* 37, n. 32, argues that Charon's remark, that rumours of conspiracies were common only when Androkleidas was alive, would otherwise have been pointless.

46. Plut. *Pel.* 6.1–3.

47. The discrepancies are: i) in *de gen. Soc.* (577B) Phillidas is already secretary; in *Pel.* (7.3) Phillidas is appointed after the conspiracy starts; ii) in *de gen. Soc.* (576CD) the advance man of the volunteers coming from exile requests lodgings for them from the conspirators at Thebes; in *Pel.* (7.2.3, 8.4) he merely reconfirms previously made arrangements; iii) Charon on his return from his interview with Archias tells only Pelopidas what happened (*Pel.* 10.2); in *de gen. Soc.* (595B) he tells everyone; iv) Kephisodoros is killed by Leontiades in *Pel.* (11.5); in *de gen. Soc.* (597F) he is fatally wounded by Leontiades and dies after seeing his enemy slain; v) The party assigned to attack Archias and Philip were all dressed as women with garlands in *Pel.* (11.1,2); but though they all wore chaplets, only a few were dressed as women in *de gen. Soc.* (596CD).

48. DeVoto, "The Liberation of Thebes," 104, argues, following Accame, that the source for Nepos and Diodorus, Ephorus, paralleled Plutarch's source. This is not correct, as we shall see.

49. Cf. How and Wells, *Comm. Hdt. ad* 5.20, Vol. 2, 7, following Macan.

50. Cf. the British raid in 1941 on a German party where Rommel was thought

to be a guest. He was not, but the leader of the raid, Roger Keyes, received a posthumous V.C.

51. See Introduction. Buckler, *Theban Hegemony*, 267, denies that Xenophon made any "outright misstatement of fact." This does not mean that he cannot be mistaken. Cf. Cawkwell, e.g., in the Penguin Xenophon, *A History of My Times*, 31–33, 45f. Fuscagni, in Sordi, *Storiografia e propaganda*, 35. DeVoto, "The Liberation of Thebes," 105, 109f. V. Gray, *The Character of Xenophon's* Hellenica (Baltimore, 1989), 65–72, emphasizes the story-telling elements in Xenophon's version of the incident, including the use of the number seven.

52. Plut. *Pel.* 8, *de gen. Soc.* 597CD; Diod. 15.81; Nepos *Pel.* 2.5.

53. So Hack, *Rise of Thebes*, 52 and n. 75; cf. Hamilton, *Agesilaus*, 155.

54. So also deVoto, "The Liberation of Thebes," 111.

55. Pherenikos is mentioned in *Pel.* 5.3 as one of the important figures of the faction of Ismenias who fled to Athens. He sent word that the Twelve were coming (*de gen. Soc.* 576C) and was classed with Pelopidas as an essentially just man (577A).

56. Cf. von Stern, *Xenophons Hellenika*, 24f. DeVoto, "The Liberation of Thebes," 114, suggests that the omission arises from his unwillingness to mention the massacre of the lakonizing Thebans. In my view it may stem from Plutarch's, or his source's, sense of symmetry in drawing a parallel with the liberation of Athens by Thrasyboulos, who used a force of Athenian exiles, but no Boiotians, in the liberation of Athens. Even if non-Theban Boiotian exiles are to be added to the 300 or so Thebans, it would still be a fairly small force, though hardly as small as Nepos' (*Pel.* 2.3) 100.

57. Isok. 14.3; Aeschines 3.138f.

58. Hack, *The Rise of Thebes*, 58 and n. 88, gives a summary of the discussion and argues for volunteers, as does J.T. Roberts, *Accountability in Athenian Government* (Madison, 1982), 81–83; Kallet-Marx, 140f., argues for official Athenian sanction.

59. Xen. *Hell.* 7.3.7, where it is clear that Hypates was killed extra-legally.

60. Plut. *de gen. Soc.* 597F.

61. For the location of the stoas and the jail see Symeonoglou, 138f.

62. In the Introduction to Xenophon, *A History of My Times*, tr. R. Warner (Penguin Classics, 1979), 22–28. Cf. Buckler, *Theban Hegemony*, 263–68; Gray, *The Character of Xenophon's* Hellenica, vii–x, 1–9.

63. Von Stern, *Xenophons Hellenika*, 18, suggests possibly Phillidas. He prefers Xenophon to Plutarch and considers the latter is following a Boiotian-based rewriting of history (23–25, 28f.). The inconsistencies and improbabilities that he points out are not particularly inconsistent or improbable.

64. Cf. Hani, in the Budé edition of Plutarch's *Moralia* 8, 42f.; von Stern, *Xenophons Hellenika*, 51f.

65. For Kallisthenes see n. 25; for other sources cf. G. Shrimpton, "The Theban Supremacy in Fourth-Century Literature," *Phoenix* 25 (1971): 310–18; Westlake, 122f.

66. Plut. *de gen. Soc.* 577C, *Pel.* 8.1; Schachter, *Cults, s.v.* "Aphrodisia" 38–40.

67. Hack, *The Rise of Thebes*, 51f.

68. This may be behind the number of less than 100 in Nepos *Pel.* 2.3 for all the conspirators, if it is not his source's estimate of the number of participants at Thebes in the coup.

69. Xen. *Hell.* 3.5.1; Plut. *de gen. Soc.* 577A, 594B.

70. So also deVoto, "The Liberation of Thebes," 109f.

71. Plut. *de gen. Soc.* 577A.

72. For the bitterly cold weather and snow Plut. *de gen. Soc.* 594D 596C.

73. Schachter, *Cults,* 38–40, makes the ladies a little too reputable if they were to be counterparts of Aphrodite to the men's Ares.

74. Nepos, *Pel.* 2.3, with his total of less than 100 is surely wrong or is referring to the conspirators in Thebes.

75. Plut. *de gen. Soc.* 598E.

76. Plut. *de gen. Soc.* 578AB.

77. For the length of the siege see Chapter VI.

78. Plut. *Pel.* 13.1 mentions the first three, 14.1 notes Gorgidas. Four had been the number of Theban Boiotarchs from 427, and the symbolism would not have been lost on the other Boiotians, especially the Plataians. Several scholars reject the idea of the assumption of the title in 378 (e.g., Cawkwell, "Epaminondas and Thebes," 275f., Beloch, *GG* 3.1.145, n. 2) on the grounds that it was premature to indulge in constitutional reform on the morrow of a revolution. But that is usually when it is done. Sordi, "La restaurazione della lege beotica nel 379–8 A.C.," 79–91, esp. 79–85, argues that two and not four Boiotarchs were elected, with the other two as polemarchs. This seems based on the assumption that without Plataia it would not have been legal to have four Boiotarchs. I doubt that revolutionary enthusiasm would have been restrained by such considerations. See Buckler, "The Re-establishment of the *Boiotarchia*," 50–57 and nn.16–18 for a strong case for Boiotarchs.

79. The elections for the Boiotarchs were undertaken in an *ekklesia*, as Plut. *Pel.* 12.4–13.1 indicates, not in a *boule*; it is significant that pro-democrats from other Boiotian cities made their way to Thebes, Xen. *Hell.* 5.4.46. Cf. Polyb. 6.43.4–7, 44.9.

80. Cf. Isok. 14.13–14, 19. Hack, *The Rise of Thebes*, 240, thinks that the refer-

ences are to events after 379, since he does not believe that there were any garrisons in Boiotia until after the loss of Thebes.

81. Xen. *Hell.* 5.4.10.
82. Plut. *de gen. Soc.* 586EF.
83. Xen. *Hell.* 5.4.46 notes a pro-democratic faction at Thespiai that came out and joined a Theban force in the area; in 5.4.55 he notes *stasis* in Thespiai; perhaps between the remaining democrats and the ruling oligarchs, if it was not between rival factions of oligarchs.
84. Xen. *Hell.* 5.4.49.
85. Diod. 15.26.3f.

VI *The Boiotian League Restored, 378–375 B.C.*

1. Diod. 15.25.3, 27.1–3; Plut. *Pel.* 13.2.
2. As pointed out in the last chapter there is no ground for concluding that Kallisthenes was Plutarch's *principal* source for the *Pelopidas.*
3. E.A. Barber, *The Historian Ephorus* (Cambridge, 1935), 17–47; R. Drews, "Ephorus and History Written *Kata Genos,"AJP* 84 (1963): 244–55, and "Ephorus' κατὰ γένος History Revisited," *Hermes* 104 (1976): 497f.
4. For the general worth of Isokrates for this period Buckler, "The Re-establishment of the *Boiotarchia*," 52, is correct; but Isokrates does in his sequence here support Xenophon. Even a rhetorician can, on occasion, get things right. There is no support here for Hamilton's suggestion (*Agesilaus*, 166) that the embassy was sent out *after* Kleombrotos' invasion.
5. What Deinarchos means by "at their own risk" is uncertain. He might mean private, unofficial efforts carried out by the philo-Boiotian Athenians; or he might be implying something about the risks in following the policy that led the two generals to trial and condemnation. The defence that the generals had been authorized to manoeuvre on the frontier would probably not have had much weight with the Assembly when it was in panic over the prospect of a Spartan invasion.
6. As Cawkwell, "The Foundation of the Second Athenian Confederacy," 56–60, pointed out.
7. Xen. *Hell.* 5.4.4 indicates that the coup was on the last day of the feast of Aphrodite, probably Boukataios 1, the beginning of the new year. *Hell.* 5.4.10f. is held to indicate that the siege was short, a couple of days at the most. For the Boiotian calendar, Roesch, *Études,* 33–54. See Kallet-Marx, 135 and n. 35; Hamilton, *Agesilaus*, 167. deVoto, "The Liberation of Thebes," 114f., relies on Plutarch for a three-week siege and follows Plutarch's chronology, wrongly.

8. So Kallet-Marx, 141.

9. Hack, *The Rise of Thebes*, 58, n. 88, gives a good summary of the scholarship and decides for unofficial Athenian involvement, as also Rice, *Why Sparta Failed*, 99f. and Hamilton, *Agesilaus*, 156f. But cf. R.J. Buck, "The Athenians at Thebes in 379/8 B.C.," *AHB* 6 (1992): 103–9.

10. Cawkwell, "The Foundation of the Second Athenian Confederacy," 58.

11. Burnett, 16; Roberts, 82.

12. Cawkwell, "The Foundation of the Second Athenian Confederacy," 56–58, and esp. n. 2, and Kallet-Marx, 144f., support an official despatch of Athenian troops much as argued here, though the latter suggests the Council as the agency.

13. For Chabrias see W.K. Pritchett, *The Greek State at War* (Berkeley, 1974), 2.72–77.

14. For the pass see Pritchett, *Studies in Ancient Greek Topography*, 1.120f.

15. Rice, *Why Sparta Failed*, 93–96; Hack, *The Rise of Thebes*, 68f., n. 17, 71–75; Kallet-Marx, 146. This does not mean, *pace* Cawkwell, "The Foundation of the Second Athenian Confederacy," 59 and n. 1, that there was a clause in the King's Peace requiring the return of exiles.

16. So Rice, *Why Sparta Failed*, 94, and Hack, *The Rise of Thebes*, 74f.

17. Hack, *The Rise of Thebes*, 78, n. 22; Rice, *Why Sparta Failed*, 95f.; Hamilton, *Agesilaus*, 164f.

18. Xen. *Hell.* 5.4.14. Burnett, 17, places it in January, 378.

19. Xen. *Hell.* 5.4.18; Gomme, "The Topography of Boeotia," 204f. Pritchett, *Studies in Ancient Greek Topography*, 1.120f., 4.91.

20. Xen. *Hell.* 5.4.14; Prandi, *Platea*, 125.

21. Munn, 111–14. See also A. Philippson, *Die griechischen Landschaften*[2], rev. E. Kirsten (Frankfurt, 1951), 1.2.500–512. Symeonoglou, 140, 198, and Map A, puts Kynoskephalai immediately to the west of the Kadmeia, across the Dirke near Site 262. This seems much too close to Thebes for what Xenophon says. For a general description of the area, P.W. Wallace, *Strabo's Description of Boiotia* (Heidelberg, 1979), 69, 93.

22. Xen. *Hell.* 5.4.14–18; Frazer, *Paus.* 5.160; Roesch, *Thespies*, 217–19; Wallace, 159f. Sphodrias, rather than Diodorus' Sphodriates, is the usually accepted version of his name. R.A. Tomlinson and J.M. Fossey, "Ancient Remains on Mount Mavrovouni, South Boeotia," *BSA* 65 (1970): 257–59 (= *Papers in Boiotian Topography and History* [Amsterdam, 1990], 145–47), suggest that the site of Mavrovouni might be the Spartan base in Thespian territory, at least until Agesilaus fortified Thespiai. It also protected the harbour at Kreusis, an important landing point for the Peloponnesians.

23. Hack, *The Rise of Thebes*, 79f.; Rice, *Why Sparta Failed*, 97f.; Hamilton, *Agesilaus*, 166.

24. E.g., Grote, 10.95, though he does not exclude the possibility of bad weather; Beloch *GG* 3.1.146.

25. Grote 10.95; von Stern, *Geschichte der spartanischen und thebanischen Hegemonie,* 65; G. Glotz and R. Cohen, *Histoire grecque* (Paris, 1939), 3.116.

26. Xen. *Hell.* 5.4.17. The route ran by Kreusis, past Ayios Vasilios to Aigosthena.

27. Kallet-Marx, 141, rightly points out that the verb does not imply that they acted solely on their own initiative.

28. Xen. *Hell.* 5.4.22.

29. Cf. Prandi, *Platea*, 124.

30. Cf. S. Accame, *La lega ateniese del secolo IV a.C.*, 31; H. Bengtson, *Griechische Geschichte*[2], (Munich, 1960), 266; J.L. Cargill, *The Second Athenian League* (Berkeley, 1981), 59; Kallet-Marx, 140f.; Hamilton, *Agesilaus*, 169–74.

31. Hack, *The Rise of Thebes*, 86f.; Rice, *Why Sparta Failed*, 112–18.

32. Cawkwell, "The Foundation of the Second Athenian Confederacy," 47–60. Cf. Hack, *The Rise of Thebes*, 90 and n. 50; Rice, *Why Sparta Failed*, 100, 106.

33. Kallet-Marx, 147f.

34. Cartledge, *Agesilaos*, 297f.

35. Besides Grote, 10.99 and n. 2, others who do not accept Theban machinations include Schober, *RE* 2.10 (1934), *s.v.* "Thebai," 1470; Reincke, *RE* 19 (1937), *s.v.* "Pelopidas," 377; Ed. Meyer, *GdA* 5.378; Beloch, *GG* 3.1.234–236; Cary, *CAH,* 6.68; Hack, *The Rise of Thebes*, 87f. and n. 47; Rice, *Why Sparta Failed*, 102–5; R.E. Smith, "The Opposition to Agesilaus' Foreign Policy, 394–371 B.C.," *Historia* 2 (1953–54): 281; A. MacDonald, "A Note on the Raid of Sphodrias," *Historia* 21 (1972): 38–44; Buckler, *Theban Hegemony*, 17. A few like Ryder, 54, n. 2, blame Sphodrias himself.

36. Cargill, *Second Athenian League*, 59; Burnett, 11; Cloché, *Thèbes de Béotie*, 121; Accame, *La lega ateniese del secolo IV a.C.,* 18–25; Bury, *History*, 561–63; Hamilton, *Agesilaus*, 169 and n. 59.

37. Kallet-Marx, 149f.; Hamilton, *Agesilaus*, 169.

38. There is some controversy about this. Whether the name is a proper noun Emporos or "emporos," a merchant, is unknown. Keil changed the reading to Diemporos, accepted by von Stern, *Xenophons Hellenika*, 38f. and others; Kallet-Marx, 151, points out that Emporos is an attested Boiotian name (cf. *SEG* 3 [1929], 333), and there is no need to change the text.

39. Plut. *Ages.* 16f.

40. Hack, *The Rise of Thebes*, 95f.; Hamilton, *Agesilaus*, 173f.
41. Cargill, *Second Athenian League*, 52–56, rightly is sceptical of any inferences drawn from it in its present state.
42. Cargill, *Second Athenian League*, esp. 14–47.
43. Munn, 106–38. See also Anderson, 133.
44. For the strategy of destroying the enemy's ripening crops see Anderson, 2f.; Munn, 121; V.D. Hanson, *Warfare and Agriculture in Classical Greece* (Pisa, 1983), 30–35 and *The Western Way of War* (New York, 1989), 33f., points out the ineffectiveness of the actual "devastation." Munn, 114f., puts the invasion late in the spring, in light of 121, n. 47, sometime between mid-May and late June.
45. deVoto, "Agesilaos in Boiotia," 77.
46. Diod. 15.32.1, which is supplementing Xenophon here. Munn, 134f., argues that after Kleombrotos' campaign the garrisons in Plataia and Thespiai were able to prevent troops from Thebes or Athens from occupying the heights. It seems to me more likely that with so many possible routes over Kithairon it was impossible for the Athenians and Boiotians to post a protective force before the Spartan line of approach was clear, and the despatch of the Spartan vanguard, or in the next year a force from Thespiai, forestalled the deployment of any hostile blocking force.
47. Diod. 15.32.2.
48. So Munn, 114–17.
49. Xen. *Hell.* 5.4.39.
50. Xen. *Hell.* 5.4.41.
51. Diod. 15.32.5–6; Anderson, 133; Munn, 117–21; deVoto, "Agesilaos in Boiotia," 77.
52. Hanson, *Warfare and Agriculture in Classical Greece*, 21, 79f.; deVoto, "Agesilaos in Boiotia," 77f.
53. Xen. *Hell.* 5.4.41; Diod. 15.33.4. Munn, 121; deVoto, "Agesilaos in Boiotia," 78.
54. Xen. *Hell.* 5.4.42–45; Diod. 15.33.5.
55. DeVoto, "Agesilaos in Boiotia," 78 cites Polyainos.
56. Cawkwell, "Epaminondas and Thebes," 259 and n. 6, argues that the Athenians took it very seriously, since their alliance was with Thebes, not the Boiotian League (cf. ll. 24 and 79 of the Decree of Aristoteles, *IG*[2] 2.43, dated March, 377), and they sent envoys to "persuade the Thebans of whatever good they can." (ll. 74f.) Perhaps this applies here.
57. Xen. *Hell.* 5.4.47. Some have inferred from this that there was no garrison

in Plataia. It is more probable that, in the absence of mercenaries with the main force, Thespiai had at least some troops available, as it was the Spartan main base. The special relation of Plataia to Athens may have made it necessary to keep the Plataian garrison firmly in place. See Hack, *The Rise of Thebes*, 103, n. 15.

58. So Munn, 122, n. 48, to explain Xenophon's remark (*Hell.* 5.4.49) that Agesilaos "completed in one day a two-day march for an army." For the location of Skolos see Munn, 122f.; Buck, *History of Boeotia*, 17f.; Fossey, "Therapnai and Skolos in Boiotia," *BICS* 18 (1971): 106–8 (=*Papers in Boiotian Topography and History*, 125–29); Schachter, *Cults* 2.133 and n. 2.

59. DeVoto, "Agesilaos in Boiotia," 79, goes beyond the evidence in having Agesilaus reassuring Hypatodoros in Tanagra.

60. D.W. Roller, "The Location of Xenophon's Γραὸς Στῆθος," *AJA* 82 (1978): 107–9, argued for the walls of Tanagra, rebutted by Munn, 124–26.

61. Also called in Polyainos 2.1.12 Ῥεὰς ἕδος, Rhea's throne, corrected to Graos or Graias by various editors on the basis of Steph. Byz. *s.v.* Τάναγρα.

62. Munn, 126–33; other possible locations include Monovigla, 16 km from Thebes, Roller, 107–9, and Psilorakhi or Mikro Psilorakhi, Bölte, *RE* 7.2 (1912), *s.v.* Γραὸς Στῆθος, 1827f.; de Voto, "Agesilaos in Boiotia," 79f.

63. Xen. *Hell.* 5.4.54; J.G.P. Best, *Thracian Peltasts and their Influence on Greek Warfare* (Groningen, 1969), 109. On 97 he suggests that such forces were probably from allied states, such as Lokris.

64. Xen. *Hell.* 5.4.58. The ailment is described as a rupture of a vein in one leg causing a swelling in the other accompanied by severe pain. He was bled, and the flow could not be stopped. The severe haemorrhage doubtless weakened him, and continued medical bleedings doubtless slowed down his recovery.

65. Xen. *Hell.* 5.4.56f.; Frontinus, *Strat.* 4.7.19. Cartledge, *Agesilaos*, 377.

66. Xen. *Hell.* 5.4.59. The idea that Kleombrotos was half-hearted or unwilling to antagonize Thebes (Rice, *Why Sparta Failed*, 140f.) goes beyond the evidence. Xenophon makes it clear that Kleombrotos' opinion, that it was impossible to cross Kithairon in the face of enemy occupation, was well-founded. Xenophon carefully points out that great pains were always taken to try to occupy Kithairon before the invasion. Cf. Munn, 137f.

67. Xen. *Hell.* 5.4.61. Diod. 15.34 puts it in the wrong year. Rice, *Why Sparta Failed*, 141f., may be right in arguing that the followers of Kleombrotos supported this policy.

68. Xen. *Hell.* 5.4.61 is very sketchy, and Diod. 15. 34.3–4 gives a more detailed

description. Demosthenes 20.77 probably exaggerates with 49 captured. The victory at Knidos was by a Persian fleet, even if commanded by Konon and manned by Athenians.

69. Xen. *Hell.* 6.1.2–17.

70. Xen. *Hell.* 5.4.62f.; Diod. 15.36.5; Buckler, "Dating the Peace of 375/4 B.C.," 353–56; Hack, *The Rise of Thebes*, 112f.

71. Xen. *Hell.* 6.1.1. For Tanagra see Buckler, "The Re-establishment of the *Boiotarchia*," 56; C.J. Tuplin, "The Fate of Thespiae during the Theban Hegemony," 327, n. 3. Roesch, *Thespies*, 44, seems to prefer 374, but without much argument, for the re-establishment of the League, as does V.J. Gray, "The Years 375–371 BC: A Case Study in the Reliability of Diodorus Siculus and Xenophon," *CQ* 74 (1980): 309. She points out the difficulties as to which cities were in and which out of the League, 306 and n. 3.

72. It is not reported by Xenophon, but it is found in Plut. *Pel.* 16f.; Diod. 15.37; Pritchett, *Studies in Ancient Greek Topography*, 4.104–22; Anderson, 162–64.

73. For the location of Tegyra near Polyira see Buck, *History of Boeotia*, 8; Lauffer, *RE* Supp. 14 (1974) *s.v.* "Orchomenos," 327; Pritchett, *Studies in Ancient Greek Topography* 4.104–9; J. Knauss, *Kopais 2: die Melioration des Kopaisbeckens durch die Minyer im 2. Jt. v. Chr.* (Munich, 1987), 186–93; Buckler, *"Plutarch and Autopsy,"* 4804. Others put it further east at Pyrgos, as does Fossey, *Topography*, 367–72, *q.v.* for earlier bibliography.

74. Diod. 15.81.2; Plut. *Pel.* 16.1; Pritchett, *Studies in Ancient Greek Topography*, 4.121, n. 46.

75. Cargill, *Second Athenian League*, 68–75, argues that it was conquered by Athens, and that the Spartan fleet was trying a rescue attempt. It explains economically Xenophon's remarks about Timotheos' conduct in not enslaving the inhabitants or banishing individuals (5.4.64); hardly the treatment ever meted out to an ally.

76. Xen. *Hell.* 5.4.65; the date from Polyainos, *Strat.* 3.10.4, 12 Skirophorion.

77. Xen. *Hell.* 6.2.1–2. J. Buckler, *"Dating the Peace of 375/4 B.C.,"* 353–61, dates the Peace to Autumn 375.

VII   The League to Leuktra, 375–371 B.C.

1. For the date of autumn, 375, see Buckler, "Dating the Peace," 353–61; Cawkwell, "Notes on the Peace of 375/4," 88–91. Gray, "The Years 375 to 371 B.C.," 306–26; Hamilton, *Agesilaus*, 190–95.

2. Xen. *Hell.* 6.2.1; Diod. 15.38.

3. G.L. Cawkwell, "Notes on the Peace of 375/4," 84–95; C. Vial in the Budé edition of Diodorus, *Diodore de Sicile, Livre XV* (Paris, 1977), 136f.; Hack, *The Rise of Thebes*, 119, n. 57 and 127–31. Gray, "The Years 375 to 371 B.C.," 309f., accepts both the Theban reconquest of Boiotia and the liberation of the dissident towns when the Peace was signed.

4. Judeich, 171–97, argues vigorously for a bilateral peace, not a King's Peace, I think rightly.

5. Isok. 15.110; cf. Ryder, 59 and n. 3.

6. Lauffer, "Die Diododordublette XV 38–50 über die Friedenschlüsse zu Sparta 374 und 371," 315–48, with refs. 315; M. Fortina, *Epaminonda* (Turin, 1958), 23; Ryder, 124; G. Cawkwell, "Epaminondas and Thebes," 257 (but cf. Cawkwell in the Penguin Classics translation of Xenophon, 308). For other examples of Ephoros' doublets, from the fifth century, see Buck, "Boiotian Historiography," 87–93.

7. Hack, *The Rise of Thebes,* 126–139, and Rice, *Why Sparta Failed,* 148f., following Curtius, 4.394–96, and Meyer, *GdA*, 5.387. Cawkwell in the Penguin Classics translation of Xenophon, 307.

8. Cawkwell, "Notes on the Peace of 375/4," 84–88 and "Epaminondas and Thebes," 257, says late 373. Hack, *The Rise of Thebes*, 147f., says the Peace lasted little more than a year, ending it in 374. Ryder, 61, says about a year and a half, i.e., in 373. V.J. Gray, "The Years 375 to 371 B.C.," 315–21, sets the renewal of hostilities in 373, as does Hamilton, *Agesilaus*, 116.

9. There were Boiotian (Theban) ships in the allied fleet (*IG* 2^2, 1607, 50, 155), and a Theban presided over the Allied Council in 373/2 (H. Bengtson, *Die Verträge der griechisch-römischen Welt.* Rev. ed. [Munich, 1975], 268).

10. Paus. 9.1.4–8. Cf. Prandi, *Platea*, 127; Ryder, 61, n. 5; M. Sordi, "La restaurazione della lega beotica," 84; Roesch, *Thespies*, 45. Diod. 15.46.6 claims that it was done to forestall an alliance with Athens, but cf. Xen. *Hell.* 6.3.1; Isok. 12.29.

11. Xen. *Hell.* 6.4.10; Diod. 15.46.6 says that Thespiai "was devastated" (ἐξεπόρθησαν); Roesch, *Thespies*, 45, says that only the governing oligarchy was expelled, but the unreliability of the Thespian hoplite contingent before Leuktra is most economically explained by the idea that the whole citizen body suffered losses, oligarchs and democrats alike. Cf. C.J. Tuplin, "The Fate of Thespiae," 327–34.

12. Isok. 14.9. Tuplin, "The Fate of Thespiae," 321–41, suggests without much conviction that at first Thespiai may have had full membership in the League (335–37). Tuplin goes on to argue that Thespiai was reduced to a very sub-

ordinate status,and underwent a *dioikismos* (338f.), as do Buckler, Stern and Underhill.

13. Tuplin, "The Fate of Thespiae," 336f., after J. Buckler, "The Thespians at Leuktra," 76–79. They both rely unduly on the hyperbole of the Athenian orators.

14. Xen. *Hell.* 6.3.1; cf. Tuplin, "The Fate of Thespiae," 329f.

15. Paus. 9.13.8. J. Buckler, "The Thespians at Leuktra," 76–79.

16. Diod. 15.57.1; Hack, *The Rise of Thebes*, 151f.; 223; Tuplin, "The Fate of Thespiae," 338. J.H. Thiel, "De synoecismo Boeotiae," 26f., notes the special status for Orchomenos. For χώρα in this sense see, e.g., Xen. *Ann.* 5.6.13; *Cyr.* 2.1.23.

17. Diod. 15.79.3–6. Cf. Plut. *Comp. Pel. et Marc.* 1; Buckler, *Theban Hegemony*, 182–84.

18. Several of the references to synods in Diod. are not clear (e.g., 15.80.2, 16.85.3), but 16.25.1 clearly refers to an assembly of citizenry, as do *IG* 7.2407, 2408 and *BCH* 98 (1974): 644f., with the phrase ἔδοξε τοῖ δάμοι Βοιωτῶν.

19. Xen. *Hell.* 7.3.5 mentions an assassination on the acropolis "with the rulers and the boule sitting there." Not all agree, however, that this is the federal boule, but several argue that it is a Theban council. See D.P. Orsi, "La boulé dei Tebani," *QS* 25 (1987): 125–44, for earlier authorities and bibliographies.

20. Cf. G.H.R. Horsley, "The Theban Hegemony," in *Hellenika: Essays on Greek Politics and History*, G.H.R. Horsley, ed. (North Ryde, N.S.W., 1982), 155.

21. J.A.O. Larsen, *Representative Government,* 1f., 21, 46. For Mantinea Arist. *Pol.* 1318b23–28.

22. Diod. 15.38.3; 15.50.4; 15.70.2.

23. E.g., Isok. 14.8.9 (for Thespiai and Tanagra); see also *Hell. Oxy.* 16.3 (for the relationship of Skolos, Skaphai and Erythrai to Thebes); Thuc. 2.15.2 uses the verb in connection with the synoecism of Attica; in 4.76.3 for the association of Chaironeia with Orchomenos.

24. Polyb. 5.94.1; Plut. *Comp. Phil. et Flam.* 1. The word is not mentioned by G.R. Stanton, "Federalism in the Greek World." In *Hellenika: Essays on Greek Politics and History*, G.H.R. Horsley, ed. (North Ryde, N.S.W., 1982), 183–90.

25. Cf. *LSJ s.v.h.*; Tuplin, "The Fate of Thespiae," *passim*, but the conclusions drawn here are not those of Tuplin.

26. The modern concept of sovereignty is not Greek, but the ideas of self-government, freedom and of the supreme controlling power being vested in a state are.

27. Bersanetti, 51 and n. 4; Sordi, "La restaurazione della lega beotica," 83, 89–91; Thiel, 23f., emphasizes the point by terming Boiotia at this time a synoecism rather then a federation. Dio Chrysostom 45.13, for what he is worth, says that Epaminondas made a synoecism of all Boiotia with Thebes. An analogy drawn between the non-Theban Boiotian cities and the perioecic states of Sparta on the basis of Isok. 8.115 is not apt, since Sparta was not a democracy, and the perioecic states did not have any part at all in the Spartan government.

28. E.g., Xen. *Mem.* 3.5.3.

29. As Thiel, 24, states, "Thespienses igitur ἀπολίδες sunt quoniam συντελοῦσιν εἰς τὸ κοινὸν Βοιωτῶν, neque hinc efficiendum Thespias a Thebanis deletas esse."

30. It is argued by some, e.g., Buckler, *Theban Hegemony*, 18, and Hack, *The Rise of Thebes,* 164, 166, that there is no evidence that Thebes terminated the political integrity of the *subject* Boiotians, a statement that is self-contradictory. Cf. Meyer, *GdA* 5.381.

31. P. Roesch, *Études,* 415f., notes that between 378 and 338 there were 43 Thebans, 3 Skaphleans, 11 Plataians, 9 Thespians, 3 Orchomenians, 1 Thisbean and 1 Tanagran mentioned in inscriptions.

32. Paus. 9.13.8. Buckler, "The Thespians at Leuktra," 76–79.

33. Cf. Gardner, Table 10.3.

34. H. Beister, "Untersuchungen zu der Zeit der Thebanische Hegemonie" (Ph.D. Diss., Munich, 1970), 1–12. This Ismenias is not the martyred leader of his faction, but probably a son or kinsman.

35. Buckler, *Theban Hegemony*, 30–33, gives an excellent summary of the powers and authority of the Damos. Sordi, "La restaurazione della lega beotica," 83, 88f. See also Roesch, *Études*, 271.

36. *IG* 7.2407, 2408. Cf. Diod. 15.52.1, 15.53.3; Paus. 9.13.7. Roesch, *Études,* 287–90.

37. The only election attested is that in 378, and it could be argued, though I think erroneously, that it was a special happening. Removals from the Boiotarchy by the Assembly are referred to in Diod. 15.72.2.

38. See, e.g., Busolt-Swoboda, 2.1423, n. 5; Larsen, *Greek Federal States*, 175; Roesch, *Thespies*, 44f., 100; Sordi, "La restaurazione della lega beotica," 82. For the special status Tuplin, "The Fate of Thespiae," 338, and *infra,* 117f.

39. Cf. Hack, *The Rise of Thebes*, 165; cf. Buckler, *Theban Hegemony*, 28.

40. *SEG* 25 (1971): 553 is an honorary decree for a worthy from Pellene (which might incline one to place it in the 360s) usually dated to mid-fourth century B.C. It is a decree of the κοινὸν Βοιωτῶν, and it lists Boiotarchs from

Thespiai and Tanagra. Surely these are used as demotics rather than indicating constituent cities which these officials represent.

41. Plut. *Pel.* 24.2–3; 25.2; 34.7; *Mor.* 194A–C; Paus. 9.14.5; Diod.15.81.4; cf. Thiel, 25f.; Sordi, "La restaurazione della lega beotica," 83.

42. Roesch, *Études*, 282–86; Buck, *History*, 88. Cf. e.g., *IG* 7.2858.

43. Cf. Thiel, 25f.; Buckler, *Theban Hegemony,* 30, 33; Hack, *The Rise of Thebes,* 166f.

44. Aristoph. *Acharn.* F.J. Frost, "Peisistratos, The Cults and The Unification of Attica," *AncW* 21 (1990): 3–9, argues that the union of Attica, much more successful than that of Boiotia, was only strongly established as late as Peisistratos. For pro-democratic farmers, P. Harding, "In Search of a Polypragmatist," in *Classical Contributions: Studies in Honour of M.F. McGregor,* G.S. Shrimpton and D.J. McCarger, eds. (Locust Valley, 1981), 41–50; cf. A.J. Podlecki, "Apragmosyne," *AHB* 5 (1991): 84f.

45. Quoted in Arist. *Rhet.* 3.4.3.

46. Paus. 9.24.2–4. Tuplin, "The Fate of Thespiae," 333f., argues that the testimony of Pausanias is inaccurate and should be rejected, following Buckler, "The Thespians at Leuktra," 76–79. The latter wishes to reject completely the story of the migration to Keressos as a historical myth, but 371 seems late for such creation, and a local strong-point might be more secure for a disaffected citizenry than a site like that of Thespiai with its walls demolished.

47. Plut. *Pel.* 18–19; Anderson, 158–61.

48. Buck, *History,* 93f.; Anderson, 158f. Sordi, "La restaurazione della lega beotica," 85–88.

49. Plut. *Pel.* 19.3. For Delion Diod. 12.70.1. Cf. Anderson, 158f.

50. Plut. *Pel.* 19.3f., 20.2.

51. Diod. 12.70.1.

52. For homosexual traditions in "professional" hoplite service, Hanson, *The Western Way of War,* 124.

53. Cf. Plut. *Pel.* 25; Hack, *The Rise of Thebes*, 171f.

54. Xen. *Hell.* 6.3.1. Hack, *The Rise of Thebes,* 178f. Hamilton, *Agesilaus*, 199–202.

55. Xen. *Hell.* 6.4.1,2 and Plut. *Ages.* 28.3 for the presence of Kleombrotos in Phokis. Xenophon 6.3.1 also notes that the Athenians were disturbed at the Theban interest in Phokis. For the Theban mission to Sparta Xen. *Hell.* 6.3.1 and Plut. *Ages.* 27.3.

56. Ryder, 64.

57. Xen. *Hell.* 6.3.4–6; Tuplin, "The Fate of Thespiae," 329–31.

58. Xen. *Hell.* 6.3.18; Ryder, 67–69, 127–30.

59. Ryder, 69; E. Bickermann, "Les préliminaires de la seconde guerre de Macédoine, la Paix de Phoenicé," *RPh* 9 (1935): 64, argued that such treatment implied subordination.

60. Xen. *Hell.* 6.3.19; Plut. *Ages.* 28.1–2. Diod. 15.50.4–6 says that the Boiotians were not included in the negotiations at all. This should be rejected, since the Boiotians were invited as members of the Second Athenian Confederacy, just as all the other members were, to sign along with all the rest.

61. Plut. *Ages.* 28.2; Paus. 9.13.2; Xen. *Hell.* 6.3.19. Hack, *The Rise of Thebes,* 185; Rice, *Why Sparta Failed,* 167.

62. Plut. *Ages.* 28.5. See C.J. Tuplin, "The Leuktra Campaign," *Klio* 69 (1987): 77–84, and Beister, "Untersuchungen," 71f., for scepticism over the dates.

63. Xen. *Hell.* 6.4.2.

64. Xen. *Hell.* 6.4.3.

65. Xen. *Hell.* 6.3.20.

66. Diod. 15.51.3 talks of sending an ultimatum, but this is rejected by most authorities. Cf. Ryder, 69.

67. Paus. 9.13.3 and Frazer, *Paus.* 5.50. Diod. 15.52.7.

68. Paus. *loc. cit.* It is unknown whether he was a Boiotarch or not, but since there are seven named in this passage of Pausanias, it seems unlikely. Cf. Beister, "Untersuchungen," 39.

69. Paus. 9.13.6. Athens is mentioned in this context as a possible refuge for women and children. Though it may not have been as friendly as formerly, it was clearly not conceived of as allied to Sparta. Bakchylides was probably near the pass of Dryoskephalai. Pritchett, *Studies in Ancient Greek Topography,* 1.121.

70. Principally Xen. *Hell.* 6.4.3–15; Plut. *Pel.* 20–23; Diod. 15.52–56; Paus. 9.13.3–12.

71. As Tuplin pointed out, the mss. of Diod. 15.52.1 all read Chaironeia or Cheroneia, changed by Wesseling to Koroneia.

72. So A.R. Burn, "Helikon in History," *BSA* 44 (1949): 321, Beister, "Untersuchungen," 40f. and map on 72, and Buckler, *Theban Hegemony,* 55–59, from autopsy and Paus. 9.13.3 and Xenophon's "mountainous and unexpected route (6.4.4)."

73. Diod. 15.53.1. So Pritchett, *Studies in Ancient Greek Topography,* 1.56f., but it is hardly "mountainous and unexpected."

74. V.D. Hanson, "Epameinondas, the Battle of Leuktra (371 B.C.), and the 'Revolution' in Greek Battle Tactics," *ClasAnt* 7 (1988): 190–207; Tuplin,

"The Leuktra Campaign," 72–107; Buckler, *Theban Hegemony*, ch. 3, esp. 55–65; Anderson, 192–204; Pritchett, *Studies in Ancient Greek Topography*, 1.49–58.

VIII Boiotia, 432–371 B.C.

1. There is no convincing evidence for an attempt at democratic government by the faction of Ismenias. Some of the followers of that faction installed a democracy after coup of 379/8, but they had been long associated with such democrats as Thrasyboulos of Steiria and had just spent three years in Athens.
2. Polyb. 5.94.1; Plut. *Comp. Phil. et Flam.* 1.
3. So Roesch, *Thespies*, 46f., following Cloché, *Thèbes de Béotie*, 197f.
4. Busolt-Swoboda, 2.1431; Roesch, *Thespies*, 46f.
5. Cf. Stanton, 187, for sympolity.
6. The evidence for its institutions is largely derived from epigraphical evidence. Roesch, *Thespies* and *Études*, are excellent discussions.
7. Schachter, *Cults*, 2.216, for changes of ownership. Roesch, *Études,* 266–75.
8. Roesch, *Thespies*, 125f.; *Études*, 287–90, 362; Busolt-Swoboda, 2.1435.
9. Roesch, *Thespies*, 126–33.
10. Roesch, *Thespies*, 105; *Études*, 287–90.
11. Cloché, *Thèbes de Béotie*, 241; Roesch, *Thespies*, 104f.
12. Roesch, *Thespies*, 135–41; *Études*, 424, 429.
13. Cloché, *Thèbes de Béotie*, 241.

Appendix

1. C. Bearzot, "Problemi del confine attico-beotico: la rivendicazione tebana di Oropo," *CISA* 13 (1987) 80–99; "Il ruolo di Eretria nella cintesa attico-beotica per Oropo," in *Boiotika,* Beister and Buckler, eds., 113–22.
2. J.M. Camp, "Notes on the Towers and Borders of Classical Boiotia," *AJA* 95 (1991): 200 and n. 27.
3. G.D. Rocchi, *Frontiera e confini nella Grecia antica* (Milan, 1988), 183–86.
4. Buck, *History*, 123; Bearzot, "Problemi," 81f., 85; F. Dürrbach, *De Oropo et Amphiarai Sacro* (Paris, 1890), 27.
5. Thuc. 8.60.1; Lysias 20.6. Cf. Bearzot, "Problemi," 84; Camp, 200 n. 7; Dürrbach, 30.
6. Bearzot, "Problemi," 86f.
7. U. von Wilamowitz-Moellendorff, "Oropos und die Graer," *Hermes* 21 (1886): 91–115, esp. 97f.
8. Dürrbach, 30f.; J. Wiesner, *RE* 35 (1939) *s.v.* "Oropos," 1173.

9. Meyer, *Theopomps Hellenika*, 101f. and P. Salmon, "Les districts béotiennes," *REA* 58 (1956): 64, argue that Oropos must have been annexed after the outbreak of the Corinthian War in 395, since anything earlier would have been prevented by respect for Sparta. Dull, "Reassessment of the Boeotian Districts," 33, points out that such a date is impossible, since "annexation of Oropos after asking Athens for an alliance seems to excel even the proverbial Boeotian stupidity," and no such incident is mentioned in the later bitterness over Oropos.

10. As Dürrbach, 31, points out.

11. Bearzot, "Problemi," 85–87.

12. C.D. Buck, *The Greek Dialects*^{2}, no. 14.

Bibliography

Accame. S. *La lega ateniese del secolo IV a.C.* Rome, 1941.

————. *Ricerche intorno alla guerra corinzia* (*Collana di studi greci* 20). Milan, 1957.

Anderson, J.K. *Military Theory and Practice in the Age of Xenophon.* Berkeley, 1970 .

Badian, E., "Plataea Between Athens and Sparta: In Search of Lost History." In *Boiotika*, H. Beister and J. Buckler, eds., 95–112. Munich, 1989.

Barber, E.A. *The Historian Ephorus.* Cambridge, 1935.

Bearzot, C. "Problemi dei confini attico-beotico: la rivendicazione tebana di Oropo." *CISA* 13 (1987): 80–99.

————. "Il ruolo di Eretria nella cintesa attico-beotico per Oropo." In *Boiotika*, H. Beister and J. Buckler, eds., 113–22. Munich, 1989.

Beister, H. *Untersuchungen zu der Zeit der Thebanischen Hegemonie.* Munich, 1970.

————. "Hegemoniales Denken in Theben." In *Boiotika*, H. Beister and J. Buckler, eds., 131–53. Munich, 1989.

Beister, H. and J. Buckler, eds., *Boiotika: Vorträge vom 5. Internationalen Böotien-Kolloquium.* Munich, 1989.

Beloch, K.J. *Griechische Geschichte,* second edition. Berlin and Leipzig, 1922.

Bengtson, H. *Griechische Geschichte,* second edition. Munich, 1960.

————, ed. *Die Staatsverträge des Altertums II. Die Verträge der griechisch-römischen Welt von 700 bis 338 v. Chr.* Revised ed. Munich, 1975

Bersanetti, G.M. "Pelopida." *Athenaeum* 27 (1949): 43–101.

Best, J.G.P. *Thracian Peltasts and Their Influence on Greek Warfare.* Groningen, 1969.

Bickermann, E. "Les préliminaires de la seconde guerre de Macédoine, la Paix de Phoenicé." *RPh* 9 (1935): 64.

Bintliff, J. and A. Snodgrass, "Mediterranean Survey and the City." *Antiquity* 62 (1988): 57–71.

———. "From Polis to Chorion in South-west Boeotia." In *Boiotika*, H. Beister and J. Buckler, eds., 285–99. Munich, 1989.

Bölte, E. *RE* 7.2 (1912), *s.v.* Γραὸς Στῆθος, 1827f.

Bonner, R.J. "The Boeotian Federal Constitution." *CP* 5 (1910): 405–17.

Botsford, G.W. "The Constitution and Politics of the Boeotian League." *PSQ* 25 (1910): 271–96.

Bruce, I.A.F. "Internal Politics and the Outbreak of the Corinthian War." *Emerita* 28 (1960): 75–86.

———. *An Historical Commentary on the* Hellenica Oxyrhynchia. Cambridge, 1970.

Buck, R.J. *A History of Boeotia*. Edmonton, 1979.

———. "Boeotian Swine as Political Theorists." *EMC* 25 (1981): 47–52.

———. "Boeotian Oligarchies and Greek Oligarchic Theory." In *Proceedings of the Third International Conference on Boiotian Antiquities*, Fossey, J.M. and H. Giroux, eds., 25–32. Amsterdam, 1985.

———. "The Sicilian Expedition." *AHB* 2 (1988): 73–79.

———. "Boiotian Historiography, 479–432 B.C." In *Boiotika*, H. Beister and J. Buckler, eds., 87–93. Munich, 1989.

———. "Group Voting in Boiotia." *AHB* 4 (1990): 61–64.

———. "The Athenians at Thebes in 379/8 B.C." *AHB* 6 (1992): 103–9.

Buckler, J. "Dating the Peace of 375/4 B.C." *GRBS* 12 (1971): 353–62.

———. "The Thespians at Leuktra." *WS* 90 (1977): 46–49.

———. "The Re-establishment of the *Boiotarchia* (378 BC)." *AJAH* 4 (1979): 50–64.

———. *The Theban Hegemony, 371-362 B.C.* Cambridge, Mass., 1980.

———. "The Alleged Theban-Spartan Alliance of 386 B.C." *Eranos* 78 (1980): 179–83.

———. "Plutarch on Leuktra." *Symb Oslo* 55 (1980): 75–93.

———. "Plutarch and Autopsy." *ANRW II*, 33 no. 6 (1992): 4788–4830.

Burn, A.R. "Helikon in History." *BSA* 44 (1949): 313–23.

Burnett, A.P. "Thebes and the Expansion of the Second Athenian Confederacy." *Historia* 11 (1962): 1–17.

Burstein, S.M. *Outpost of Hellenism: the Emergence of Heraclea Pontica on the Black Sea*. Berkeley, 1976.

Bury, J.B. *History of Greece*, third edition. London, 1959.

Busolt, G. "Die Neue Historiker und Xenophon." *Hermes* 43 (1908): 278.

Busolt, G. and H. Swoboda. *Griechische Staatskunde,* third edition. Munich, 1926.

Camp, J.M. "Notes on Towns and Borders of Classical Boiotia." *AJA* 95 (1991): 193–202.

Cargill, J.L. *The Second Athenian League: Empire or Free Alliance*. Berkeley, 1981.

———. "The Second Athenian Confederacy." Ph.D. diss., U. of California, Berkeley, 1977.

Cartledge, P. *Agesilaos and the Crisis of Sparta*. Baltimore, 1987.

Cary, M. "Heraclea Trachinia." *CQ* 16 (1922): 98f.

———. "The Second Athenian League." Chap. 3 in *CAH*, first edition, vol. 6 (1927), 55–79.

Cawkwell, G.L. "Notes on the Peace of 375/4." *Historia* 12 (1963): 84–95.

———. "Epaminondas and Thebes." *CQ* 66 (1972): 254–78.

———. "The Foundation of the Second Athenian Confederacy." *CQ* 67 (1973): 47–60.

———. "Agesilaus and Sparta." *CQ* 70 (1976): 62–84.

———. "The Imperialism of Thrasybulus." *CQ* 70 (1976): 270–77.

———. Preface to Xenophon, *A History of My Times*, tr. by R. Warner. Harmondsworth, 1979.

Clarke, G. "A History of Boeotia, 405–395 B.C." M.A. thesis, Alberta, 1986.

Cloché, P. "La Politique thébaine de 404 à 396 avant J.-C." *REG* 31 (1918): 315–43.

———. *Thèbes de Béotie*. Namur, 1952.

Cook, M.L. "Boeotia in the Corinthian War: Foreign Policy and Domestic Politics." Ph.D. diss., U. of Washington, 1981.

———. "Ancient Political Factions: Boiotia 404–395." *TAPA* 118 (1988): 57–85.

———. "Ismenias' Goals in the Corinthian War." *Teiresias*, Supp. 3 (1990): 57–63.

Demand, N. *Thebes in the Fifth Century*. London, 1982.

———. *Urban Relocation in Archaic and Classical Greece*. Norman, Okla., 1990.

deVoto, J. "Agesilaos in Boiotia in 378 and 377 B.C." *AHB* 1 (1987): 75–82.

———. "The Liberation of Thebes in 379/8 B.C." In *Daidalikon: Studies in Memory of R.V. Schoder S.J.,* R. Sutton, ed., 101–16. Wauconda IL, 1989.

———. "Pelopidas and Kleombrotos at Leuktra." *AHB* 3 (1989): 115–18.

Drews, R. "Ephorus and History Written *Kata Genos*," *AJP* 84 (1963): 244–55.

———. "Ephorus' κατὰ γένος History Revisited," *Hermes* 104 (1976): 497f.

Ducat, J. *Les kouroi du Ptoion*. Paris, 1971.

———. "La confédération Béotienne et l'expansion Thèbain à l'époque archaïque." *BCH* 97 (1973): 59–73.

Dull, C.J. "A Study of the Leadership of the Boeotian League from the Invasion of the Boiotoi to the King's Peace." Ph.D. diss., Wisconsin, 1975.

———. "A Reassessment of the Boeotian Districts." In *Proceedings of the Third International Conference on Boiotian Antiquities*, Fossey, J.M. and H. Giroux, eds., 33–39. Amsterdam, 1985.

Dürrbach, F. *De Oropo et Amphiarai Sacro*. Paris, 1890.

Forrest, W.G. "Central Greece and Thessaly." Chap. 41 in *CAH*, second edition, vol. 3, part 3 (1982), 286–320.

Fortina, M. *Epaminonda*. Turin, 1958.

Fossey, J.M. "Therapnai and Skolos in Boiotia," *BICS* 18 (1971): 106–8 (=*Papers in Boiotian Topography and History*, 125–29)

———. *The Topography and Population of Ancient Boiotia* (two volumes in one). Chicago, 1988.

———. *Papers in Boiotian Topography and History*. Amsterdam, 1990.

Fossey, J.M. and H. Giroux, eds., *Proceedings of the Third International Conference on Boiotian Antiquities*. Amsterdam, 1985.

Frost, F.J. "Peisistratos, The Cults and The Unification of Attica." *AncW* 21 (1990): 3–9.

Fuscagni, S. "Callisthene di Olinto e la 'Vita di Pelopida' di Plutarco." In *Storiografia e propaganda*, M. Sordi, ed., 31–55. Milan, 1975.

Gardner, P. *A History of Ancient Coinage*. Oxford, 1918.

Garnsey, P. *Famine and Food Supply in the Graeco-Roman World*. Cambridge, 1988.

Glotz, G. and R. Cohen, *Histoire grecque*. Paris, 1939.

Gomme, A.W. "The Topography of Boeotia." *BSA* 18 (1911–12): 189–210.

Gomme, A.W., A. Andrewes and K.J. Dover, *A Historical Commentary on Thucydides*, 5 vols. Oxford, 1945–81.

Gray, V. J. *The Character of Xenophon's Hellenica*. Baltimore, 1989.

———. "Two Different Approaches to the Battle of Sardis in 395 B.C.," *CSCA* 12 (1979): 183–200.

———. "The Years 375–371 B.C.: A Case Study in the Reliability of Diodorus Siculus and Xenophon." *CQ* 74 (1980): 301–12.

Griffith, G.T. "The Economic Union of Corinth and Argos (392–386 B.C.)." *Historia* 1 (1950): 236–56.

Grote, G. *History of Greece*, new edition in 10 vols. London, 1888.

Hack, H.M. "Thebes and the Spartan Hegemony, 386–382 B.C." *AJP* 99 (1978): 210–27.

———. "The Rise of Thebes: A Study of Theban Politics." Ph.D. diss.,Yale, 1978.

Hamilton, C.D. "The Politics of Revolution at Corinth, 395–386 B.C." *Historia* 21 (1972): 21–37.

———. *Sparta's Bitter Victories*. Ithaca, 1979.

———. *Agesilaus and the Failure of Spartan Hegemony*. Ithaca, 1991.

Hammond, N.G.L. "The Main Road from Boeotia to the Peloponnese." *BSA* 49 (1954): 103–22.

Hanson, V.D. *Warfare and Agriculture in Classical Greece*. Pisa, 1983.

———. "Epameinondas, the Battle of Leuktra (371 B.C.), and the 'Revolution' in Greek Battle Tactics." *ClasAnt* 7 (1988): 190–207.

———. *The Western Way of War*. New York, 1989.

Harding, P. "In Search of a Polypragmatist," *Classical Contributions: Studies in Honour of M.F. McGregor* , G.S. Shrimpton and D.J. McCarger, eds., 41-50. Locust Valley, 1981.

Hardy, W.G. "The Hellenica Oxyrhynchia and the Devastation of Attica." *CP* 21 (1926): 346–55.

Harrison, E. "A Problem in the Corinthian War." *CQ* 7 (1913): 128–34.

Head, B.V. "On the Chronological Sequence of the Coins of Boeotia." *NC* 1 (1881): 177–275. Reprint. Chicago, 1974, paginated 1–99.

———. *Historia Nummorum*. London, 1910.

Henry, W.P. *Greek Historical Writing. An Historiographical Essay Based on Xenophon's* Hellenica. Chicago, 1966.

Herman, G. *Ritualised Friendship and the Greek City*. Cambridge, 1987.

Higgins, R. *Tanagra and the Figurines*. Princeton, 1986.

Horsley, G.H.R. "The Second Athenian Confederacy." In *Hellenika: Essays on Greek Politics and History*, G.H.R. Horsley, ed., 131–50. North Ryde, N.S.W., 1982.

———, ed., *Hellenika: Essays on Greek Politics and History*. North Ryde, N.S.W., 1982.

Judeich, W. "Athen und Theben vom Königsfrieden bis zur Schlacht bei Leuktra." *RhM* 76 (1927): 171–97.

Kagan, D. "Politics and Policy in Corinth (421–336 B.C.)." Ph.D. diss., Ohio State, 1958.

———. "The Economic Origins of the Corinthian War (395–387 B.C.)." *PdP* 80 (1961): 321–41.

———. "Corinthian Politics and the Revolution of 392." *Historia* 11 (1962): 447–57.

————. *The Peace of Nikias and the Sicilian Expedition.* Ithaca, 1981.

Kallet–Marx, R.M. "Athens, Thebes and the Foundation of the Second Athenian League." *ClasAnt* 4 (1985): 127–51.

Kelly, D.H. "The Theban Hegemony." In *Hellenika: Essays on Greek Politics and History*, G.H.R. Horsley, ed., 151–63. North Ryde, N.S.W., 1982.

Kelly, T. "Cleobulus, Xenares, and Thucydides' Account of the Demolition of Panactum." *Historia* 21 (1972): 159–69.

Knauss, J. *Kopais 2: die Melioration des Kopaisbeckens durch die Minyer im 2. Jt. v. Chr.* Munich, 1987.

————. *Kopais 3: Wasserbau und Geschichte Minysche Epoche - Bayerische Zeit.* Munich, 1990.

Larsen, J.A.O. "The Boeotian Confederacy and Fifth-century Oligarchic Theory." *TAPA* 86 (1955): 41–50.

————. *Representative Government in Greek and Roman History.* Berkeley, 1955.

————. *Greek Federal States: Their Institutions and History.* Oxford, 1968.

Lauffer, S. "Die Diodordublette XV 38–50 über die Friedenschlusse zu Sparta 374 und 371." *Historia* 8 (1959): 315–48.

————. *RE* 23.2 (1959), s.v., "Ptoion," 1505–78.

Lauffer, S. and D. Hennig. *RE* Supp. 14 (1974), *s.v.* "Orchomenos," 290–355.

Lendon, J.E. "The Oxyrhynchos Historian and the Origins of the Corinthian War." *Historia* 38 (1988): 300–313.

Lerat, L. *Les Locriens de l'Ouest.* Paris, 1952.

Loening, T.C. *The Reconciliation Agreement of 403/2 B.C. in Athens. Hermes* Einzelschriften 53, Stuttgart, 1987.

MacDonald, A. "A Note on the Raid of Sphodrias." *Historia* 21 (1972): 38–44.

Maidment, K.J. ed. and translator, *Minor Attic Orators* I. Loeb, London, 1941.

McKay, K.L. "The Oxyrhynchus Historian and the Outbreak of the Corinthian War," *CR* 3 (1953): 6–7.

McKechnie, P.R. and S.J. Kern, eds., *Hellenica Oxyrhynchia.* Warminster, 1988.

Meyer, E. *Geschichte des Altertums.* Stuttgart and Berlin, 1884–1902.

————. *Theopomps Hellenika.* Halle, 1909.

Moggi, M. *I sinecismi interstatali Greci.* Pisa, 1976.

Moretti, L. *Ricerche sulle leghe greche.* Rome, 1961.

Morrison, J.S. "Meno of Pharsalos, Polycrates and Ismenias." *CQ* 36 (1942): 57–78.

Munn, M.H. "Agesilaos' Boiotian Campaigns and the Theban Stockade of 378–377 B.C." *ClasAnt* 6 (1987): 106–38.

Ober, J. *Fortress Attica.* Leiden, 1985.

Orsi, D.P. "La boulé dei Tebani." *QS* 25 (1987): 125–44.

Parke, H.W. "Herippidas, Harmost at Thebes." *CQ* 21 (1927): 159–65.

Perlman, S. "The Causes and the Outbreak of the Corinthian War." *CQ* 14 (1964): 65.

Philippson, A. *Die griechischen Landschaften*, second edition, rev. E. Kirsten. Frankfurt, 1951.

Podlecki, A.J. "Apragmosyne," *AHB* 5 (1991): 81–87.

Powell, A. "Mendacity and Sparta's Use of the Visual." In *Classical Sparta: Technique Behind Her Success*, A. Powell, ed., 173–92. Norman, Okla., 1989.

Prandi, L. "Problemi di confini attico-beotico: Eleutherai." *CISA* 13 (1987): 50–79.

———. *Platea: momenti e problemi della storia di una polis (Serie di antichità e tradizione classica*, 11). Padua, 1988.

Pritchett, W.K. *The Greek State at War,* Vol. 2. Berkeley, 1974.

———. *Studies in Ancient Greek Topography*. Berkeley, 1965–.

Proietti, G. *Xenophon's Sparta. Mnemosyne* Supp. 98, Leiden, 1987.

Reincke, K. *RE* 19 (1937), *s.v.* "Pelopidas," 375–80.

Rice, D.G. "Why Sparta Failed: A Study of Politics and Policy from the Peace of Antalcidas to the Battle of Leuctra, 386–371 B.C." Ph.D. diss., Yale, 1971.

———. "Agesilaus, Agesipolis and Spartan Politics." *Historia* 23 (1974): 164–82.

———. "Xenophon, Diodorus and the Year 379/78 B.C.," *YCS* 24 (1975): 95–130.

Roberts, J.T. *Accountability in Athenian Government*. Madison, 1982.

Robinson, C.A. "Topographical Notes on Perachora." *AJA* 31 (1927): 96.

Rocchi, G.D. *Frontiera e confini nella Grecia antica*. Milan, 1988.

Roesch, P. *Thespies et la confédération béotienne*. Paris, 1965.

———. *Études béotiennes*. Paris, 1982.

Roller, D.W. "The Location of Xenophon's Γραὸς Στῆθος." *AJA* 82 (1978): 107–9.

Ryder, T.T.B. *Koine Eirene*. Oxford, 1965.

Salmon, P. "Les districts béotiennes," *REA* 58 (1956): 51–70.

———. *Étude sur la confédération béotienne (447/6–386)*. Brussels, 1976.

Schäfer, A. *Die Berichte Xenophons, Plutarchs und Diodorus über die Besetzung und Befreiung Thebens*. Munich, 1930.

Schachter, A. *The Cults of Boiotia*. vols. 1–. London, 1978–.

Schober, F. *RE* 2.10 (1934), *s.v.* "Thebai," 1423–92.

Seager, R. "Thrasybulus, Conon, and Athenian Imperialism." *JHS* 87 (1967): 95-115.

———. "The King's Peace and the Balance of Power in Greece, 386–362 B.C." *Athenaeum* 52 (1974): 36–63.

Shrimpton, G.S. "The Theban Supremacy in Fourth-Century Literature." *Phoenix* 25 (1971): 310–18.

Shrimpton, G.S. and D.J. McCarger, eds., *Classical Contributions in Honour of M.F. McGregor.* Locust Valley, 1981.

Smith, R.E. "The Opposition to Agesilaus' Foreign Policy, 394–371 B.C." *Historia* 2 (1953–54): 274–88.

Snodgrass, A.M and J.L. Bintliff, "Surveying Ancient Cities." *Scientific American* 264 (1991): 88–93.

Sordi, M. "Aspetti del federalismo greco arcaico: autonomia e egemonia nel koinon beotico." *A&R* 13 (1965): 55–75.

———. "La restaurazione della lega beotica nel 379–8 a.C." *Athenaeum* 51 (1973): 79–91.

———, ed. *Storiografia e propaganda.* Milan, 1975.

Stanton, G.R. "Federalism in the Greek World." In *Hellenika: Essays on Greek Politics and History,* G.H.R. Horsley, ed., 183–90. North Ryde, N.S.W., 1982.

Starr, C.G. *Political Intelligence in Classical Greece.* Leiden, 1974.

Stern, E. von. *Geschichte der spartanische und thebanischen Hegemonie vom Königsfrieden bis zur Schlacht bei Mantinea.* Dorpat, 1884.

———. *Xenophons Hellenika und die böotische Geschichtsüberlieferung.* Dorpat, 1887.

Strauss, B.S. *Athens After the Peloponnesian War: Class, Faction and Policy 403–386 B.C.* London and Sydney, 1986.

Symeonoglou, S. *The Topography of Thebes.* Princeton, 1985.

Tainter, J.A. *The Collapse of Complex Societies.* Cambridge, 1988.

Ténékidès, G. *La notion juridique d'independance et la tradition hellénique.* Athens, 1954.

Thiel, J.H. "De synoecismo Boeotiae post annum 379 peracta." *Mnemosyne* 54 (1926): 19–28

Tomlinson, R.A. "Two Notes on Possible *Hestiatoria.*" *BSA* 75 (1980): 221–28.

Tomlinson, R.A. and J.M. Fossey, "Ancient Remains on Mount Mavrovouni, South Boeotia," *BSA* 65 (1970): 243–63 (= *Papers in Boiotian Topography and History,* 130–56).

Tuplin, C.J. "Pausanias' and Plutarch's Epaminondas." *CQ* 78 (1984): 346–58.

———. "The Fate of Thespiae during the Theban Hegemony." *Athenaeum* 64 (1986): 321–41.

———. "The Leuktra Campaign." *Klio* 69 (1987): 77–84.

Underhill, G.E. *A Commentary on the Hellenica of Xenophon.* Oxford, 1900.

Urban, R. *Der Königsfrieden von 387/86 v. Chr. Historia,* Einzelschriften 68, Stuttgart, 1991.

Vial, C. Commentary to *Diodore de Sicile, Livre XV,* Budé translation, Paris, 1977.

Wallace, P.W. *Strabo's Description of Boiotia.* Heidelberg, 1979.

Westlake, H.D. "The Sources for the Spartan Debacle at Haliartus." *Phoenix* 39 (1985): 119–33.

Wilamowitz-Moellendorff, U. von. "Oropos und die Graer," *Hermes* 21 (1886): 91–115.

Ziegler, K. *Plutarchos von Chaironeia.* Munich, 1964.

Index